FOUNDATIONS OF MODERN ECONOMICS SERIES

Otto Eckstein, *Editor*

PUBLISHED

American Industry: Structure, Conduct, Performance, 3rd Ed., *Richard Caves*
Prices and Markets, 2nd Ed., *Robert Dorfman*
The Price System, *Robert Dorfman*
Money and Credit: Impact and Control, 3rd Ed., *James S. Duesenberry*
Public Finance, 3rd Ed., *Otto Eckstein*
Economies and the Environment, *Matthew Edel*
Managerial Economics, *Farrar and Meyer*
Labor Economics, *Richard B. Freeman*
Economic Development: Past and Present, 3rd Ed., *Richard T. Gill*
Evolution of Modern Economics, *Richard T. Gill*
Economic Systems, 2nd Ed., *Gregory Grossman*
Student Guide, *Hartman and Gustafson*
International Economics, 3rd Ed., *Kenan and Lubitz*
National Income Analysis, 3rd Ed., *Charles L. Schultze*

GREGORY GROSSMAN   *University of California, Berkeley*

Economic Systems

SECOND EDITION

PRENTICE-HALL, INC.   *Englewood Cliffs, New Jersey*

Library of Congress Cataloging in Publication Data

GROSSMAN, GREGORY.
    Economic systems.

    (Foundations of modern economics series)
    Bibliography: p.
    1. Comparative economics. I. Title.
HB90.G76 1974   330.12   73–21915
ISBN   0–13–233486–0
ISBN   0–13–233478–X (pbk.)

PRENTICE-HALL FOUNDATIONS

OF MODERN ECONOMICS SERIES

Otto Eckstein, *Editor*

10   9   8   7   6   5   4   3   2   1

PRENTICE-HALL   INTERNATIONAL   INC.,   *London*
PRENTICE-HALL OF AUSTRALIA, PTY., LTD., *Sydney*
PRENTICE-HALL   OF   CANADA,   LTD.,   *Toronto*
PRENTICE-HALL OF INDIA PVT. LIMITED, *New Delhi*
PRENTICE-HALL   OF   JAPAN,   INC.,   *Tokyo*

Foundations

of Modern Economics Series

Economics has grown so rapidly in recent years, it has increased so much in scope and depth, and the new dominance of the empirical approach has so transformed its character, that no one book can do it justice today. To fill this need, the Foundations of Modern Economic Series was conceived. The Series, brief books written by leading specialists, reflects the structure, content, and key scientific and policy issues of each field. Used in combination, the Series provides the material for the basic one-year college course. The analytical core of economics is presented in *Prices and Markets* and *National Income Analysis*, which are basic to the various fields of application. Two books in the Series, *The Evolution of Modern Economics* and *Economic Development: Past and Present*, can be read without prerequisite and can serve as an introduction to the subject.

The Foundations approach enables an instructor to devise his own course curriculum rather than to follow the format of the traditional textbook. Once analytical principles have been mastered, many sequences of topics can be arranged and specific areas can be explored at length. An instructor not interested in a complete survey course can omit some books and concentrate on a detailed study of a few fields. One-semester courses stressing either macro- or micro-economics can be readily devised. The instructors guide to the Series indicates the variety of ways the books in the Series can be used.

The books in the Series are also being used as supplements to the basic textbooks, to permit a fuller curriculum on some toipcs. Intermediate level courses are using volumes in the Series as the core text, and are combining it with various readings.

v

This Series is an experiment in teaching. The positive response to the first two editions has encouraged us to continue to develop and improve the approach. New books are being added and the previous books revised and updated. The thoughtful reactions of many teachers who have used the books in the past have been of immense help in preparing the third edition.

The books do not offer settled conclusions. They introduce the central problems of each field and indicate how economic analysis enables the reader to think more intelligently about them, to make him a more thoughtful citizen, and to encourage him to pursue the subject further.

Otto Eckstein, *Editor*

Contents

viii

Preface

The positive reception that the first edition of this little book found at universities and colleges in the United States and abroad, has encouraged the author to bring out a more up-to-date version. The revision of the book's content has been prompted by both the rapid change in the factual material pertaining to the various economies, and the lively evolution of the theoretical and conceptual aspects of the broad field that economists now generally call "comparative economic systems." But if—as someone said—the problem with history is knowing where to begin, the problem with writing a concise textbook on economic systems is knowing where to stop. The first edition required a very parsimonious handling of topics and empirical examples. Fortunately, the publisher has kindly allotted somewhat more space for the present edition. Accordingly I have expanded (and in some instances significantly revised) the conceptual portions of the book, and have added separate sections on three important and distinctive communist economies, those of Hungary, Cuba, and China. The concluding chapter has also been in part rewritten and expanded.

The author of a textbook on economic systems, even one as brief as the present, cannot possibly accomplish his job without help or advice from many specialists. I am particularly fortunate in this regard, though of course none of the persons listed below is to be held responsible for anything in the book. The persons whose kind assistance it is my pleasure to gratefully acknowledge are: Jean Bénard (Paris), Roberto M. Bernardo (Guelph University), Otto Eckstein (Harvard), Bernard Cazes (Paris), Pieter deWolff (Amsterdam), Edwin M. Epstein (Berkeley), Alexander Eckstein (Ann Arbor), Hans-Werner Gottinger (Bielefeld), Charkes A. Gulick (Berkeley), Lovell Jarvis (Berkeley), Silvana Malle (Verona), Svetozar Pejovich (Ohio University), Carl Riskin (Columbia University), Andris Trapans (Berkeley), Benjamin Ward (Berkeley), Tong-eng Wang (Berkeley). Special thanks are due Professor Morris Bornstein (Ann Arbor), the reviewer of the manuscript for the publisher, who generously offered a large number of specific suggestions for improvement.

Gregory Grossman

Criteria and

Values

CHAPTER ONE

INTRODUCTION

If you live in the United States, the food you buy is probably grown on a family farm, handled by private middlemen, processed by private companies, and sold to you by an independent grocer or a chain store. You have never met the farmers, the middlemen, and the processors, and you do not care to meet them. Nor do they care to meet you. But you do care that they and the grocers keep producing and selling the goods you want, and they and their employees and stockholders care that you keep buying what they have to sell. They do what they are doing for profits and wages, which they get by supplying you with what you are prepared to buy at prices you are prepared to pay.

The groceries that your counterpart in the Soviet Union buys have been grown on a state farm or a collective farm; they were processed and moved by state enterprises and were probably sold in a state store. The individual workers received wages for their work, or in the case of the collective farmers, a share of the net income; but they did what they did primarily because they were directed in great detail by the government and its planners.

The city dweller in that other communist colossus, China, gets his or her groceries at the end of a process of production and distribution that is basically similar to, but in some significant respects different from, that in the Soviet Union. Moreover, in both countries, a considerable proportion of foodstuffs is purchased by consumers directly from peasants.

In Yugoslavia, another communist country but with a radically

1

different economic system from the Soviet or the Chinese, the food is grown by peasants, free to grow what they want. But it is processed, transported, and sold by socialist enterprises in which, however, the workers and their representatives themselves decide what and how to produce without any direct orders from the government. They do so for the sake of profits, which in large measure go into their own pockets, and which they get (as do American firms) by meeting consumer demand in the market. And, finally, most of the population of the world still gets most of its food from the family's own field, or rice paddy, or livestock herd, without the intermediation of any outsiders.

These five instances illustrate the strikingly different ways in which people in different societies obtain their daily bread. Such differences, of course, are not limited to food; they extend to all the goods and services produced and consumed, to the distribution of income and wealth among the members of each society, to the growth and development of the economy, to the provision of society's collective needs, to the support of the needy and the individual's protection against insecurity, and so forth. The *way* these things are done has a lot to do with *how well* they are done and *what* gets done at all. Moreover, the way these things are done has a lot to do with how people order their social and political affairs in general, and with what they believe is right, just, and fair. And conversely, the way we do things affects our beliefs.

To put it differently, every economy has to accomplish certain basic tasks: determine what, where, how, and how much is to be produced; allocate the aggregate amount of goods and services produced (the gross national product) between private consumption, collective consumption, replacement of capital stock used up in the course of production, and further growth of the economy; distribute its material benefits (the national income) among the members of society; and maintain economic relations with the outside world. These things may be done spontaneously, with no central direction or planning, or they may be done with some measure of central control, but done they must be in any functioning economy.

The simplest arrangement is for every household to take care directly of its own economic needs and be entirely independent of the rest of the community or society: to produce its own food, clothing, shelter, and other things; to distribute these within the family according to some customary notions; to take care of its own young, old, and invalids; and to fall back on its own resources in the face of insecurity. Instances of such a *subsistence economy* in its extreme form, with no exchange between households at all, would be hard to find nowadays; though less extreme forms, in which exchange does occur but on a very small scale, still exist in many parts of the underdeveloped world.

Whatever romantic qualities may attach to it, the subsistence economy has one fatal flaw—it is doomed to very low labor productivity and therefore to a very low level of consumption. Higher levels of living require higher labor productivity, which can be attained only with division of labor, specialization, exchange, and hence considerable interdependence among individuals or families. A modern, industrial productive economy implies an extremely high degree of interdependence, a fact that the reader can easily confirm to his own satisfaction by stopping to reflect for a moment on the very small proportion of his material needs he supplies directly for himself or his family.

An economy in which individuals and families are substantially interdependent is usually called a *social economy*. It is only with the social economy, and mostly with the more advanced kinds, that this book concerns itself. In order to accomplish its tasks, a social economy resorts to what the social scientist calls *institutions*—an institution in its broadest sense being a set of "norms, rules of conduct, or established ways of thinking."[1] Property, the business corporation, the family household, the government, money, the income tax, sharecropping, the tipping of waiters, planning, profit-making, the labor union—these are all examples of economic institutions.

The set of institutions that characterizes a given economy comprises its *economic system*. To facilitate analysis, we may also deal with imaginary economic systems in which the institutions are kept deliberately "pure" and relatively simple. Imaginary systems of this kind, usually called *models*, can be very helpful in understanding real or potential institutions and systems.

Two more quick definitions: By *economic unit*, we mean a group of individuals such as a household, a firm, a labor union, or a government bureau brought together for a common economic purpose. By *economic agent*, we mean someone who performs a particular kind of economic function; for example, a consumer, a worker, an entrepreneur, an investor, or a planner.

In studying economic systems, there is always the danger that we will fall victim to our own preconceptions, prejudices, and biases, or fall into nasty semantic traps. We shall gain little unless we try hard to keep our minds open. Being objective does not mean abandoning all preferences and values; this would be as unnecessary as it is unlikely. It does, however, mean making a strong effort to understand the logic, historical origins, and purposes of all kinds of institutions and ideas, whether we or our fellow citizens like them or not; avoiding easy labels; and, most of all, taking nothing for granted.

PERFORMANCE CRITERIA

Comparing economic systems we inevitably ask which is best. But what does "best" mean in this context? It is difficult enough to tell which of several automobiles is best. Some of the criteria we apply to cars—purchase price, credit terms, operating cost, resale value—can be brought to the same denomi-

---

[1] Walter S. Buckingham, Jr., *Theoretical Economic Systems: A Comparative Analysis* (New York: The Ronald Press Co., 1958), p. 90.

nator, dollars and cents, discounted to the same point in time, and combined into a single figure for each car, which can then be compared with corresponding figures for other cars. But other criteria—appearance, comfort, ease of handling, safety, snob appeal—cannot be reduced to a common denominator; and insofar as they enter into our decision, they do so through our subjective preferences. The preferences of different persons need not be alike, which is why there are so many different cars on the road.

Even more than evaluating cars, evaluating economic systems involves subjective preferences as well as rational appraisal. But unlike the criteria that apply to cars, the criteria that apply to economic systems include many of the basic philosophic issues—welfare, progress, freedom, security, efficiency—on which reasonable men have disagreed for centuries and no doubt will continue to disagree for many more. Only the dogmatic will insist on applying a single yardstick to measure the performance of all economic systems. In the final analysis, it is up to each of us to decide which combination of features in an economic system we like best. Yet, in contrast to cars, each of us cannot have for himself the economic system he wants if it is different from the one that obtains in his society (unless, of course, the system of his choice exists in another country and he is willing to emigrate). To change an economic system, or to improve the existing one, or to preserve it, we have to resort to political action. Indeed, this is what a great deal of political action in a democracy is about.

A cautionary note. It is legitimate to compare ideal or pure systems, or actual economies, among themselves, or an actual system with *its own* ideal. It is not legitimate to compare an actual economy with an ideal model of a different kind (say, American reality with an abstract model of socialism, or Soviet reality with an ideal capitalism), though exactly this trick is often resorted to by none-too-scrupulous or simply careless politicians and propagandists.

Plenty

Clearly, one of the first things we should like to know about economies with different systems is how much they produce or provide in goods and services, overall and per person. Here we have a variety of measures to choose from: for example, gross national income and consumption. We may wish to break these measures down even further—for instance, into industrial and agricultural output, or into private goods and collective goods, or into goods that are meant to contribute to national defense and those that are not. We may also be interested in labor productivity: national product per gainfully employed person, or industrial production per man-hour. And let us not forget leisure (time free from work), an important product in every economy.

The particular criteria we employ will depend on the questions we wish to answer, unless the inadequacies of statistical data force us to resort to less appropriate measures, which is often the case. It should be noted, though, that the purely technical statistical problems of carrying out international compari-

4

sons of this sort are very complex, and the numerical results, in which the man in the street often has considerable and understandable interest, can at times be properly interpreted only by those skilled in economic statistics.

Furthermore, the implications with regard to economic *systems* are not always obvious. Just because one country's production per capita is only, say, one-half of another country's does not mean that its system is correspondingly worse. A given economy's production per person depends not only on its economic institutions but also on a large number of historical, political, cultural, geographic, natural, and demographic circumstances as well. Because the American national product per capita is much higher than the Soviet does no more by *itself* prove the superiority of "capitalism" over "socialism" than the fact that the national product per capita of "socialist" Czechoslovakia is much higher than that of "capitalist" Greece proves the reverse.

Growth

Today, more than in any previous era, growth is considered to be a major criterion of successful economic performance; indeed, in the eyes of many people in the world, it is the most important criterion.[2] In most of the hundred-odd underdeveloped countries, economic development, meaning primarily growth of production, often constitutes the major national purpose, at times to the point of obsession in the eyes of those of us who are more comfortably situated. In many of these countries, the success of their governments and institutions tends to be largely measured in terms of the growth that they produce or permit; while alternative systems vying for emulation and goodwill in these countries—capitalism and socialism, democracy and dictatorship—tend to be measured by the same yardstick.[3]

Yet it is not simply the challenge from communism and the competition of the two politico-economic systems in the eyes of the "third world," nor solely the imperatives of national defense, that have prompted the advanced Western countries to seek a steady and substantial rate of economic growth. There are sound domestic reasons for such an aim. Take the problem of poverty, for instance. Rich as these nations are overall, none of them, not even the United States, is without significant—at times, shocking—pockets of poverty that are difficult to justify on social and moral grounds in otherwise relatively affluent societies. The elimination of such poverty calls for: (1) structural changes, such as the movement of people out of, or the creation of jobs in, depressed sectors; (2) enlargement of employment opportunities in general; and (3) redistribution

---

[2]A comprehensive discussion of economic growth in its historical and policy aspects may be found in Richard T. Gill's *Economic Development: Past and Present* 2nd ed., (Englewood Cliffs, N.J.: Prentice-Hall, Inc., 1973), another volume in the *Foundation of Modern Economics Series*.

[3]What has already been said about the difficulties of measuring relative outputs applies even more to measuring comparative growth, where we introduce the time dimension and with it a whole set of additional conceptual and statistical difficulties.

of income in favor of those individuals who, for various reasons, cannot benefit from the first two types of measures. All these measures, however, are politically much more feasible when the national income is growing rapidly than when it is growing slowly or not all.

On the other hand, it would be wrong to assume that growth alone helps solve social problems. It may also be the chief cause of their appearance and aggravation, especially at early stages of industrialization when many of the old traditions, institutions, attitudes, and economic interests are destroyed or impaired. For this reason, economic development, especially rapid industrialization, may be resisted by various groups in society, and not necessarily only for selfish or unenlightened reasons.

Finally, economic growth tends to contribute to a deterioration of the environment, as every industrialized country by now has discovered to its sorrow. But here, too, the relationship is not simple, for the additional economic and political resources required to combat and reverse the process of environmental deterioration can be most easily found if the total economic pie is increased. To stop all growth is not the wisest way to combat pollution.

Stability

Economic stability usually refers to the avoidance of two kinds of closely interrelated phenomena: periodic fluctuations in employment and output in the whole economy or some of its sectors (business fluctuations, business cycles), and persistent and significant upward or downward movement of prices in general (inflation or deflation). It may also refer to large fluctations in the growth *rate* from year to year.

Inflation favors debtors and penalizes creditors (which is not the same as favoring the poor and penalizing the rich, for rich usually owe much more than the poor). It changes the relative well-being of economic classes, cuts into some forms of savings, and introduces greater uncertainty into economic decisions. Deflation is at least as bad. Recessions and depressions reduce the national product and real income of the whole society and throw people out of work, thus setting in motion human and social tragedies and costs. The propensity of the economy to be unstable is clearly in large part a function of its institutions, and different economic systems may well differ on this score.

Security

In the more developed countries of today the individual household's economic security is typically no longer at the mercy of a fickle nature, as it had been until recently since the beginning of time, and as it still is in most of the underdeveloped world. But modern man has gained this security at the price of an immeasurably greater dependence on the rest of society. His insecurity now stems primarily from the unpredictability of social phenomena. Fortu-

6

nately, these are not completely beyond society's control, nor need the individual be entirely without social protection against unexpected adversity.

A major type of individual economic insecurity derives from economic instability. But even in the absence of a depression or inflation, and often for no fault of his own, a person may lose his job, property, or earning power. Many such unfortunate events, especially if they have purely personal causes, cannot very well be prevented under any economic system. Insofar as they are the byproducts of progress or of spontaneous shifts in consumer demand, it may not even be desirable to prevent them entirely, lest progress or the freedom of consumer choice be obstructed. And in addition there are the many and often tragic risks of sickness, invalidity, death of the breadwinner, and so forth.

By and large public opinion in modern, advanced countries (and even in many poorer countries) nowadays agrees that people should not bear the full brunt of adverse social forces and "acts of God" over which they have no control. It is this emphasis on the protection of the individual against various risks that is one of the main distinguishing features of the twentieth century as compared with former centuries. Those states that underwrite a wide range of such risks, and perhaps furnish a large number of other services to their citizens, are usually referred to as "welfare states," although the term tends to be used very loosely. In regard to individual security, economic systems vary, first, in the extent to which they are (or are not) welfare states, and second, in the extent to which they do or do not attempt to prevent the social causes of insecurity, such as business fluctuations.

Efficiency

Few of us are against efficiency, and even fewer are for its opposite, waste. The economist recognizes three kinds of efficiency. First, there is technical efficiency, the most effective use of a given resource (labor, material, machine, and so on) or bundle of resources *in a particular job*. Waste is exemplified by labor idling on the job, excessive fuel burned under a boiler, materials spoiling because of neglect, or a motor running unnecessarily. It may seem at first glance that technical efficiency has little to do with economic system—at least we take the desire to avoid it for granted. But in point of fact the avoidance of technical inefficiency depends a great deal on incentives to managers and workers, which in turn rests on socioeconomic institutions. For instance, technical inefficiency is a very serious problem in Soviet-type economies, as we shall see in Chapter 6. More subtly, economic systems may be associated with different attitudes toward thriftiness and work discipline.

There are two kinds of economic efficiency, static and dynamic. *Static economic efficiency* subsumes technical efficiency and represents the best allocation of available resources among all the alternative uses in a given time span. In other words, economic efficiency obtains when no possible reallocation of resources can increase the output of one or more final goods without at the same time decreasing the output of one or more final goods. It is of course an ideal that is probably not even closely approached by any actual economy, but nonetheless the notion is a very useful one for analytical purposes.[4]

How efficiently a given economy (or an economic model) actually does (or might) operate depends on the nature of prices, the rules for decision-making that obtain among managers and planners, the degree of centralization of decisions, the degree of competition, the fiscal structure, and many other factors. Clearly, these in turn largely depend on the economy's institutions.

Dynamic efficiency, on the other hand, relates economic growth to the increase in resources that supposedly occasions this growth. Thus, two economies may both increase their stock of capital by some percentage, their labor forces by some percentage, and so forth, and yet the rate of growth of the national product in the two cases may be quite different. As with differences in productivity, the difference in dynamic efficiency may also stem from differences in the ease with which the two economies adopt economically rational innovations, or in the extent to which their *static* efficiencies change as they grow, and so forth. These, in turn, may derive primarily from the systems' institutions.

Equity and Justice; Equality

Rare is the man who does not have some notion of what is or is not fair or just in the distribution of income, wealth, power, and opportunity among individuals and groups in society. Almost equally rare is the man who does not feel strongly about it. We are all prone to judge political and economic systems by the criterion of distributive justice and equity. At bottom, every "ism" assumes some standard of social justice (as it also assumes some image of human nature), and every reform or revolution, or opposition to them, is motivated primarily by distributive considerations.

But considerations of equity and justice are not the only ones applicable in this connection. Income, wealth, and power are the inevitable rewards—to some degree in *any* society—to those who succeed at the game of production. Being rewards, they also serve as incentives for productive activity. Hence, a social policy of holding down the inequality of distribution of income, wealth, and power—however desirable on other grounds—may in some measure depress efficiency, productivity, or growth. Most of us will probably agree that there is no objective formula that will balance the ethical requirements of distributive justice against the needs of production and material well being. Each of us has to find the answer within himself; our attitudes toward different institutions and economic systems will be shaped accordingly. On the social plane, it is the political process that translates ethical norms (whose?) into reality.

[4]Chapter 7 of Robert Dorfman's *Prices and Markets*, this series, (Englewood Cliffs, N.J.: Prentice-Hall, Inc., 1967) addresses itself at greater length to what we here call static economic efficiency. Note that efficiency in this sense is not the same as productivity, which depends on the level of technology and the quality of available resources, as well as on the efficiency with which these two are utilized.

An important form of equality is the *equality of opportunity*: an equal chance for everyone to exercise his or her abilities in the economic sphere. This means not only the absence of social discrimination on grounds over which the individual has no control, but also a positive social policy of providing equal access to ability-developing facilities (education and so forth). Needless to say, equality of opportunity is an ideal that appeals to many people in all countries (though it is yet to be fully realized in any country). But it does not necessarily lead to equality of income, wealth, or power. On the contrary, insofar as individual abilities and motivations differ, and insofar as rewards are scaled according to performance, full equality of opportunity would still result in unequal distribution of benefits.

Economic Freedoms

Much belabored and abused, the word "freedom" may mean different things and refer to many different conditions. We use the word here in the sense of absence of social obstacles to effective *choice*, and for the moment we concern ourselves only with "economic freedom"—or, better, "economic freedoms," since there are several.

Choice may be exercised by different kinds of economic units and economic agents. Let us begin with *households*: If in their capacity as consumers they are free to buy any goods available for purchase (of course within the limits of their purchasing power or credit), the condition known as *freedom of consumer choice* exists. This freedom is absent if, to a significant extent, consumers are limited in their purchases by rationing (as in wartime in the United States or elsewhere) or if they are doled out goods in predetermined amounts (as happened in Russia during so-called period of War Communism, 1918–21). If individuals are essentially free to accept any job within the limits of their abilities and to quit any job, they enjoy *freedom of choice of job*. In most societies this freedom is less fully realized than the freedom of consumer choice because of professional degree requirements, formal licensing of professions, restrictions imposed by unions, military service, and so on. These two freedoms, plus the freedom to make use of whatever other resources the household may dispose of, make up *freedom of household choice*.

Similarly, a business enterprise may have the freedom to acquire any resources it wishes and can pay for, to use any technology (within the limits imposed by patent laws), to produce any products, to sell them at any price it can charge, and to invest in any way it pleases. If it can do all these things, it enjoys maximum *freedom of enterprise*. In reality, it usually cannot do all these things as it pleases. It may be restricted by labor laws and collective bargaining contracts, zoning regulations, sanitary and building codes, provisions of the corporate charter, price controls, and so forth ad infinitum. Freedom of enterprise is always relative. Still, in some countries or economic systems there is so much more of it than in others that we can meaningfully speak of "free enterprise

9

economies (or systems)." Notice that free enterprise is not identical with private enterprise. *Private* enterprise need not be very free; it was not under the Nazis in Germany. On the other hand, a publicly owned enterprise may be just as free in its business activities as its private counterpart, as exemplified by two French automotive concerns: Renault, a nationalized company, and Peugeot, a private one.

An important though sometimes overlooked aspect of the freedom of enterprise is the freedom to create new economic institutions in response to new needs and independently of the initiative of the state (though usually not without the latter's eventual involvement). Familiar examples from just the recent past are the multipurpose credit card, the overseas charter flight, the condominium in real estate, computer time-sharing arrangements, and the independent non-profit research institute. This aspect of the freedom of enterprise is closely related to the "self-organizing" feature of an economic system, to be discussed in the next chapter.

Freedom of household choice and freedom of enterprise may be valued *per se*. Americans, especially, in line with our individualistic and libertarian tradition, feel that individuals (or households) and businesses should be free to spend their own money as they see fit and to do as they wish with the resources at their command, so long as they do not thereby seriously impair society's interests and well being.

However, many would also add that people and businesses cannot be regarded identically for this purpose, because in the final analysis businesses exist for people, and not vice versa. Furthermore, many would insist that among businesses one must sharply distinguish between small, personal enterprises and large (and typically bureaucratic and impersonal) corporations.[5] By virtue of its size, importance, impact on the economy, and impersonal nature, the large corporation is often regarded as a quasi-public body.

But in addition to being valuable in their own right, freedom of household choice and freedom of enterprise have also *instrumental* importance. They are highly useful social devices that permit consumers to get the most for their incomes and facilitate (though not ensure) efficient use of resources and the exercise of initiative by business firms. In their absence, society has to resort to methods of rationing goods and enforcing controls, which may be both expensive to administer and detrimental to the economy's efficiency (though under some circumstances they may be necessary).[6]

[5] Although the corporation is a "legal person" in that it can sue and be sued, it can hardly be identified for most purposes with an individual or a small, private business. To do so would be to commit what Thurman W. Arnold has called "the personification of the corporation"; see his The Folklore of Capitalism (Garden City, N.Y.: Blue Ribbon Books, 1937), Chap. 8. This book, though by now somewhat dated in its factual material, is still a most stimulating discussion of the myths and fallacies that often block our understanding of economic matters. A more recent critique along similar lines is Dow Votaw's "The Mythology of Corporation," California Management Review, 4:3 (Spring 1962), pp. 58–74.

[6] Institutionally, the opposite of free consumers' choice is the rationing of consumer goods, typi-

Economic Sovereignty

Who ultimately decides what will be produced by the economy? If it is consumers—say, by exercising effective demand in the market—and if production is closely attuned to consumer preferences, then the economist says that *consumers' sovereignty* prevails.[7] In fact, because the preferences of households as resource owners (especially as suppliers of labor) also affect production, it is better to speak of *household sovereignty*. On the other hand, most things may be produced in response to the explicit preferences or wishes of the country's political leaders—as for instance in the Soviet Union—in which case we speak of the dominance of *leaders' preferences* or of *leaders' sovereignty*.[8]

Consumers' sovereignty should not be confused with freedom of consumer choice. Sovereignty refers to the ultimate source of production decisions; consumer choice, to the method by which the produced consumer goods are distributed to households. For example, central planners may themselves determine what and how much is produced, thus denying sovereignty to consumers, but may rely on free choice at the retail level—on a "take it or leave it" basis—to distribute consumer goods to individual households, of course within the limits of each household's income. Such a combination of the absence of consumers' sovereignty with the presence of freedom of consumer choice obtains in the USSR.

Although it is sometimes said that consumers' sovereignty prevails in a country such as the United States, the statement can be accepted only with major qualifications. (1) Numerous factors—taxes, monopoly power, limitations on resource mobility—interpose themselves between consumer demand and production, so that the latter is far from perfectly attuned to the former. (2) In certain cases governments interfere directly with consumption; for example, forbidding the use of narcotics or requiring a minimum amount of education for each citizen. (3) Only some two-thirds of the final demand in the American economy

---

cally by means of ration cards or coupons, as in the United States during World War II. Although warranted in emergency situations, rationing is inconvenient for consumers, encourages black-marketeering and other violations of law, seriously impairs legitimate economic incentives, and is costly for society to administer and enforce. For these reasons even communist regimes prefer to maintain freedom of consumer choice in normal times. Note that a consumer (or other buyer) has freedom of choice only if the market price of every relevant good is no lower than its equilibrium price (that is, the price at which its demand and supply are equal). If the market price is below the equilibrium level, then (by definition) there is not enough of the good to satisfy all effective demand; hence, some buyers are unable to exercise their choice to buy it.

[7]Note that consumers' sovereignty has only limited bearing on consumer welfare. For instance, the Soviet consumer exercises less economic sovereignty than the Ethiopian consumer but is materially much better off by almost any standard. The most important single determinant of material well being per capita is overall productivity per capita.

[8]Also sometimes referred to as *planners'* preferences and *planners'* sovereignty, terms which are less accurate because the major choices are not up to planners but up to their political superiors, and possibly up to the voters.

originates with consumers (this being the share of personal consumption in the gross national product). Over one-fifth of the gross national product is taken up by all levels of government; this part of final demand is determined by the public as voters and not as consumers. The remainder of the gross national product, about 15 percent, goes for private (mostly business) investment, which in turn looks forward to future demand by consumers, government, and business.

Whether consumers' sovereignty is a desirable feature of an economic system or not has been debated a good deal among economists, especially among proponents of different kinds of socialism during the 1930s and '40s. Democratic socialists, in common with other democratically inclined social scientists and statesmen, consider it desirable, despite the several qualifications just listed. Authoritarian socialists, especially communists, put little stock in it. Generally speaking, the arguments have been as follows. *Pro consumers' sovereignty*: (1) Production is for people, for consumers, and therefore their desires and preferences should be decisive in the final analysis. (2) Consumers know best what's best for them, although they may need a good deal of education on this score as well as protection against quackery and fraud. (3) Disregard for consumers' sovereignty may open the door to other kinds of authoritarianism, especially political dictatorship. *Against consumers' sovereignty* the arguments have been: (1) Consumers often do not know what is best for them because they lack the necessary scientific and technical information, or because they do not care. (2) Tastes of different consumers are not independent but are swayed by fads and fashions. (3) Nor is consumer demand spontaneous, for it is heavily influenced by advertising and other pressure from producers. (4) The average consumer does not appreciate the distant future sufficiently and does not save enough for later generations.[9] (5) Consumer demand depends heavily on the distribution of income and wealth—that is, the consumers' "dollar ballots" are of unequal urgency to them and it is improper to speak of consumer sovereignty without reference to income distribution. The upholders of consumers' sovereignty admit many of these strictures but prefer to deal with the problems in ways other than rejecting consumer sovereignty outright—for example, by consumer education, letting society (government) add to the level of saving in the economy, and redistributing incomes through taxation and other democratic means in order to make the "dollar ballots" more comparable.

Protection of the Environment

In the course of just a few years the general public in the United States and much of the rest of the world has become very conscious of the deterioration of man's environment as a concomitant of economic "progress." More and more, economic activities and institutions are judged from the standpoint of the protection of the environment, and are—rightly—condemned insofar as they

12

[9]This point is of course more important in the poorer countries that badly need to build up their productive capital.

contribute to the pollution of air and water, the littering and scarring of the landscape, the congestion and noisiness of urban life, and the destruction of irreplaceable resources and wildlife. Intuitively we might expect that different economic systems would perform differently in this regard, and a priori theorizing may support such expectations. Yet in fact, by far the most important determinant of the degree of environmental disruption seems so far to have been the degree of industrialization (together with population congestion) rather than the economic system as such, whether "socialist" or "capitalist." We shall have more to say on this in the last chapter.

Other Criteria

The criteria that we have discussed so far have been, if not narrowly economic, primarily so. But man does not live by bread alone; he does not judge alternative socioeconomic systems only by their material aspects. He tests them in the crucible of his ethical, religious, and political beliefs. Material success itself may be looked upon with suspicion as distorting human values and standing in the way of what is considered to be the ideal of a good society on ethical grounds. Thus, the "utopian socialists" of the first half of the nineteenth century and the Christian socialists of the twentieth century rejected what they believed to be the excessive materialism, money-grubbing, and social injustices of capitalism.[10]

On the other hand, communists of Soviet persuasion not only extol material affluence for their "socialist" societies, but deliberately and consistently appeal by means of "material incentives" to individuals' self-interest in order to get done the work of their economies. Since the byproducts of such a policy is a considerable inequality of incomes and the perpetuation of selfishness on the part of individuals, the policy has been severely criticized by communists of the Chinese ("Maoist") and Cuban ("Castroist") persuasions, as we shall see in Chapter 6.

Proponents of capitalism, on their part, have upheld it not only for its material results but also for its likely beneficial effects on individual initiative, individual self-reliance, and political freedom. At times they have even admitted that on economic grounds alone capitalism may leave something to be desired but have held the loss to be a small material price to pay for the strengthening of political freedom.[11]

The case for capitalism as a promoter of political freedom is essentially

[10]One of the most eloquent—and by now classic—indictments of capitalistic materialism from a Christian-ethical standpoint is The Acquisitive Society (New York: Harcourt, Brace & Co., 1920) by the late eminent British economic historian and Fabian socialist R. H. Tawney.

[11]A good statement of this position may be found in Henry C. Wallich's The Cost of Freedom: Conservatives and Modern Capitalism (New York: Harper & Brothers, 1960). Less moderate statements in defense of capitalism as a promoter of political freedom will be found in two classic works, both by University of Chicago economists: Friedrich A. Hayek, The Road to Serfdom (Chicago: University of Chicago Press, 1944), and Milton Friedman, Capitalism and Freedom (Chicago: University of Chicago Press paperback, 1962).

13

twofold. First, the rise and spread of political liberty in the modern world has largely paralleled the rise and development of capitalism. Secondly, liberty fares best in those societies in which power is least concentrated; the market and private property are effective institutions for keeping power unconcentrated (chiefly, by reducing the power of the state). Moreover, the market mechanism is impersonal; it amounts to a "rule of law (economic rules) and not of men" in the economic sphere. On the other hand, obviously capitalism does not *guarantee* liberty; even today in many countries it goes hand in hand with dictatorship.

VALUES

The performance criteria just listed are not merely yardsticks for comparing different economic systems or means for attaining other things. As we have already repeatedly stressed, most of them may be and often are desired for their own sakes as *goals* or *ends* of social life, and as such they become social *values*. Unlike the choice among purely instrumental means, the choice between alternative ends or values cannot be made on the basis of a rational calculus. Values cannot be reduced to a common denominator, nor can one value be logically demonstrated to be superior to another. Insofar as accepted, they are accepted as matters of faith, belief, philosophy, or whim.

Values often tend to be interdependent. Some social ends conflict with one another; we can realize one of them more fully only if we give up a measure of another. At other times they complement one another; striving for one of them, we also facilitate the realization of another. We have already taken note of the interdependence of such social ends as growth, egalitarianism, and the protection of the environment.

In fact, most people tend to accept the same individual values. Most people in all societies are for plenty, for freedom, for individual security, and so forth. Where they differ is in the relative importance attached to them and in the willingness to sacrifice a measure of one (for themselves or for others) for a measure of the other. On this score they may not only differ, but often differ violently. Of course, a ruthless dictatorship can suppress the outward expression of values other than its own, but this is not the same thing as converting everyone to the official creed. And conversely, a society will outwardly subscribe to a single set of values only if there is a dictator to define, interpret, and enforce them. Not even every dictator can accomplish this, as was discovered in the communist world after Stalin's death.

14

The System:

Institutions and Problems

CHAPTER TWO

THE ECONOMY AS A SYSTEM

Although different economic systems are characterized by different institutions, not any assemblage of institutions constitutes an economic system. Implicit in the term "system" is the notion that the various parts and components (economic units and agents, institutions) not only interconnect and interact but do so with a certain degree of mutual consistency and coherence. In other words, the system must be a functioning whole—though it need not function perfectly or to our liking.

A crucial requirement is that the system be capable of adjusting to disturbances and adapting to changing conditions. Economies that are not subject to disturbances do not exist; even the simplest economies have to face the vagaries of nature and of conflict with the outside world. Advanced social economies are of course subject to many additional kinds of disturbance, such as demographic changes, growth of physical production facilities, discovery and depletion of natural resources, technological advance, changing expectations, changing values and tastes—both individual and collective, fluctuations in the supply of money, and so forth. Some disturbances are minor, others are major; but in all cases the economy has to respond to them in order to remain a functioning and acceptable social system. It may respond by *adjusting* the flow of resources among the many lines of activity (reallocation of resources) and redistributing income and wealth among the economic units and agents, without significantly revising the institutions. Or it may respond by *adapting* the institutions to the new conditions as well as adjusting in the above sense.

Thus, the economy is also a system in the other, formal, sense of the word.[1] The system as a whole produces a certain output (in the case of the economy, goods and services, distribution of income and wealth, "quality of life," and so on). Disturbances in the output or in the conditions are first sensed and then signalled to various spots in the system by means of "feedback," and then, insofar as adjustment takes place, signals go out to adjust the operation of various parts and components. Naturally, the adjustment need not be completed after a single round, as the one we have sketched; full adjustment to the initial disturbance may take several or many rounds (iterations), if it is completed at all. In the meantime, many other disturbances may occur to affect the process of adjustment.

The adjustment may be automatic in the sense that it is brought about by the responses of many economic agents to signals in, say, a market, and is not consciously willed and carried out by man. For example, in a well-functioning market, a growing shortage of some good in relation to its demand brings about a rise in the price of the good. This price rise then acts as a signal to buyers of the good to use less of it (because it is now more expensive in relation to incomes and to other goods) and to shift resources to its production (because this is now more profitable). Thus, the economy adjusts itself to the initial disturbance—and to the many other disturbances that occur in the course of the adjustment process. This then is a case of automatic adjustment (control) or self-regulation.

Alternatively, the adjustment may take place as a result of a conscious decision on the part of some human beings who are charged with this task. For example, if the disturbance is a fall in business activity and employment owing to a decline in spending in the whole economy, the adjustment may be sought by the Federal Reserve Board, which would take certain measures to increase the amount of purchasing power in the hands of the public. Another example might be drawn from the Soviet economy, which generally does not possess a self-adjusting market mechanism. Instead, the adjustment has to be a conscious decision by some planner (or possibly many planners), who receive information on disturbances, evaluate it, perhaps solicit additional information, and then may issue orders to shift resources, increase or decrease the consumption or the production of some goods, and so forth. At times, even in the Soviet Union, the adjustment may be in part automatic and in part not.

[1]This is not the place to discuss formal "systems analysis" or the related science of "cybernetics." The interested reader is referred to the entries under these two captions in the *International Encyclopedia of the Social Sciences* (New York: The Macmillan Co., 1968). He may also find useful the following two collections of readings: Walter Buckley, ed., *Modern Systems Research for the Behavioral Scientist* (Chicago: Aldine, 1968), and F. E. Emery, ed., *Systems Thinking* (Penguin Books, Inc., 1969. paperback). A brief introduction to systems analysis on the firm level, but suggestive for the economy as a whole, is James C. Emery, *Organization Planning and Control Systems* (New York: The Macmillan Co., 1969, paperback).

Whether automatic or not, the process of adjustment utilizes the pattern of communication within the system and the flow of information—messages—through the channels of communication; these are of crucial importance. A very important type of message is a price; this kind of message essentially says to economic agents that each of them can have a unit of a given good (or so much money) if he gives up so much money (or a unit of the good). The adjustment process also depends on the objectives that each economic agent pursues: say, profit in the case of the business firm, income in the case of the worker, full employment or price stability in the case of the national economic planners, and so forth.

Adaptation

However, at times the response to a disturbance may take the form of the creation of a new institution or institutions or the substantial reform of old institution(s). In this case the system adapts itself to the changed conditions; it reorganizes itself. Of course, the disturbance may be also the lure of new opportunities for profit or for other economic advantage. For example, the appearance and rapid diffusion in recent years of the all-purpose, bank-issued credit card (a new kind of institution) was in response to the perception of new profit possibilities by the major banks. At times, the adaptation or reorganization is so far-reaching that we may properly speak not only of new institutions but of new systems. Thus, the appearance around 1930 of the Soviet economic system as we now know it was the result of a complete redesign of the whole economic system in the USSR.[2]

As in the last example, or in the case of the creation of the Federal Reserve System in the United States in 1914 for the purpose of preventing future financial crises, the adaptation was a deliberate decision of the political leadership of the country in question. Obviously, many of the major institutional and systemic changes occur in this way. However, many also occur through the direct initiative and action of the very economic agents who operate the new institutions to their own advantage. In these cases we may speak of the adaptation through self-organization. We have already touched on this phenomenon in the preceding chapter under "Economic Freedoms" and have given some examples from the recent past there. Many other examples could be cited, such as the creation of new kinds of business firms by promoters and investors (unless this necessitates enabling legislation or action by the state, which is sometimes the case), the banding of workers together in unions, and so on. These are all familiar examples of what is sometimes called self-organization in the economic system. Different economic systems differ greatly on this score; for instance, the Soviet-type economy provides almost no (legal) possibility for self-organization

---

[2]The reader may wonder what the "disturbance" was in this case. It was essentially the huge gap between the economic backwardness and international weakness of the country, on one hand, and the ideological promise and power-political aspirations of the ruling group (the Communist Party and the then dictator, Stalin), on the other.

in this sense, the American economy provides a great deal, and many other economies are to be found in between.[3]

COORDINATING MECHANISMS

A most important aspect of adjustment in the economic system is the coordination of the activities of thousands and millions of individual units.

Every economic unit in a social economy is dependent on innumerable other units to furnish it with consumer goods, labor services, materials, fuel, and markets for its products. Without some mechanism to provide the minimal amount of coordination of the activities of the separate but interdependent economic units, a modern economy would not be able to meet even the most basic needs of its citizens. Moreover, this mechanism should not only bring the various factors of production into productive use, but should ensure that their employment be tolerably full and efficient. Finally, it should distribute incomes to consumers—that is, to all of us—in a tolerably equitable way.

There are three such coordinating mechanisms, generally speaking: tradition, the market mechanism, and command.

Tradition

By tradition we mean generally accepted, customary, and persistent specific patterns of relationship among economic units or agents. In relatively primitive economies a very large part of economic life is often so governed: exchange between individuals or tribes; the individual's occupation within the existing division of labor; the tribute paid to authority; and so forth. Thus, in a medieval manor, tradition determined such basic relations as the payment of serfs to the lord in labor, produce, or money; his reciprocal obligations to the serfs; and the support he furnished to other members of the manor community (priests, artisans, servants). As this example shows, the origin of the traditional relationship may be traceable to certain power relations or initial bargains, but with time these become crystallized into customary relationships that are generally accepted most of the time. In a modern economy, the role of tradition is relatively much smaller but by no means negligible. Private charity and philanthropy, tipping, many aspects of employer-employee relations, the exchange of gifts and favors, the ethics and limits of competitive behavior, professional standards—these and many other norms of behavior are governed in large measure by tradition.

---

[3]No value judgment is meant by this statement. Self-organization is not necessarily the best way of bringing about systemic adaptation, though often it is. It is a social method of bringing about adaptation, although insofar as it is an aspect of economic freedom it may also be invested with value in its own right.

As a mechanism for regulating the division of labor and the distribution of benefits and burdens in society, tradition has many advantages, perhaps the most important of which is the predictability of the relations and behavior patterns in question. It saves the need for renegotiating individual transactions, while at the same time avoiding the unpleasant element of compulsion that may often attach to command. Its chief drawback is obviously the slowness with which it adjusts to changing conditions—technological innovations, new products, new tastes and mores, changing notions of justice and equity—if it adjusts to them at all. It is thus often an obstacle to progress, especially in the early stages of industrialization when the traditional ties and norms of behavior are still strong.[4] Yet at times the preservation of some measure of tradition may actually facilitate orderly transition to a modern economy and society by taking the edge off social instability and individual insecurity occasioned by rapid modernization.[5]

Market Mechanism

However, in all more or less advanced economies (other than those of the Soviet type), it is chiefly the market mechanism that allocates resources among various lines of activity; adjusts production, consumption, and resources to one another; distributes incomes; and brings about economic growth. The market mechanism (sometimes also called "the price mechanism" or "the price system"[6] or simply "the market") has been at the center of economists' attention for centuries, yet there is no standard definition of it. We may say that the *market mechanism* operates in a social economy when the following three conditions are met: (1) The individual economic units by and large decide themselves what, how, where, and when they produce and consume. (2) They do so largely with reference to the terms on which alternatives are available to them—that is, with reference to *prices* in the broadest sense of the word. (3) Prices respond, more or less, to the forces of demand and supply for the individual goods or factors. The end result tends to be the equilibration of demand and supply and the co-ordination of the economic activities of innumerable individual units and agents.

Too much should not be read into this definition. For instance, it says nothing about whether firms are privately or publicly owned; nor about the degree or character of competition among the firms or households; nor about the rules that the individual economic agents follow in making their decisions; nor about the presence and extent of government intervention in the economy

---

[4]Cf. the discussion by Richard T. Gill, *Economic Development: Past and Present*, 2nd ed. (Englewood Cliffs, N.J.: Prentice-Hall, Inc., 1973), pp. 30–31.

[5]Such has been the case with the highly paternalistic employer-employee relations that have persisted in Japan despite very rapid industrialization over the better part of a century. See James C. Abbeglen, *The Japanese Factory* (Glencoe, Ill.: The Free Press, 1958).

[6]This is the phrase preferred by Robert Dorfman in his book in this series *The Price System* (Englewood Cliffs, N.J.: Prentice-Hall, Inc., 1964), to whom we leave the analytical treatment of the operation of the market mechanism.

19

(so long as this intervention does not eliminate the market mechanism); nor about the price-forming process or degree of price responsiveness and flexibility; nor, finally, about the efficiency with which the economy's resources are used or allocated, or whether they are fully employed. But the definition does indicate that the economic units are largely independent or autonomous with regard to the decisions in question, and that they deal with one another primarily through voluntary exchange of goods and services. More or less automatically and impersonally, in highly complex economies as well as in relatively simple ones, day after day, the market mechanism—Adam Smith's "invisible hand"—directs and coordinates the decisions and activities of millions of independent, dispersed economic units and agents. With all its problems and imperfections, it is surely one of the most remarkable of social institutions. We shall return to inquire into some of the characteristics and problems of the market mechanism in Chapters 4 and 5.

Command

Yet the same directing, resource allocating, coordinating, and income-distributing functions can be accomplished in a social economy by means that are in a sense the very opposite of the automatic and impersonal market mechanism; namely, by means of the *command principle* (or "command" for short). In this instance, the individual economic units (though probably only the firms and not the households) are ordered what, when, where, how, and how much to produce and consume. If done rationally at all, these commands (directives, orders, targets, "plans") derive from some sort of conscious attempt ("planning") to coordinate the activities of the individual units and to direct the economy as a whole toward certain definite goals.

The command principle implies several important things: relatively little independence or autonomy on the part of the individual economic unit; the presence of superior authority that issues the commands and is capable of eliciting a minimal degree of compliance; very probably a hierarchical organizational structure; and a minimal amount of *coordinative planning* on which the commands are based.

FORMS OF PROPERTY

Another, and much more venerable, way of distinguishing economic systems is according to the form of property ownership that predominates in the given economy. This is, for instance, the classic Marxist distinction, one that has influenced many non-Marxists as well.

Strictly speaking, *property* refers to a bundle of rights over tangible or intangible assets that permits the owner (within certain important limits to be presently noted) the right of use and disposal over them. In the case of *private* property, this right rests with private individuals; but the notion can be extended to include ownership by other nongovernmental bodies, such as cooperatives and mutual societies. In this section we are concerned only with ownership of productive assets (means of production). The ownership of strictly consumers' goods by households is a form of private property that is often designated as "personal property." Only in some extreme and quite rare types of communist communities—though not in the present-day communist countries—is the individual not allowed to own property. As we have mentioned, whether the means of production in an economy are predominantly owned privately or by public (governmental) bodies is one of the most important distinguishing features of economic systems, even if—contrary to what is still maintained by the more extreme partisans on both sides—the factor of ownership does not determine everything of importance about an economic system.

The bounds of private property are not always sharp. From the *social* standpoint, the difference between certain specific privately and publicly owned production facilities is not very great. Think of a private urban bus line, subject to close control by municipal or state regulating authorities, and a bus line owned by a specially created public transit district. Here the rights attaching to private property (the bus company, though not necessarily the individually owned shares of stock in the company) are so circumscribed by government as to make the distinction between public and private enterprise quite tenuous. The situation is typical of many public utilities regulated by state, federal, or other public authorities.

This example leads to a more general observation. The use of privately owned assets is always and in many ways subject to innumerable restrictions and limitations imposed by various public authorities. In the United States these include, among many others, property and income taxes, which cut into the benefits obtainable from private ownership; zoning regulations; building, housing, safety, and sanitary codes; nuisance abatement regulations; and labor laws and regulations, which may substantially limit the use of property through restrictions on the employment contract. In certain cases the owner of the property is legally obligated to furnish its services regardless of his wishes; for example, in the case of common carriers and public utilities (where the state, on the other hand, allows a certain return on capital in the setting of rates) and under the various state and federal antidiscrimination statutes. Lastly, the state always has the power of eminent domain—that is, of forcing the owner to sell his property to the state or a division thereof for legitimate public purposes against (supposedly) fair compensation.

The brief list in the preceding paragraph is sufficient to show that in fact there is no such thing as an absolute right of private property. Nor is there likely to be in any actual society, however strongly it may be ideologically committed to private property and private enterprise, because of the great variety of social goals and values that in practice must be mutually reconciled and compromised.

Turning now to the social functions that the institution of private property performs, we might mention, first, that it plays a major role in determining the

21

distribution of wealth, income, and power in society. In doing so it also helps determine the degree of decentralization of economic decisions. Second, private ownership is a most important device for preserving and maintaining society's capital (that is, physical production facilities and stocks of goods, as well as claims on other countries), for the obvious reason that every owner looks after his own. This is its custodial function. Third, the desire to accumulate private property is a very powerful stimulus—historically, the most important one—for the continued increase in society's real capital, and for all economic activity. And last, private property performs the important *social* function of providing the individual and his dependents with economic security—provided of course he owns some to begin with and does not lose it at the crucial time (such as during a stock market crash)—and in this way contributes to the individual's overall sense of independence.

In all these respects the institution of private property is only a means to certain ends, not an end in itself. As a means it is usually not without rivals. For instance, much new capital formation in capitalist countries—let alone the communist countries—is undertaken by government nowadays. Even in such a staunchly capitalist country as the United States, about a fifth of all capital formation is in the public sector. Examples are roads, streets, schools, and public housing. Moreover, most of this capital stock is seemingly no worse maintained for being publicly owned.

KINDS
OF ECONOMIC SYSTEMS

According to Mechanism

One way to distinguish economic systems is according to the prevailing coordinating mechanism. Although it is possible to devise abstract models of economic systems that contain only one of the three social mechanisms, actual contemporary economies (except the most primitive) contain all three in varying proportions. However, one of the social mechanisms usually predominates; accordingly, we speak of a *traditional economy, a market economy,* or *a command economy.*

Because in this book we limit our attention to modern economic systems, we shall not be concerned with the traditional economy hereafter. Rather, we shall focus our attention on the market economy and the command economy, always remembering, though, that custom or tradition as a social mechanism may exist to an appreciable extent in either.

According to Ownership

22

Another major way in which economic systems differ is according to the prevailing ownership of productive assets. *"Capitalism"* is, of course, a system in which productive assets are privately owned—though private property is not a simple and clear-cut concept, as we shall presently see. "*Socialism*" has many definitions; for the moment we shall think of it as an economic system in which most productive assets are publicly owned, usually by the state or some division thereof. The term "mixed economy" is often applied to an economy in which there are substantial amounts of both private and public ownership side by side.

It used to be thought that every capitalist economy would be governed by the market mechanism, and every socialist economy would forswear the market mechanism in favor of command. True, virtually all capitalist economies that have existed in history have been market economies; but the Nazi economy in Germany (say, between 1936 and 1945) may be called a capitalist command economy. And although most socialist economies—those under communist control—have been command economies most of the time, there is the important historical case of the USSR in the twenties, and the even more important contemporary instances of Yugoslavia since the early fifties and Hungary since the late sixties, all of which have been socialist market economies (see Chapter 8).

But before taking up several economic systems in detail we should look at certain institutions and problems.

MOTIVATION

In the last analysis, social economies function because individuals do what has to be done to make them function. But why do they do it? What motivates them? What is the source of economic drive and how does it relate to the other institutions? These are among the most fundamental questions to be asked about any economic system, and the answers to them reach deep into the philosophical underpinnings of man and society. In part for this reason— that is, because the problem quickly transcends the usual bounds of their discipline—economists have not studied these questions very much. They generally take the source of economic drive as given, usually assuming that it is the quest of personal material gain. For most of the economist's purposes this is a good enough approximation. But for some purposes it will not do; for example, what motivates the manager of a nationalized firm who earns a fixed salary? Or the communist planner? Moreover, in recent years two societies have sprung up— Castroist Cuba and Communist China—whose *official* values deliberately reject personal material gain and stress concern for the common good as the leading motive for economic activity and the source of economic drive. The student of comparative economic systems must therefore take into account a wide variety of possible motives for economic activity.

Generally speaking, there are three ways in which an individual may be made to perform for society, whether in the economic sphere or in other spheres of social activity. First, the individual may be materially rewarded for his performance. The reward—usually a sum of money—may be earned by the individual directly in the market, as in the case of private profit, or it may be given

23

to him by his employer or superior, either in the form of a regular wage or fee or as an extraordinary bonus or promotion for good performance. To the individual the reward is an incentive to perform; it is of course a *material incentive*. From the standpoint of society the reward is a form of power over the individual —*remunerative power*. By varying the size of the reward and the link between performance and reward (or, rather, expected reward) society can bring about certain patterns of behavior on the part of its members. The individual responds *calculatively*; that is, by calculating to determine which behavior will bring him the greatest material gain in the face of the existing structure of rewards. Naturally, for society to achieve its purposes in this way individuals must be acquisitively motivated. If they are not, or if society does not want them to be self-serving, then other forms of power may have to be applied to attain social objectives. For instance, society may invoke *moral incentives*—a somewhat imprecise phrase that denotes the use of rewards with little intrinsic value but with a strong symbolic appeal (such as medals, honorary titles, certificates of merit, public acclaim and esteem, and the like).

Second, the individual may be forced by society to do something; to pay taxes, to contribute labor, to serve in the army or other nonvoluntary organizations; to perform penal labor; to be a slave. The individual's motive is fear of punishment for noncompliance. In these cases society exercises *coercive power* over him, and he usually responds with varying degrees of nonenthusiasm (alienative involvement). Third, the individual may be induced to perform for the sake of the common good or a "higher" goal than just self-interest; he is moved by certain sentiments or ideals. Here society exercises *normative power* over the individual.[7]

In reality it is not always easy to draw the line between the three kinds of personal motives and the three forms of social power and individual involvement. In any given situation there is likely to be a mixture of these elements. Thus, even the most crassly acquisitive persons are rarely completely insensitive to sentiment and ideals, let alone to the threat of punishment by society. And although in all countries the individual's economic performance is elicited through material incentives, it is rare that society's remunerative power is not somehow tempered or reinforced by its coercive and normative power. Nonetheless, it is useful to distinguish between the several concepts as we are doing in this section.

Material Incentives

The concept "material incentive" is sometimes misunderstood to refer to the *average* level of income; in other words, it is assumed that the country with the higher average income relies more on material incentives than the country

---

[7]The classification and most of the terminology in the two preceding paragraphs derive from Amitai Etzioni's *A Comparative Analysis of Complex Organizations* (Glencoe, Ill.: The Free Press, 1961), Chap. 1; see also pp. 80–82 and throughout.

with the lower average income. This is not necessarily so, for the term refers to *differences* in the remuneration of different jobs or other economic activities. The greater the degree of material incentive, the greater the difference in the reward of skilled as against unskilled work, trained as against less trained labor, for responsibility and initiative, and for working at the geographic-economic frontier (say, Alaska or Siberia). More generally, "material incentive" is the additional material reward to do what society (or someone in society) values more. It varies directly—but not necessarily proportionately—with the economic value that the activity contributes to society.[8]

The differences in reward must be seen over the long run as well as over the short run. In the short run they pertain to the alternatives open to the individual with given skills, experience, and other personal attributes. In the long run, on the other hand, individuals may acquire additional or new education, training, skills; they may change their lines of work and places of residence. And in doing so they may well be guided in large measure, though usually not exclusively, by the comparative long-run prospects of earnings. Thus, material incentives help determine not only the employment structure in the short run, but also the occupational composition of the labor force in the long run.

The forms that material incentives take are many, but most of them are well known to the reader; differences in wages and salaries, special pay under certain conditions (such as overtime), tips (presumably a reward for the rendering of better service), commissions to salesmen and brokers, bonuses to managers for managing better (whether in capitalist corporation or a socialist firm), and—last but not least—profit in its innumerable variants. To repeat, it is the differences in the rewards for different economic activities and efforts that matter, and to what extent other means (coercion, indoctrination) are also used for this purpose. The average level of earnings is not the key here.[9] On the contrary, people often respond to the opportunity to earn more if they are poor than if they are economically comfortable.

This is not the place to enter upon a lengthy discussion of what determines the extent of differences between wages and salaries for different kinds of work, let alone profits and similar nonlabor earnings. Suffice it to say that the economist's old friends, demand and supply, are as important as any factors, in socialist (communist) as well as in capitalist countries. (Socialist countries, too, have labor markets insofar as some freedom of choice of job obtains,[10] and where there are markets there are forces of demand and supply at work.) Thus,

---

[8]At this point we abstract from the important question of how and by whom the individual's economic contribution to society is valued.

[9]To offer one example: In Czechoslovakia, under the communist regime, the dispersion of labor earnings has been remarkably narrow and therefore material incentives have been presumably very weak. In addition, private profit has been virtually nonexistent. But the average level of earnings in Czechoslovakia is quite high by world standards.

[10]Regarding freedom of choice of job see above, p. 9–10. Note that owing to terminological differences, the official view in the communist countries is that there are no "labor markets" there.

if demand shifts in favor of those economic agents whose services are already relatively well rewarded—the more skilled, the better educated, those with entrepreneurial talent—earnings differentials in the society will tend to widen. This is what often happens in the process of industrialization and modernization under various economic systems. On the other hand, changes in demand can also work in favor of the lower-remunerated elements of the labor force, thus diminishing income inequalities. An example is the rising demand for food in the world in recent years, which has tended to benefit farmers and peasants in both communist and noncommunist countries, and thus to reduce the gap between them and the rest of the population.

On the supply side, anything that limits the number of people in a certain line of work—whether by their own combination (for example, unionization) or by government action (for example, licensing of professions)—tends to raise their earnings relative to those of others. But in the long run, by far the most important force that tends to reduce the dispersion of wages and salaries is the freedom of access to education, training, acquisition of skills, and economic opportunities in general. This is why the inequality of labor earnings tends to be least in the countries in which education and training are most broadly distributed, again in socialist and capitalist countries alike.

It goes without saying that the distribution of labor earnings is not the only determinant of the distribution of income. We can hardly overlook property incomes, a large element in the capitalist countries, where it tends strongly to contribute to income inequality, a rather minor element in all but a few communist countries. (However, *illegal* private income, which is not quite property income but may be akin to it, seems to be quite significant in the USSR and other East European countries, and no doubt contributes to income inequality there.) On the other hand, the inequality of income distribution can be mitigated by taxation and other deliberate measure. Without going further into this matter, and before returning to the question of incentives and controls, let us observe that material inequality may be substantially reduced but is very difficult to eliminate, even with the strongest of intentions, and even in the absence of important private property, as the recent experiences of China and Cuba suggest (Chapter 7).

In sum, consistent use of material incentives is doubtless a most powerful force to induce people to get the economy's work done. Indeed, so powerful that, despite some ideological doubts, the Soviet Union (and most of the other communist countries that have been following its model) have been fully resorting to material incentives. In this they can fall back on Marx's own words regarding the distribution of rewards in the first socialist stage of the postcapitalist society ("to each according to his labor") and on Lenin's emphatic prescriptions.

But heavy reliance on material incentives also brings about severe drawbacks if equalitarianism is at all part of one's guiding values. To begin with, it tends to contribute to income inequality; especially so when the economy is undergoing rapid structural transformation, so that some occupational specialties and skills are quite scarce and can, therefore, command higher remuneration. This is indeed a problem for communist (and other left-revolutionary) regimes, which on one hand push for a rapid industrialization and modernization of the economy and the society, and on the other have an ultimate goal of equality in mind.[11] Second, and perhaps even more serious for such revolutionary regimes, is that material incentives work by appealing to man's acquisitive and selfish traits. But these are precisely the traits that man is supposed to lose if the revolutionary transformation is to be fully successful.

Can he lose them with time if they are not only the basis of most economic effort, but the effort itself is necessary to build up the productive capacity for the ultimate society of equality and abundance? The Soviets, following Marx and Lenin, say "yes." Their Chinese and Cuban critics say "no," they insist that other means of eliciting effort must be used lest the central goal of reshaping man—his thoughts, his attitudes, his behavior—be hopelessly undone by the continued appeal to man's traditional traits through material incentives.

Coercive and Normative Controls

What are these other methods? In Chapter 7 we shall see how the problem has been approached in Communist China and Castroist Cuba. Here, suffice it to refer to what was said at the beginning of this section; namely, that the two alternatives to the exercise of remunerative power by society are coercive power and normative power. Now, coercion is rather poorly suited to elicit effort, let alone initiative, in a complex, more or less modern economy. It is necessarily crude, and does not permit the measure of coercion to be adjusted to the desired result. Worse, it alienates the individual, turns him into an unwilling producer, a malingerer, and frequently a saboteur. It is not well suited to ensure that even the simplest and most routine tasks are properly done, not to mention the jobs requiring high skill and initiative that an advanced economy depends on. Thus, we need not dwell on coercion further at this point.[12]

Normative power is something else. By this we mean of course appeal to "higher" values than just one's own material benefit with the aid of education, indoctrination, and the manipulation of appropriate slogans and symbols. It is

---

[11]Another problem that may appear in almost any economic system when rapid industrialization relies heavily on material incentives is inflation. Under such conditions it is necessary to pay higher wages in order to attract people into the employed labor force and into new industries, occupations, and regions. The rapidly rising money wages feed an inflationary price-wage spiral.

[12]This is not to say that coercive power has not been important in even relatively advanced economies and even in peacetime. The most outstanding recent instance is, of course, the Soviet Union, where many millions have worked at forced labor, especially since about 1930. Since the mid-1950s, following Stalin's death in 1953, the number of forced laborers in the Soviet Union has been much smaller than before, but it was still estimated at 1.2 million as late as 1973 (cited in The Economist [London], March 3, 1973, p. 32). Most of this labor has been employed at jobs requiring relatively low skill, but some of it has been used in such responsible and skilled tasks as operating railroads and even conducting advanced scientific research. The latter instance is the setting for Aleksandr Solzhenitsyn's famous novel, The First Circle (New York: Harper & Row, 1968).

often combined with the personal ("charismatic") influence of a leader, such as Lenin, Mao, or Castro. Quite likely, though, both the normative power and the charismatic influence are applied together with large doses of material incentive, as in the Soviet Union, or at least with appreciable doses, as in China and Cuba.

But the extreme use of normative power is fraught with major problems, too. First, there are serious political implications. If everyone is to put his shoulder to the wheel and push hard for the sake of The Cause rather than for his own pecuniary benefit, then the cause must be defined by a supreme authority; a single ideology must be upheld and constantly reinterpreted; the population must be educated in one set of values; and deviant behavior must be ferreted out and punished. In other words, the political corollary is a dictatorial and authoritarian—perhaps totalitarian—order, with repression of dissent, with the secret police, and the like. Certainly small, voluntary communities such as religious orders, communitarian groups, or the Israeli *kibbutz* can operate on the basis of the individual's subordinating his interests to the group and to an ideal. But even the record of such small groups over the past two centuries is mixed, with a high ratio of failure. It remains to be shown that whole countries can do so without paying a heavy political price,[13] or that this price in the long run will be supported by a modern industrial society.

Next, normative methods can at times be very powerful in mobilizing and channeling economic effort, but they tend to be crude and blunt. They cannot be measured and applied with any precision. They deal with black-and-white contrasts rather than with the grays—economic trade-offs and the finer balancing of costs and results—that characterize a more sophisticated economy. They vest power in the type of person who is good at manipulating and mobilizing large numbers of people rather than in the technical specialist or the professional planner and manager. They focus attention on some tasks and lead to the neglect of many others.[14] In short, they tend to be wasteful and inefficient. This is no doubt a major reason that such methods, though still used, have generally declined in importance in the Soviet Union as its economy has become more complex and sophisticated.

Further, the ideological and political atmosphere generated by heavy reliance on normative methods may well be hostile to prudent planning, careful economic calculation, business-like management, and rational accounting and pricing—for whatever set of social ends. This much is also suggested by the experience of various communist countries. To be sure, economic rationality

---

[13]Certainly the examples of China and Cuba do not show it. On one hand, both are dictatorial and authoritarian societies. On the other hand, in both the use of normative power has been significantly supplemented by both remunerative power (material incentives) and coercion. See the discussion of both countries in Chap. 7.

[14]A good example of this is the campaign to harvest and produce 10 million tons of sugar in Cuba in 1970. The campaign to reach this goal enveloped and mobilized virtually the whole country. In fact, only 8.5 million tons were produced. Nevertheless, the effort caused serious neglect and high cost in the rest of the economy, as later stressed by Fidel Castro himself.

and efficiency are not everything, but a modern economy does suffer in their absence.

Lastly, we should note that it is possible for a society to use relatively little of all three forms of power (remunerative, coercive, and normative) in order to elicit economic performance from its members. This seems to have been the case in communist Czechoslovakia since, say, the middle fifties. Wages and salaries have been differentiated very little, and, consequently, material incentives have been quite weak. But there has also been very little reliance on both coercive and normative methods in the economic sphere (though not in the political sphere). The results, in the opinion of many expert observers, have not been favorable to productivity and efficiency.

Economic Drive

After all is said and done, a great deal remains to be explained about the motivation of economic agents, and especially about the source of drive for the development and transformation of a dynamic economy. Material incentive surely is a potent force in everyday situations. But does it sufficiently explain the less common forms of behavior, even if on the face of it there is clear pecuniary gain to the chief protagonists? Why do people act as entrepreneurs, promoting and expanding businesses, or as managers of large enterprises, or as planners or industrializing statesmen? In regard to private enterprise we usually credit the *profit motive* (backed up by the institution of private property) with being the most important, if not the sole, source of drive. But what complex of psychological, cultural, and social elements lies behind the profit motive? Is it rooted in the "Protestant Ethic," as the great German sociologist Max Weber brilliantly, but not entirely convincingly, argued?[15] Is it a natural desire of the typical "economic man," as the classical economists assumed? And besides, how far will the profit motive push people along the lines of economic activity? We do not fully know the answers to these questions.

We do know that the profit motive in the usual sense is not the only motive force in economic life. The manager of a large corporation, who is the dominant type of manager and entrepreneur in the United States today, gets relatively little direct benefit from the profits that his organization earns. He takes his reward in salary and bonuses, partly in the dividends on the relatively small amount of the company's stock he may own, and no doubt also significantly in esteem. Others in executive positions—such as managers of public enterprises in the West and of firms in the Soviet Union, civil servants, national planners—work, often extremely conscientiously and ably, for their salaries, occasional

---

[15]*The Protestant Ethic and the Spirit of Capitalism*, translated by Talcott Parsons (New York: Scribners, 1930). A convenient summary of the controversy in this matter and suggestions for further reading will be found in Robert W. Green, ed., *Protestantism and Capitalism: The Weber Thesis and its Critics* (Boston: D. C. Heath and Co., 1959).

bonuses, professional pride, ideological convictions, national ideals, and various other nonprofit motives.

POWER, ORGANIZATIONS, BUREAUCRACY

We have noted the three kinds of power that society uses to bring about the compliance and proper performance of individuals: remunerative, coercive, and normative. But how does power arise in specific situations? This is an important point in comparing and contrasting economic systems.

Power is the capacity to influence the actions of others in a predictable way. Its distribution (or maldistribution) is clearly one of the chief criteria by which economic systems are judged. Its sources are many, since anything that can significantly influence the behavior of people can be translated into power by someone else.

A major source of power in any society is control of assets, whether private or public. To an orthodox Marxist, property ownership is *the* source of power in the final analysis. To be sure, in a capitalist society private property is an important source of power. Yet its very prevalence may cause power to be diffused. Moreover, not all property interests coincide. The conflicts among them, as well as among them and labor and other large organized interests, are not only among the major conflicts in a democratic capitalist society but ensure the very dispersal of power (pluralism) that in the long run is the best safeguard of political democracy.

Another major kind of power is the power of coercion that inheres in government. It assumes an extreme form when both the government and most productive property are under the control of the same individual or group, as in the communist countries; that is, when remunerative and coercive power coalesce throughout the whole society.

In modern societies power also rests with important positions in administrative bureaucracies; with those in control of information flow (national intelligence services, the press and other communication media, sometimes also with the statistical services); with those in possession of scientific and technical expertise; with control over armed forces or other organs of coercion; with the ability to bring to bear the weight of large numbers of individuals (as in the case of labor unions, mass political parties, or other large organized groups); with moral authority (for example, clergymen or some philosophers and statesmen) or the ability to manipulate ideological symbols (as in the case of politicians and demagogues); and with sheer personal qualities. The fact that one kind of power may dominate another—money may influence legislators or bureaucrats, and business or labor can be dominated by a strong government—does not basically vitiate the fact that there is more than one *source* of power.

30

Organizations; Bureaucracy

Most important in any modern economy is the institution we usually call "formal organization." Business firms, except the very smallest, are instances of formal organizations, as are government departments, schools, labor unions, some churches, and so forth. An understanding of the way organizations function and the problems they face is therefore very important for the appreciation of economic systems. For instance, the Soviet-type command economy is one huge formal organization that takes in just about the whole economy with the exception of the household sector.

The mechanism that gets things done in a formal organization is generally referred to as a *bureaucracy*. The characteristics and problems of bureaucracies have been the objects of intensive study by social scientists in recent years, following the pioneering theoretical work on the subject in the early part of this century by Max Weber. An abstract model of a bureaucracy[16] contains the following feature. It has different levels of authority; its work is governed by definite and impersonal rules; each official in a bureaucracy has his own job and his own rules to apply; the officials are selected and appointed according to their qualifications for the jobs, and promoted according to their skill at applying the rules.

Such a bureaucracy is, theoretically speaking, a very efficient means for performing tasks in society, in that its work is expert, predictable (given the rules), and presumably speedy. But even the idealized model contains some drawbacks. The officials may see the problems that they tackle in only partial perspective and the rules may not keep pace with changing conditions. Actual bureaucracies may of course have many other defects that need not be spelled out here. Yet for many social tasks there is no practicable alternative to bureaucratic handling; consider military organizations, government departments, or large business firms.

Interestingly, the economy is one social sphere in which there does exist a successful alternative to the bureaucratic organization of complex tasks; namely, the market mechanism. In the economic sphere, in contrast to other social spheres, it is possible (1) to quantify the alternatives facing a decision-making unit—that is, to express them in terms of prices; and (2) to define the goals of the unit in more or less definite and quantitative terms—for example, profit-making. When these two conditions are met, the market mechanism can take over. Thus, a large American corporation may so decentralize its operations that its various divisions become virtually autonomous and are related to

---

[16]On the Weberian model of a bureaucracy see, for example, Joseph A. Litterer, ed., *Organizations: Structure and Behavior* (New York: John Wiley & Sons, Inc., 1963). See also Robert K. Merton et al., *Reader in Bureaucracy* (Glencoe, Ill.: The Free Press, 1952). A stimulating book that attempts to systematize the behavioral principles and characteristics of bureaucracies is Anthony Downs's *Inside Bureaucracy* (Boston: Little, Brown & Co., 1966, paperback).

one another through a kind of internal market mechanism. The General Motors Corporation is a classic example of such corporate decentralization.[17] Or a Soviet-type command economy may dismantle its hierarchical structure, largely eliminate the command principle, and "marketize" itself, which is what happened in Yugoslavia in the early 1950s and in Hungary in 1968.[18]

CENTRALIZATION-
DECENTRALIZATION

Economic systems differ very markedly in the degree of centralization that attends decisions and functions within them. As we have seen, a market economy is a decentralized system in comparison with a command economy, but the degree of centralization (or decentralization) in each of these may also vary greatly. In a command economy, as in any formal organization, centralization (decentralization) means essentially the moving of decisions and functions to some higher (lower) level(s) in the formal hierarchy. In a market economy, where there is no overall formal hierarchy, centralization of economic decisions and functions means either (1) their transfer from the independent economic units to some governmental body, or (2) their transfer from a lower governmental level to a higher one (for example, from the local authority to the state government, or from the state to the federal government), or (3) to a higher level within the given governmental hierarchy.

So far we have been speaking of the centralization of *decisions* (otherwise known as the "centralization of authority") in the system. But we can also regard the problem of centralization from the standpoint of information. Does the information flow, in some sense, from the periphery to the center, from the bottom rungs of a hierarchical ladder to its top, and then back again? Or is it exchanged primarily among entities on more or less the same level? In a formal organization in which decisions are quite centralized the flow information is also usually quite centralized, for those who take the decisions sooner or later will also require and obtain a lot of information. This frequently is accompanied by a shrinking of the flow of information "horizontally" (on the same level). On the other hand, it is quite possible for information to be highly centralized but many decisions to be taken decentrally. An example is a central bank's macroeconomic regulation by means of the discount rate. The central bank continuously receives a great deal of information about the condition of the economy. This information is centralized in our sense. But to regulate the economy the

---

[17]The best-known study of decentralization in the General Motors Corporation is Peter F. Drucker's *The Concept of the Corporation* (New York: John Day, 1946; Mentor Books, paperback, 1964).

[18]On the other hand, there may also be good reasons for preserving a bureaucratic structure even where the organization could conceivably "marketize" itself internally. These reasons are typically related to the advantages of centralization, which are about to be taken up in this section.

central bank decides to change the discount rate at which it is prepared to lend. The discount rate and the many other interest rates that generally move with it are givens (parameters) for the many thousands of economic agents when they make their calculations and take their own decisions. The economy therefore responds in a certain and more or less predictable way. In this case, decision-making authority is decentralized, though information is centralized.

There is always a cost attached to obtaining and processing information and maintaining communication lines, and, other things equal, the more centralized the organization (or economy), the greater this cost. In fact, a large part of the resource commitment in any type of modern economy is devoted to this end.[19] The choice between more and less centralized economic institutions therefore hinges in some measure on the corresponding information cost. It follows that a major technological advance in this area, such as the invention and development of electronic computers for the storage and high-speed processing and retrieval of information, coupled with up-to-date means of high-speed communication, tends to make a greater degree of centralization more attractive. Some large U.S. corporations have been lately centralizing operations thanks to computers, and there is great interest along these lines in the Soviet Union, where the handling of information is voluminous and costly, and where the preference for centralization is strong on doctrinal and political grounds.

Advantages of Decentralization of Decisions

In the Western democratic countries, however, and especially in the United States, there is a strong general preference for decentralizing economic decisions and functions in society, in common with the preference for political decentralization. The reasons are not only, perhaps not mainly, economic. Thus, decentralization of economic functions within the context of a market economy tends to contribute to the dispersion of power, which in turn, as we have seen, tends to strengthen the bases of political and personal freedom. For those who make the decisions, it tends to make their work more satisfying, heightens their sense of responsibility and independence, promotes initiative and resourcefulness, and presumably contributes to the mature discharge of democratic responsibilities. These are realized best in a market economy and with a high degree of freedom of choice and opportunity.

But there are also more strictly economic considerations in favor of decentralization. Generally speaking, as we have mentioned, decentralization means shorter channels of communication; hence, lower cost, greater speed, and less risk of distortion in handling information—most important considerations where adaptation to changing conditions (fluctuations in demand, technical innova-

---

[19]Cf. Joseph L. Bower, "Planning Within the Firm," *The American Economic Review: Papers and Proceedings*, 60:2 (May 1970), pp. 186–94. Although the author does not expressly refer to the Soviet system, those familiar with it will immediately recognize the resemblance between it and Bower's corporate firm.

tions) and speed of response play an important role, especially in competitive situations. This is what we mean when we say that those "on the spot" can decide many things much better and much faster than can their superiors in a formal organization or some government official in a bureau. It is precisely with regard to this kind of adaptation, flexibility, and speed of response that the Soviet economy, with its very long lines of communication, tends to perform quite poorly. Moreover, to the extent that excessive centralization dampens incentives, initiative, and responsibility, it tends to justify itself and perhaps even to prompt further centralization. Here, again, the Soviet example is apposite.

Advantages of Centralization of Decisions

It would be wrong, however, to consider that all the advantages lie on the side of decentralization, as our prodemocratic biases might lead us to think, or that the arguments for centralization rest primarily on antidemocratic or power-grabbing instincts. Without ruling out these factors, we ought to recognize some very weighty reasons for centralization, whether within formal organizations (including the command economy) or in market economies.

One important reason is the need to safeguard or promote public interest and priorities. In all societies and organizations, the interests and values of particular individuals or groups need not coincide with those of the larger whole, nor is it always possible to so structure incentives and behavior rules as to channel their autonomous activities invariably into socially desirable directions. The more demanding the public interest and the greater the gap between official values and the interests of particular groups or individuals, the less adequate are individuals' incentives from the standpoint of society and the greater the need to centralize functions to avoid subverting the public interest and social priorities. It is partly in these terms that one can explain much of the extreme centralization in communist economies. But the same causes operate elsewhere, too; for example, in private business corporations.[20]

A closely related instance is the use of direct measures by central authorities to effect a quick, large-scale transfer of resources from one use to another, as in the case of the mobilization of men and productive capacity in wartime or for rapid industrialization under very adverse conditions. True, in some such cases—though not in all—the owners of the resources could be "bribed" to transfer them, but only at the price of a socially unacceptable redistribution of income and at the risk of setting off (or aggravating) an inflation.

Yet another reason for centralizing decisions relates to what the economist calls external economies and diseconomies. These are instances in which the full social benefits or costs of an activity do not or cannot enter into the individual

---

[20]The student may wish to list for himself by way of exercise the occupations and institutions in the American economy that are primarily concerned with collecting, processing, and transmitting the information on which economic decisions are based. Then consult Fritz Machlup, *The Production and Distribution of Knowledge in the United States* (Princeton: Princeton University Press, 1962).

firm's calculations simply because they are not "appropriable" by the firm. A private electric power company that builds a dam for power-generating purposes may thereby also diminish the risk of flood damage downstream, but nobody pays the company for the latter benefit and it does not enter into the company's calculations whether to build the dam at all. On the other hand, a factory that pollutes a river may cause considerable damage downstream, but these social costs would find no reflection in its own profit and loss statement.[21] In the first case the power company may find it uneconomic from its own standpoint to build the dam, although the broader social calculus would favor it. A possible solution in this case would be to have some public authority build the dam. In the second case, the factory may not be justified from a social standpoint, although it may be profitable by itself. A good deal of centralization—through government regulation, taxation or subsidies, nationalization, or outright prohibition—is prompted precisely by such instances and aims to bring private and social costs or benefits closer together.

Another frequent reason for the centralization of certain economic functions or decisions in a democratic society no less than in any other is the need to avoid socially disruptive, harmful, or politically unacceptable results that bargaining in the marketplace (or refusal to bargain by some party) may bring about. In this general class fall such activities of government in all democratic advanced countries as intervention in labor disputes and legal provisions for orderly procedure for their resolution, support of farm incomes, antimonopoly legislation, and so forth. We shall return to these forms of government intervention in our discussion of the market economy in Chapter 5. Although the political procedures and administrative techniques may be different, governments, including those in charge of command economies, also have to face the general problem of resolving conflicts between broad socioeconomic groups (even if these groups may not openly organize to advance their interests, as they do in democracies).

In no society or organization are the circumstances that prompt centralization or decentralization quite static. Conditions, values, problems change constantly, sometimes at an almost imperceptible pace, sometimes in large jumps. The issue is never finally resolved.

[21]External economies and diseconomies are sometimes called "neighborhood effects" or simply "externalities." The example of the dam is discussed at greater length by Otto Eckstein in *Public Finance* (Englewood Cliffs, N.J.: Prentice-Hall, 1967), this series, pp. 9–11.

Ideologies and "Isms"

CHAPTER THREE

An *ideology* is a set of ideas, more or less shared by a social group (for example, a nation or class), that (1) represents a certain picture of social reality, and (2) sets up desirable values and goals for society to strive for, or preserve. We may not always be aware of it, but few of us are without a set of notions and ideas that in their totality form some kind of ideology. In any society there is a constant interaction among reality, ideology, and the socioeconomic institutions (system).

Needless to say, ideologies do not fall from the sky. They arise in specific historical contexts, in response to definite circumstances and needs and in relation to other sets of ideas. But it would be an oversimplification to hold that they merely express the self-interests of individuals and groups, if only because such self-interest is not always easy to identify. Nor do ideologies remain stable; rather, they tend to evolve in response to changing circumstances, sometimes so imperceptibly that the process is not evident to contemporaries. An ideology that remains unbending in the face of a changed reality—that is, a *dogma*—cannot hope to survive very long, and action based on it cannot hope to be successful in the long run. The durable ideologies are the flexible and adaptable ones, which often also means the less precise ones.

An *industrializing ideology*—an important phenomenon among the less industrialized countries in the modern world—typically sees highly developed industry (especially "heavy" industry) as the key to domestic prosperity and to national power and prestige in the world. It is frequently used to justify radical changes in society, to elicit political support and even heavy sacrifices for the sake of industrialization from the population, and to legitimize a given developmental strategy and a given politico-economic system. A very common key ingredient of such an ideology is *nationalism*, often coupled with fear or envy of powerful

36

neighbors or colonial powers. Examples are Imperial Germany and Tsarist Russia before the First World War, and Japan before the First and Second World Wars, and dozens of underdeveloped countries today. Even present-day communism—which has become largely an extreme form of industrializing ideology nearly everywhere it is in power—is heavily suffused with nationalism. In systemic terms, as a rule, the more pronounced the quest for rapid industrialization and the more backward the initial conditions, the more is production stressed at the cost of equity and individual security, the higher the degree of centralization of political and social processes, the greater the role of the state, and the more extreme the economic (and political) means employed to attain and maintain rapid growth.[1]

Ours is an age of "isms": capitalism, socialism, communism, Marxism, fascism, Leninism, Titoism, revisionism, African Socialism, and so on ad infinitum. They stand for political movements, ideologies, doctrines, policies, economic and social systems, utopian dreams. Only too often they also serve as facile labels that do us dubious service. Their very proliferation attests to the growing inadequacy of most of the old labels to represent something definite, which only confirms the old truth that neither ideas nor events stand still.

Thus, it behooves us to avoid thinking in terms of discrete "grand alternatives," to try to escape from the "tyranny of the 'isms,' "[2] and to appreciate the great variety of actual—and even more so, potential—institutional patterns. Yet to recognize this much is not to dismiss entirely their analytical meaningfulness or their historical importance. We therefore devote the rest of this chapter to a brief survey of some of the most important "isms" as they bear on economic systems.

CAPITALISM

"Capitalism" is a word we constantly use but rarely stop to define with any degree of precision. For present purposes let *capitalism* denote an eco-

---

[1]A convenient, brief discussion of the major ideologies of American capitalism in the postwar era may be found in R. Joseph Monsen, Jr., *Modern American Capitalism: Ideologies and Issues* (Boston: Houghton Mifflin paperback, 1963). A more detailed treatment is in Francis X. Sutton, Seymour E. Harris, Carl Kaysen, and James Tobin, *The American Business Creed* (Cambridge: Harvard University Press, 1956; Schocken paperback, 1962). Regarding industrializing ideologies see, for example, Alexander Gerschenkron, *Economic Backwardness in Historical Perspective* (Cambridge: Harvard University Press, 1962), especially Chap. 1. For the web of relations between ideology, "industrializing elites," industrial management, and labor in the process of industrialization see also the following books: Clark Kerr, John T. Dunlop, Frederick H. Harbison, and Charles A. Myers, *Industrialism and Industrial Man* (Cambridge: Harvard University Press, 1960; Galaxy paperback, 1964); and Reinhard Bendix, *Work and Authority in Industry* (New York: John Wiley & Sons, Inc., 1956). The argument of Clark Kerr et al., is conveniently summarized in their "Industrialism and World Society," *Harvard Business Review* 39, no. 1 (January–February 1961), pp. 113–26.

[2]These phrases belong to Robert A. Dahl and Charles E. Lindblom, respectively a political scientist and an economist, who in their important book on social systems and processes, *Politics, Economics, and Welfare* (New York: Harper paperback, 1953), especially Chap. 1, take a strong position along these lines.

nomic system in which productive assets are predominantly privately owned and production is primarily for sale.[3] Advanced Western economies also contain smaller or larger publicly owned sectors; they are mixed economies, in the sense in which we have already used this term.

The private owner's object is to earn a handsome profit from the use of his productive assets. This much is obvious—and the profit motive, coupled with the institution of inheritance and bolstered by the law of contract, is the great engine of capitalism; indeed, the greatest source of economic drive in all history to date. But what is socially acceptable by way of profit-making in one epoch is not in the next. Laws and mores change. In the sixteenth century it was regarded as perfectly proper to seize on the high seas another country's treasure ships, which themselves may have been carrying precious metal that today we would regard as no better than looted or obtained through inhuman exploitation of native miners. Subsequent centuries, through most of the nineteenth, witnessed slave traffic and slave labor on a vast scale. And even as little as half a century ago, much business in this country was conducted with a disregard for the public, workers, investors, and natural resources that would be shocking and often illegal today. The progressive imposition of social—moral as well as legal—restraints on profit-making[4] need not mean an impairment of capitalism over the long run. On the contrary, by adapting the limits of private profit-making to the (themselves evolving) standards of humanitarianism and justice, and by assimilating various other measures of social welfare, capitalism has tended to gain in popular acceptance precisely in those countries that have had the longest experience with it.

Private ownership, free enterprise, production for the market, profit-making—these are not only economic phenomena. They set the tone for all aspects

[3]The second part of this definition is necessary in order to exclude subsistence economies, in which the means of production, albeit very simple, are usually also privately owned.

The beginnings of modern analysis of capitalism as a social and historical phenomenon lie primarily with Karl Marx and his associate Friedrich Engels, whose life spans covered nearly the whole nineteenth century. Their approach and conclusions, which we take up briefly later in this chapter, have profoundly influenced, whether positively or negatively, directly or indirectly, nearly all subsequent writings on capitalism. Among other writers of note we may mention two German social scientists, Werner Sombart and, again, Max Weber. (For an excellent summary of their views see Talcott Parsons, " 'Capitalism' in Recent German Literature," *The Journal of Political Economy* 36, no. 6 (1928), pp. 641–61, and 37, no. 1 (1929), pp. 31–51. In his classic work, *The Theory of Economic Development* (Cambridge: Harvard University Press, 1934; original German edition in 1911) the Austrian economist, later Harvard Professor, Joseph A. Schumpeter, placed the innovative and creative functions of capitalism at the center of his analysis. In another famous book, *Capitalism, Socialism, and Democracy* (New York: Harper, 1942), published three decades later, Schumpeter saw a mature sluggish, corporate capitalism that was on the verge of evolving into socialism. A system of "countervailing power," of large economic power blocs in balance, is the main theme of John K. Galbraith's *American Capitalism: The Concept of Countervailing Power* (Cambridge: Houghton Mifflin Co., 1952). Of approximately the same vintage but less unorthodox in approach is David M. Wright's *Capitalism* (New York: McGraw-Hill Book Co. Inc., 1951; Chicago: Henry Regnery Co., paperback, 1962). A convenient list of many recent American works on U.S. capitalism may be found in the bibliography to Monsen's *Modern American Capitalism*, cited in note 1.

[4]We noted some in our discussion of private property, above.

of society and all sides of man's life and culture. Those who have studied the appearance and development of capitalism in historical perspective—great thinkers such as Adam Smith, Karl Marx, Werner Sombart, Max Weber, John A. Hobson, Thorstein Veblen, Joseph A. Schumpeter, and John M. Keynes—stressed the characteristic spirit, mores, values, and attitudes of the capitalist society, and contrasted it sharply in these regards with preceding historical eras.

Earlier Capitalism

As for capitalism's earlier stages, the aspects of its spirit that have been frequently stressed are enterprise, venturesomeness, acquisitiveness, competitiveness, and the urge to innovate. The dominant values that have characterized capitalism (especially in the Anglo-Saxon countries) are individualism, material progress, and political liberty. Writers such as Weber and Sombart stressed rationality as a characteristic attitude (or, to them, "spirit") of capitalism that distinguished it sharply from earlier eras. By "rationality" they meant the deliberate subjugation of means to definite ends, especially to the end of pecuniary gain, a careful weighing of alternatives, the keeping of systematic records, and, on the negative side, break with tradition, superstition, and magic.

It is often thought that the ideology of early capitalism was typically that of *laissez faire*[5]—no interference in economic activity by government, whose functions would be limited to that of a "night watchman"—that is, a mere protector of life and property and (one should add) enforcer of contracts. This is not correct. Even in Britain, the most advanced capitalist country for several centuries until the last quarter of the nineteenth century, the ideology of *laissez faire* prevailed for only a relatively short span of time; say, during the second half of the nineteenth century. Before that, in England as in most other countries in Europe, the prevailing doctrine was *mercantilism*—the doctrine that the state has the right and duty to both regulate and protect private enterprise, regarded as an instrument for the state's greater power and glory. Even in the heyday of individualistic capitalism in the United States—say, between the Civil War and the Great Depression—the dominant ideology was that of not pure but modified *laissez faire*, one which, on one hand, diluted free competition with tariff protection and large federal subsidies for railroad construction, and on the other hand increasingly accepted government regulation of public utilities and "trustbusting." In Germany, France, Russia, and Japan—all relative latecomers to industrialization—*laissez faire* was regarded as a luxury that only the most advanced capitalist countries could afford. In these countries, under the impact of nationalist sentiments, active government protection and promotion of domestic private (and sometimes state-owned) industry were readily accepted and sought in the decades before the First World War. At the same time, govern-

---

[5]Literally, "let them do"—that is, leave business alone. The phrase was coined by French economists of the later part of the eighteenth century known as *physiocrats*, who opposed government interference with business.

ment enforcement of competition found little favor, and the monopoly, the cartel, and the powerful bank became the dominant capitalist institutions on the Continent.

The growth of capitalism, and particularly of capitalist industrialization, meant also the creation of large working classes in the more advanced countries. Often crowded in miserable slums in the new cities that industry spawned, working long hours for low wages and under harsh and unhealthy conditions, deprived of the stabilizing institutions of the villages whence many of them came, and for decades left out of the orderly political processes—the workers of Europe[6] were at once indispensable to the success of capitalism and its greatest social and political problem throughout this earlier phase of industrial capitalism. It was for and among them, sparked by ideas of intellectuals often of middle-class origin, that radical ideologies and political movements, especially socialism, developed to challenge the capitalist order.

Contemporary Capitalism

Capitalism's prospects did not appear very bright on the whole immediately after the Second World War. True, it had been capitalism that brought about the remarkable advances and productivity and material well being in the course of the nineteenth and early decades of the twentieth centuries. But capitalism was also associated in the minds of many with terrible wars, the business cycle culminating in the world depression of the thirties, great inequalities in income and wealth, colonialism, and much social tension. To communists, its end would inevitably arrive through revolution and class war, hastened by the alleged incapacity of capitalism to deal with its own problems. The great enhancement of Soviet power and prestige after the war, the communist takeovers in Eastern Europe and China, and the rise of large communist parties in some Western countries (notably Italy and France) made their prognosis that much more telling. Democratic socialists in the Western countries were looking forward to the peaceable demise of capitalism via the ballot box, and were much encouraged by the electoral victory of the Labor Party in Britain in 1945. Others who were neither revolutionaries nor radicals, as for instance Joseph Schumpeter[7] at Harvard, were predicting a slow but inevitable loss of vigor and enterprise on the part of the bureaucratized large capitalist firms and the consequent gradual transformation of capitalism into socialism.

Things did not work out this way. In the two decades following the war, capitalism not only proved its staying power but in addition exhibited greater dynamism and creative capacity than ever before, both in the advanced industrial countries and in a number of less-developed ones. In some countries—

[6]Thanks to its early establishment of political democracy, its very favorable population: resource ratio, its frontier of settlement, the ethnic multiplicity of its working class, and a number of other factors, the United States shared these conditions and problems to a much smaller extent, of course.

[7]*Capitalism, Socialism, and Democracy* (New York: Harper, 1942).

especially in Western Germany, Italy, Austria, France, and above all, in Japan —the growth of production and the rise in average consumption levels have been remarkably rapid. At the same time, business fluctuations and unemployment have been minimized in the advanced capitalist countries (though less in the United States and Canada than elsewhere). However, it is not our purpose here to recount economic history; the interested reader is referred to Richard T. Gill's book in the present series[8] and to the many references therein. Some of the salient systemic properties of modern capitalism we shall be taking up in Chapter 4. Rather, at this point we shall cast a brief glance at the "ism" side of the subject; that is to say, at some of the basic institutional, ideological, and attitudinal differences between the capitalism that has obtained in the advanced countries since World War II and the earlier varieties.[9]

Perhaps the most significant feature of postwar capitalism has been the politico-economic equilibrium among, and mutual acceptance of, business (especially, big business), government, and organized labor in the advanced countries. In most cases, to this pattern of coexisting forces should be added two others: agriculture and small business, both impinging on the national economic picture as much through political channels as through strictly economic ones. Business has come to accept the active intervention of government in the economy for the sake of enhancing economic stability, promoting growth, reducing insecurity, and softening the economic inequities generated by the marketplace and exacerbated by inequalities in individuals' endowments or bargaining power. In some countries, private business has also acquiesced in the presence of substantial nationalized sectors and in active economic planning by the government. Furthermore, business has accepted collective bargaining with powerful organized labor as a regular and permanent arrangement. These attitudes, bolstered by the growing sense of professionalism on the part of management in large corporations, have been reflected (particularly in America) in the new "managerial ideology," which, without abandoning the profit objective, stresses management's responsibility to various elements within and without the corporation (employees, customers, suppliers, the general public, as well as the stockholders).[10]

On its part, labor has tended to accept the existing social order and to moderate its political goals. This has been to some extent true even in those countries, such as Italy and France, where a dominant segment of the labor movement has been under communist control ever since the war. The declining militancy of the various national labor movements has in turn contributed to a bifurcation of the left in the industrialized, democratic countries. Most of the

[8]*Economic Development: Past and Present* (Englewood Cliffs, N.J.: Prentice-Hall, 1963).

[9]For a good overview of these changes as regards the United States and Western Europe, see Calvin B. Hoover, *The Economy, Liberty, and the State* (New York: Twentieth Century Fund, 1959; also Anchor paperback, 1961), Chaps. 7–9.

[10]Cf. Monsen, *Modern American Capitalism,* Sutton *American Business Creed* and the essays by Robert L. Heilbroner, Earl F. Cheit, and Paul A. Samuelson in Cheit (ed.), *The Business Establishment* (New York: Wiley, 1964).

left, including particularly the bulk of the labor movement and political parties closely associated with it, has moderated its previously radical and revolutionary programs. As a result, the socialist—and even some of the communist—parties in such countries have shifted progressively toward the middle of the political spectrum. In some such countries, the bulk of the labor movement can scarcely be described as left-of-center any more. At the same time, in nearly all the advanced, democratic countries, many small parties have sprung up in reaction to this tendency and in order to uphold various revolutionary and radical ideologies (Maoist, Castroist, Trotskyist, anarchist, "New Left", and so forth). In sum, for many advanced capitalist countries the conflict between capital and labor, though by no means extinguished, is no longer the paramount social problem it once was. Lately it has been rivaled by the problem of adjusting the less modern sectors, small-scale agriculture and small business, to the needs of a modern economy without undue human hardship or political instability, and such nonclass issues as the preservation of the environment.

ANTICAPITALIST "ISMS"

From the beginning, industrial capitalism induced a series of critical and hostile reactions which took the form of various radical ideologies and political movements, most of which fall under the very broad rubric of socialism. In turn, many (though far from all) of the socialist ideas and movements of the last hundred years have been the direct or indirect offspring of two towering intellectual and revolutionary figures of the nineteenth century, both Germans but long-time residents of England, Karl Marx (1818–1883) and his close collaborator Friedrich Engels (1820–1895). For over a century capitalism and socialism have been in continuous and close reciprocal relationship. For over half a century a third element, communism, has been interacting with the first two. In the process, all three have been substantially affected, though in different ways and to unequal degrees. The rest of this chapter takes up Marxism, communism, and socialism—their social and philosophical origins, evolution, and present state.[11]

Reactions to Early Industrialization

The negative features of early capitalist industrialization, which we have already briefly mentioned, produced several types of anticapitalistic response. There were those among the educated classes—shocked with William Blake

---

[11]We have space here only for the briefest treatment. The interested reader is referred to Carl Landauer's extensive and thorough *European Socialism: A History of Ideas and Movements* (Berkeley: University of California Press, 1959), 2 vols., which contains a long bibliography in Vol. 2. *Socialism and American Life* (Princeton: Princeton University Press, 1952), edited by Donald D. Egbert and Stow Persons, may surprise the contemporary reader as it brings out the place of socialism in the history of this country. A most readable and at the same time scholarly history of socialist ideas up to 1917 is Edmund Wilson's *To the Finland Station* (New York: Doubleday & Co. Inc., 1940; also in paperback).

(1757–1827) by the desecration of "England's green and pleasant land," or of other countries, by the "dark, Satanic Mills"—who romanticized the past and who would have, if they could, stopped and reversed the historic process.[12] There were some among ordinary workers, like the English "Luddites" of 1811–1812, who gave vent to their misery by smashing the machines. There were others, usually among the more skilled workers, who tried to organize labor unions, often in the face of police repression as well as the hostility of employers. Lastly there were the "utopian socialists"—Frenchmen like Saint-Simon (1760–1825), Fourier (1772–1837), and Cabet (1788–1858), and the indefatigable Scottish industrialist Robert Owen (1771–1858)—who saw the root of social evil in the existing institutions, and especially in private property and selfishness; who drew up blueprints for a more perfect society, usually based on communistic or cooperative principles of work and distribution of income; and who (or whose followers) set up a good number of model and typically short-lived communities.[13]

Unlike the "utopians," Marx and Engels sought to discover the inexorable laws of history and of society, to delineate the inevitable future. Accordingly, they called their variety of socialism *scientific*; for the utopian socialists and their blueprints of ideal communities, Marx[14] had nothing but scorn.

His historical determinism was only one of many ways in which Marx was a product of his own era. His belief in the powers of reason and science as applied to man, for prediction as well as for analysis, and in the perfectibility of man, he derived from the Enlightenment of the preceding generations. His political economy stemmed largely from that of the English Classical School of the late eighteenth and early nineteenth centuries. His philosophy rested on German philosophy of the same period, especially on that of Hegel (1770–1831). His emphasis on class conflict was strongly colored by the experience of early industrial capitalism. His appreciation of the role of revolutions in history was greatly affected by the imprint left by the French Revolution of 1789 and by subsequent upheavals in Europe, especially those of 1848 and the Paris Commune of 1871.

Marx was a very prolific writer. *The Communist Manifesto*, written jointly with Engels on the eve of the revolutionary events of 1848, is one of the great political documents of all time.[15] His magnum opus is *Capital* (three volumes, first published in 1867, 1885, and 1894), which presents an exhaustive analysis of the development and functioning of the capitalist economy. There are few

---

[12]An excellent discussion of such "social-minded conservatives" of that era and of other responses to early capitalism will be found in Landauer, *European Socialism*, Chap. 1.

[13]Many of these were in the United States, of which the two most famous were Owen's New Harmony (est. 1825) in Indiana and the Fourierist Brook Farm in Massachusetts during the 1840s.

[14]For the sake of brevity we shall henceforth refer to Marx alone, while always remembering Engels' close relation to him. Notice also the distinction between the adjectives *Marxian* and *Marxist*. "Marxian" pertains to Marx himself; "Marxist" pertains to "Marxism"—that is, everything that in some sense takes its origin from him and his ideas.

[15]There are many editions of this document in English. One with a very helpful introduction and annotations by Samuel H. Beer, and with important brief selections from other Marxian works, is published by Appleton-Century-Crofts, Inc. (New York: 1955) in their Crofts Classics series.

aspects of philosophy or society that Marx did not address himself to, usually at great length. Marxism is an all-embracing world-view; it purports to explain and interpret all significant aspects of social life and thought on the basis of certain basic principles and laws, and likewise to predict the future of humanity.

THE MARXIAN THEORY
OF HISTORY

The Marxian theory of history belongs to the family of economic interpretations of history (hence, "historical *materialism*"). To Marx and his followers it is the economic facts of life ("the basis") that determine the nature of other aspects of society ("the superstructure," such as law, culture, religion, art, philosophy, and so forth) at any given epoch in history. More specifically, the decisive economic factor is the given period's *mode of production*. This somewhat vague notion encompasses both society's production capacity and its level of technology ("productive forces"), and the relation of various classes (landlords, capitalists, workers) to the production process ("production relations").[16] Depending on the mode of production, there is or is not *exploitation* in a given society, exploitation being the appropriation of the product of labor of some class or classes (slaves, serfs, workers) by others (slave owners, feudal lords, capitalists). The antagonism between classes is a central theme in the Marxist view of history: "The history of all hitherto existing society is the history of class struggle," Marx and Engels wrote in the *Communist Manifesto*.

According to Marx, all mankind sooner or later must pass through the same succession of six major historical stages: primitive (tribal) communism; slavery; feudalism; capitalism; socialism; and communism.[17] Under primitive communism, and again under socialism and full communism, the means of production are owned in common, and hence at these stages there is (in Marxian terms) no division into classes and no exploitation. In the three intermediate stages—slavery, feudalism, and capitalism—the means of production are owned or controlled by small segments of the population (the "exploiting class"), with the majority of the population toiling for their benefit. Of course, when Marx and Engels were writing, there was yet no socialist society (let alone a communist one) in existence; but they were predicting its inevitable arrival, just as

[16]Indeed, in Marx, classes are *defined* in terms of their relation to production. By contrast, modern social science avoids a fixed definition of class and prefers to adapt it to the purpose of the given investigation.

[17]In the earlier Marxist writings, socialism and communism were generally regarded as two substages—the "lower" and the "higher"—of the postcapitalist stage. Also, lately there is a tendency among non-Marxist scholars to refer to communism in this sense as "full communism" in order to distinguish it from the other meanings of the word (for instance, a political movement), a convention that we shall follow henceforth.

they were predicting that those societies that had not yet arrived at capitalism would of necessity get there in time.

Socialism and Full Communism

Although in their view both socialism and full communism are characterized by the absence of private property and other common features, Marx and his followers distinguish sharply between the two. (1) *Productivity*: Under socialism society is as yet unable to produce enough to meet all its material needs; under full communism it is able to do so, it has reached "abundance."[18] (2) *The nature of man as producer*: Under full communism, it is expected, work will be man's "second nature," he will work willingly, cheerfully, efficiently, and highly productively without requiring any direct incentive, such as a wage. Under socialism, however, man is not yet sufficiently reformed in this direction; he still requires material incentives to work enough and well. Hence the famous Marxian formula expressing the principles of income distribution in the two cases: under socialism, "from each according to his ability, to each according to his *labor*"; under full communism, "from each according to his ability, to each according to his *need*." Since both scarcity and the need for individual incentive will disappear with the arrival of full communism, there will be no more use for money, prices, finance, and the like. These too will disappear under full communism, according to Marx. So will the state, for in Marx's view the function of the state is to support whatever exploiting class may be in power at a given time. No scarcity, no classes, no exploitation, no state.

Notice that the official Soviet ideology does not claim that the USSR has arrived at full communism yet. Rather, it claims to have arrived at socialism and to be building the *basis* of (full) communism.[19] We need not stop to consult our crystal ball as to whether it, or any other country, will ever arrive at full communism *in the Marxian sense*.[20] But we may remark that it is to Marx's great credit to have realized, over a century ago, that the progress of technology is pushing mankind toward ultimate abundance, and to have seriously posed the question of what society will be like when (we may add: and if) it gets there.

Marxian Historical Dynamic

Technology is the basic dynamic force in history, according to Marx. Each of the above-named historical stages corresponds to a technological level; hence their sequence and inevitability. Unlike many other stage-scheme builders—of

[18]But notice that "need" and "abundance" are very vague notions which have never been satisfactorily defined for this purpose in Marxist writings.

[19]For this reason it is not at all paradoxical (as is sometimes assumed) that the Soviet Union retains wages, other forms of individual material incentive, prices, money, and so forth. Many Western socialists deny that socialism obtains in the Soviet Union and other communist countries, because for them socialism means primarily social justice and political freedom.

[20]Of course, it is possible to arrive at something different from what Marx envisaged and still call it full communism. There is a perceptible tendency in Soviet writings toward such redefinition.

45

whom there were a good number in the nineteenth century, especially among the so-called German Historical School of economists—Marx had a definite mechanism for transition from one stage to the next. As he saw it, the progress of technology builds up and develops the "productive forces" of a country. The institutions, however—the "production relations" in particular—for a while change little. At first, the production relations "correspond" to the productive forces; they enable the technology and capacity of the economy to produce rather fully. But with time, the production relations tend to lag more and more behind the development of productive forces; eventually, they become a hindrance to the full utilization of the latter. In the meantime, the development of productive forces gives rise also to a new class, which in time seizes power and refashions society's institutions to its own liking and needs—that is, produces a new set of production relations that is again in harmony with the level of development of productive forces. But the advance of technology does not stop here; the process resumes anew, propelling society through another epoch of social tension, revolution, and the emergence of yet another historical stage—until finally socialism takes over from capitalism; the working class—the last in the historical succession of dominant classes—captures power, and through the further progress of technology *and* the reeducation of man leads society into full communism.

MARXIAN ANALYSIS OF CAPITALISM

The capitalists' success necessarily creates a large working class— in Marxist language, a *proletariat*—which has no source of livelihood other than the sale of its own labor power.[21] With time, the inexorable working of economic forces causes the other classes effectively to disappear and society comes to consist of just two mutually hostile classes: the capitalists, who are the owners, managers, and employers of labor; and the propertyless proletariat. Under capitalism, the bourgeoisie controls the state—that is to say, the ultimate instruments of force and coercion which administer society for the bourgeoisie's benefit.

As we have mentioned, *Capital* is devoted to an extensive and incisive analysis of the economics of capitalism. A basic Marxian premise is the *labor theory of value*, which rests on the axiom that all economic value is produced by labor (and not by any other factors of production), and argues that all goods produced for the market ("commodities" in the Marxian terminology) tend to have prices which are proportional to their "socially necessary labor content."[22]

---

[21]Much Marxist terminology has a quaint ring to American ears. The *proletariat* and the *bourgeoisie* are the working and capitalist classes, respectively. *Proletarian, bourgeois* are the corresponding adjectives; as nouns, they designate individual members of the two classes.

[22]Marx borrowed the labor theory of value from the English Classical School, especially David Ricardo (1772–1823), but he adapted it for his purposes—namely, to show the existence of exploitation

According to the Marxian view, labor power under capitalism is just another commodity. Hence, labor's wages conform to the same price-forming law as do prices of commodities in general; they are at the level which is just necessary for the "reproduction" of the labor force—for subsistence and bringing up the next generation of workers. (Marx postulated the existence of continuous unemployment that would prevent wages from being bid up above the subsistence level.) But under capitalism, technology is so far advanced that the average worker can produce far above his and his family's own subsistence needs. This excess, "surplus value," is appropriated by the capitalist, from which the latter derives his own consumption needs and (most important) the savings to finance further "accumulations" (investment). A part of the surplus value also goes to other property-owning classes—as interest to financiers and as rent to the owners of land and other natural resources. At the same time, the appropriation of the surplus value by capitalists constitutes his "exploitation" of the workers.

The dynamics of capitalism occupies the center of the Marxian economic analysis. Though, at first, capitalism constitutes an unprecedented engine of material progress, eventually it *must* run into greater and greater difficulties and cause growing misery to the vast majority of those living under it. Ownership of capital—and with it, by definition, all power—become more and more concentrated with time; the polarization of society is aggravated. In the course of their constant search for profits, capitalists overinvest, which leads to a long-run decline in the rate of profit, and also to sharp periodic declines, the so-called "crises."[23] And meanwhile, the proletariat becomes poorer and poorer (the so-called "immiseration theory").[24] Revolutionary feelings among the workers mount, until at some propitious moment a successful proletarian revolution overthrows capitalism.

To the cause of such a revolution Marx devoted a large part of his life. He died in 1883; Engels, in 1895. As the nineteenth century gave way to the twentieth, Marxist parties had become by far the most important radical parties in the world, except in the English-speaking countries. And at the same turn

---

under capitalism (see next paragraph in text) and the inevitability of its eventual doom. Notice that one must distinguish between (a) the source of value in a philosophical or metaphysical sense, in which case one can call it virtually anything to one's liking, and (b) value in the sense of relative price of a commodity (in relation to other commodities) as it in fact appears on the market in either the short or the long run, in which case one must refer to a positive theory of price formation (for instance, supply-and-demand), and (c) value in the normative sense—that is, what should the value (price) of a given good be given certain overall economic objectives and a certain mechanism of resource allocation in society. A modern "Western" economist would say that prices would indeed tend to be formed in a capitalist market economy as the Marxian theory of value would have it if (1) labor were the only scarce factor of production and if (2) one considered only the long run. The first condition is unrealistic; the second, not exhaustive.

[23]A careful survey of the Marxian theory of crises and some of its implications by a leading American Marxist scholar will be found in Pauḷ M. Sweezy, *The Theory of Capitalist Development: Principles of Marxian Political Economy* (New York: Oxford University Press, 1942), Chaps. 8–12.

[24]There has been considerable debate whether Marx meant that the proletariat becomes only *relatively* poorer, or also *absolutely* so. The point is of historical and theoretical importance, although for lack of space we have no choice except to bypass it here.

of the century there began a process of repeated fissioning of the Marxist movement, so that today the historical progeny of Marx and Engels include such militant parties and ideologies as Maoism and Castroism, and such moderate ones—in some cases all but rejecting their Marxist heritage—as the social democratic parties in Western Europe.

It is easy to find fault with Marx. Though his theory of history has been quite influential, most Western historians today reject its brand of economic determinism and its rigid stage scheme. His economic theory was primitive even for his own day, but he must be given credit for pioneering in the theory of business cycles. Of all the modern social sciences it is perhaps sociology that owes most—directly and indirectly—to Marx as the first modern political sociologist.[25]

Nor did his prognoses fare better. True, as he expected, industrialism grew and spread on the face of the globe, and technology continued its rapid advance. But industrial society did not become progressively more polarized into the wealthy few and the proletarian mass. Nor did the workers become progressively poorer. On the contrary, in the advanced countries, the material levels of living of the masses rose decisively, a large and generally conservative white-collar class came to play an increasingly important role in social and political life, and the revolutionary fervor of the working class has been on the wane. Marxist (communist) regimes did gain power in about a dozen countries, but almost invariably under conditions that were the very opposite of those anticipated by Marx. Withal, for better or worse, no single individual in the past hundred years has had a greater influence on history than this impecunious researcher in the British Museum, writer of ponderous German tomes little read in his own day, and contentious, ill-tempered leader of a small revolutionary sect.

LENINISM AND ITS OFFSHOOTS

Vladimir Lenin (1870–1924), founder of the Bolshevik (Communist) party of Russia and of the Communist International, leader of the successful Bolshevik Revolution in 1917, and founder of the Soviet state, was much more than a fervent follower of Marx. He was above all an innovator, adapting Marxism to new conditions and pushing its theory and practice in new directions, the importance of which for our century's history cannot be overrated.

First, drawing on a long Russian tradition of revolutionary action, Lenin

[25]See Schumpeter, *Capitalism, Socialism, and Democracy*, Chaps. 1–4, for an engaging discussion of Marx as prophet and scholar.

developed the notion of a professional, conspiratorial party, internally authoritarian and highly disciplined, as the instrument of revolution.[26]

Second, Lenin refused to admit the necessity of waiting for the maturation of capitalism in order to carry out a successful socialist revolution, as Marx's more orthodox followers insisted. According to them—and to Marx himself—the establishment of socialism in a backward, agrarian country was an absurdity. But Lenin saw that the revolutionary potential of a poor, disaffected, land-hungry peasantry could be harnessed for its own ends by a party speaking in the name of the working class. The political chaos, social upheaval, economic difficulties, and revulsion against war that characterized Russia in 1917, after three disastrous years of participation in the First World War, gave the Bolsheviks their opportunity.

The Leninist formula of seizure of power with its four basic ingredients—determined leadership by a small revolutionary elite, economic backwardness, a disaffected peasantry, and war against an invader or a colonial power—worked again during and after the Second World War in Yugoslavia, China, Vietnam, and—in a somewhat modified way—in Cuba in the late fifties. The Leninist way, rather than the classical Marxist way of revolution by the working class, is the only way in which communists have gained power in Russia or elsewhere, apart from being brought to power by dint of Soviet military force.[27] Yet the weakness of the Leninist formula is inseparable from its success. When power is seized by a highly authoritarian small party whose ideology is not shared at the time of the takeover by the bulk of the population, when especially the social class that is the instrument of victory—the peasantry—has aspirations very different from those of the communist leaders, when the new regime feels that it must engage as soon as possible in feverish industrialization at virtually any cost, and when it regards itself hostile to all or most of the world at large—under these conditions, as the history of communist regimes amply shows, political democracy has three strikes against it, and the door is open to the severest political repression and terror.

Today, Lenin is a highly revered figure among all communists despite the profound differences among them. Indeed, the greater the ideological conflict among the various factions of communists, the greater the tendency for each to build up Lenin's image while claiming fidelity to his ideas. As a result, "Leninism" today stands for whatever orthodoxy the given brand of communism may wish to uphold.[28]

[26]More correctly, Lenin elaborated and grafted onto the Marxist world-view the theory of professional conspiratorial activity that originated with Russian revolutionaries in earlier decades. The written material on Lenin and Leninism is very large. A comprehensive analysis is Alfred G. Meyer's *Leninism* (Cambridge: Harvard University Press, 1957).

[27]In Chile, a Marxist coalition including communists took power democratically as a minority regime in 1970, to be ousted in a military coup in 1973.

[28]Totalitarianism has been defined in several ways. One may think of it as a dictatorial regime which, through a single mass party and police intimidation, seeks to exercise *total* control over society and to maximally impose its ideology on the mind and the spirit of its subjects.

STALINISM, MAOISM, CASTROISM

Lenin died only six years after the Bolshevik Revolution and before the Soviet economy had completed its reconstruction from the ravages and strains of the First World War and the Civil War. The USSR as we know it today—economically, socially, and politically—is largely the creation of Joseph Stalin (1879–1953), who seized power after several years of bitter struggle against other communist leaders and ruled the country for the next quarter of a century, until his death, as the most absolute of modern dictators. Today, "Stalinism" is a virtual synonym for the highest degree of ruthless and bloody totalitarianism.[29] And, unlike Marxism or even Leninism, it is not so much a coherent system of ideas as a way of doing things.

Two latter-day offshoots of Leninism are Maoism and Castroism (also known as Fidelism), that is, the ideas and policies of Mao Tse-tung and of Fidel Castro, the dictatorial leaders of China and Cuba since the communist take-overs in the two countries. They share with Leninism the emphasis on dictatorial, single-party rule and on seizure of power long before capitalism has done its task of industrializing the country (in China, even more than in Lenin's Russia, by harnessing peasant discontent). But they differ from Leninism and Stalinism in regard to the internal structure of the economy and the preference for moral against material incentives, as will be discussed in Chapter 7.[30]

DEMOCRATIC SOCIALISM

If the authoritarian, more or less revolutionary communist parties of the world represent one major branch that grew from the Marxist trunk, the moderate, reformist, democratic socialist parties of Western Europe and some other advanced countries of the noncommunist world represent the other. It would be difficult to imagine more dissimilar political cousins than, say, the Social Democratic party of Sweden, on the one hand, and the Chinese Communist party on the other. Present-day communist regimes are primarily polit-

---

[29]A perceptive discussion of Leninism, its evolution, and its relation to other radical ideologies can be found in A. James Gregor's *Contemporary Radical Ideologies* (New York: Random House, 1968), Chap. 3 and throughout.

[30]For lack of space we do not take up the loose and highly varied congeries of ideologies known collectively as the "New Left." Much of it is Marxist in one sense or another, but much of it is not. Its chief concern is radical critique of contemporary capitalism, and often also of established communist societies, especially the Soviet. Its prescriptive aspects are much more difficult to ascertain. For an incisive critique see Assar Lindbeck, *The Political Economy of the New Left: An Outsider's View* (New York: Harper & Row, 1971, paperback). See also the discussion of this book and Lindbeck's reply on the pages of *The Quarterly Journal of Economics*, 86:4 (November 1972).

ical vehicles for the ruthless industrialization of backward countries, a job that was reserved for capitalism by Marx, while one of democratic socialism's chief functions at the present juncture is to enhance the effectiveness and distribute widely the benefits of what are otherwise essentially advanced capitalist economies. It is hard to tell which of the two is farther removed from the original Marxism.

Democratic socialism—or, as it sometimes is called, "social democracy"—has had many ideological sources. The most important of these, especially on the European continent, was Marxism, or, more exactly, its revisionist stream that arose and gathered strength in Central and Western Europe in the early years of this century. The revisionists of that era argued that Marx's prognoses regarding capitalism were not coming true. Capitalism was not heading for a certain collapse, nor were the workers becoming more miserable (rather, the contrary). On the other hand, with the growth in its numbers, the working class in the advanced countries was now in a position to play a large and increasing role in orderly political life, and with time even to seize power by parliamentary means. The revisionist position was violently opposed by the revolutionary-inclined Marxists, who saw in it an ideological heresy and a betrayal of the proletarian cause. But it did find a strong appeal, especially in Germany, among many workers, trade union leaders, and intellectuals who either subscribed to the revisionist analysis of capitalism or preferred gradual advance to violent revolution.

Another important ideological source of democratic socialism has been the ethical teaching of the various Christian (especially Protestant) religions. (In Catholic countries socialism has had a strong anticlerical aspect.) Christian Socialists, as such socialists came to be known, saw in the individualism, acquisitiveness, inequality, and other features of the capitalist order the very opposite of the good society implicit in Christian teachings. Such, for instance, has been the major philosophical basis of socialism in Britain. The mass support for socialism, where it has existed on a mass basis, has nearly always been provided by a strong labor movement allied to the Socialist party, and to some extent (particularly in Scandinavia) by a broad consumer cooperative movement. Yet the political and ideological leadership of democratic socialism—as for that matter usually also of revolutionary communism—typically has been provided by relatively small groups of intellectuals, of whom perhaps the most famous was the gradualist, non-Marxist Fabian Society in England (organized in 1882).

There is no space here to relate the history of democratic socialism—especially its bitter, and all too often desperate and tragic, battles against communism, fascism, and Nazism from the nineteen twenties on. Nor shall we dwell on the record of socialism in the United States, where it has played a significant role in the history of the labor movement but was unable to establish itself durably owing to specific American economic, cultural, and political factors.[31]

[31]See Egbert and Persons, *Socialism and American Life*; also Walter Galenson, "Why the American Labor Movement is not Socialist," *The American Review*, 1, no. 2 (Winter 1961), pp. 1–19.

Rather, we shall take a brief look at the present-day complexion and ideology of social democracy, particularly as it has lately emerged in advanced countries other than the United States, and especially in Western Europe.

To do so we first have to take a backward glance at the period between the two World Wars. During those two fateful decades the European Social Democratic (S.D.) parties were still overwhelmingly proletarian in their class-consciousness, voting strength, and policy orientation. Insofar as their ideologies originally derived from Marx—which would embrace virtually all the S.D. movements on the Continent—their basic commitment to Marxism (albeit to the revisionist version) was still very strong. Working-class solidarity and the fundamental conflict with capitalism were the twin pillars of their political programs, which of course aimed at the eventual establishment of socialism by democratic means. Capitalism was condemned for a long list of social evils: economic inequality, the poverty of the working class, unemployment, the worker's alienation from the production process, the distortion of social and cultural values, crime, war, and so forth. The values stressed by the S.D. parties were political freedom and democracy, individual security, and the elimination of economic inequalities of all kinds. It is these values, of course, that involved them in struggles with totalitarian movements and regimes (which in turn often regarded social democracy as their greatest enemy) and, during the thirties, against the Great Depression.

As the S.D. parties saw it at the time, the basic instrument for the achievement of their domestic goals was to be the nationalization of at least the most important industries or sectors of the economy. If the prime evil was private property, then the basic solution lay in taking the most important means of production out of private hands, though with compensation to the former owners, and their transfer to public ownership, preferably of course under a S.D. government. Planning, especially for full employment and a more egalitarian distribution of income, received some attention in socialist writings of the time, as did the possible use of the market economy under socialism. But these discussions remained largely on the theoretical plane, for few socialist parties came to power in the interwar period or retained power long enough or under sufficiently favorable conditions to translate their programs into action.[32]

After the Second World War, and especially after Western Europe's economic recovery, the S.D. parties came to be faced with a distinctly new situation which was soon to lead to major ideological and programatic rethinking and revising. Within each country, the chief elements in the new situation were the economic success of capitalism (or at least of a mixed economy) and major shifts in the social structure. Thus, economic growth has been very rapid in many advanced countries (for example, West Germany, France, Italy, Austria)

[32]A conspicuous exception is Sweden, where the Social Democratic party came to power in 1932, at the bottom of the depression, and successfully put through a series of employment-raising and social welfare measures.

and, by old standards, appreciable even among the laggards (for instance, Belgium, United Kingdom, Scandinavian countries), consumption levels have risen correspondingly, and (equally significantly) economic fluctuations and unemployment have been minimal. The share of white-collar employment in total employment increased rapidly, and even the blue-collar labor force, thanks to rising incomes, increasingly tended to absorb middle-class aspiration. Class consciousness tended to be blunted. A strictly working-class appeal thus carried little promise of future electoral successes. Moreover, the same socioeconomic trends rendered Marxist analysis of capitalism and Marxist attitudes increasingly irrelevant. On the other hand, even conservative governments went in for extensive social welfare programs and sometimes (especially in France) for far-reaching economic planning, thus taking some of the wind out of the socialists' sails.[33]

By the late fifties and early sixties many of the continental S.D. parties had dropped even nominal ideological allegiance to Marx. The greatest policy change has been the virtual abandonment of opposition to private property per se and of the goal of nationalization. This came about through a greater awareness of the danger of perverting socialist ideals through the excessive bureaucratization and enhancement of governmental power that may follow nationalization. Also instrumental were the instructive experience of Eastern Europe, where these negative phenomena occurred on a large scale; the disillusionment with the nationalization programs in Western Europe immediately after the war, which often created as many problems as they solved; the realization that under modern conditions the control of industry, whether for private or social ends, is more important than ownership; and a more sophisticated appreciation of the possibilities for exercising such controls without outright public ownership. And nationalization has also tended to lose in voter appeal. The new S.D. position therefore became: private ownership as a rule, public ownership only where necessary, and maximum reliance on the market economy, the latter, to be sure, supplemented by conscious governmental steering and planning and by extensive welfare measures.[34]

These developments have confronted democratic socialism with a dilemma. As an American observer has well put it: " . . . if it means the replacement of

[33]As the New Deal did to the Socialist party in the United States.

[34]At this point it is necessary to stress that the above description pertains to the general tendency among European (and similar) socialist parties. Within almost every such party there has been a "left-wing" faction that has opposed this tendency and has fought for more militant, working-class oriented, anticapitalist, and perhaps more traditionally Marxist policies. In Italy—reflecting that country's semideveloped nature—the large Socialist party has taken the "left" position, even collaborating electorally with the even more powerful Italian Communist party until the late fifties, while the "right wing" view has been represented by the much smaller Social Democratic party. Eloquent defense of right wing socialist view may be found in the writings of the prominent British Laborite C. A. R. Crosland, such as The Future of Socialism (London: Jonathan Cape, 1957) and The Conservative Enemy (New York: Schocken, 1962). A brief but forceful statement of a British "left" view is Edward H. Carr, The New Society (London: The Macmillan Co., 1951; Boston: Beacon paperback, 1957).

the mixed economy by total public ownership of the means of production and distribution, it ceases to be democratic, and that, if it means no more than a changed mix in the mixed economy, it ceases to be socialistic."[35] As we have seen, the actual trend has been toward the latter alternative, which at times may appear to be little more than a kind of "me-too-ism" with regard to the nonsocialist parties (which return the compliment by committing themselves in turn to the welfare state, high employment, and other traditional socialist goals). It has been suggested, consequently, that the S.D. parties will direct their efforts primarily toward more comprehensive economic planning (though within a market economy), equality of opportunity (as in education), and the safeguarding of political democracy against its enemies, from both the left and the right.[36]

[35]Arthur Schlesinger, Jr., in a review of Crosland's *The Conservative Enemy* in *The New York Review of Books* 1, no. 2 (1963), p. 6.

[36]Cf. Landauer, *European Socialism*, vol. 2, Chap. 47.

The Capitalist

Market Economy

CHAPTER FOUR

ANGLIA:
THE PERFECT-COMPETITION MODEL

It often helps us gain insight into a complex phenomenon by first investigating a relatively simple, if unrealistic, one. We shall therefore begin the chapter by outlining and analyzing a very simple model of the perfectly competitive market economy. This model—which we dub *Anglia* in honor of the English (but also Scottish) classical and neoclassical economists who put it on the theorist's map—has had an active life in economic theory textbooks and other academic works, bears the venerable patina of long-time pedagogic usage, and has shaped our capitalist ideologies. It is entirely imaginary; no such real economy exists, has existed, or is likely to exist. But this should not embarrass us so long as we remember its fictitious nature.

In Anglia, all resources are privately owned. Firms are managed by owner-entrepreneurs who aim to maximize profits. Households seek to maximize incomes. No firm, let alone a household, is large enough to affect in the market the prices of things that it sells and buys—in other words, there is *perfect competition*. On the government's part, *laissez faire* is observed; but property is protected, contracts are enforced, weights and measures are set, money is provided, and (moderate) taxes are collected. Firms have freedom of enterprise and households have freedom of household choice.[1] Prices move freely. The market mechanism coordinates production and distributes incomes. Labor, unor-

[1] For the meaning of these terms see p. 9–10.

55

ganized, and other factors of production receive the rewards that the market concedes them.

Invoking the criteria of Chapter 1, how may we appraise Anglia? First, the criterion of plenty: We cannot tell from the model itself how affluent Anglia's citizens are, but we may surmise that they are probably not very affluent by modern standards if their economy is so "backward"—so devoid of large-scale production and pressing socioeconomic problems—as to preserve perfect competition and avoid government intervention in the operation of the market mechanism. On the other hand, economic theory tells us that a perfectly competitive economy with profit maximization (and abstracting now from such complications as external economies and diseconomies) tends to attain *static* efficiency.[2] We need not fear lack of entrepreneurial drive, for owners are at once profit-maximizers and their own managers. Also, because assets are managed by their private owners, there will be a tendency for physical capital to be well cared for. *Dynamic* efficiency is something else again, depending as it does largely on the adoption and diffusion of technical innovations. On this score we need not be too sanguine. Although private property and competition provide the incentive for innovating, the organizational and financial resources to conduct large-scale, modern research, development, and promotion of new products may not exist in Anglia. To be sure, there may still be a good deal of the more "old-fashioned" kind of inventing and innovating. On the other hand, a good deal of innovating would also create many disequilibria in the economy, establish more or less monopolistic advantages for some firms, and thus undermine our assumption of perfect competition. Equally uncertain is the verdict on growth, which depends on dynamic efficiency and, even more, on the rate of investment in the national product. The last may or may not be relatively high, depending on the economy's saving propensity. Yet with profits held down by competition to a "normal" level, this most important source of savings may not be very large. Nor can we say much about economic stability, which would depend in part on the nature of the monetary system (which we here bypass); but the dispersion of spending and saving decisions among many decision units makes economic fluctuations not unlikely.

As for economic freedoms, they exist in our model by assumption. Household sovereignty also probably obtains to a high degree, for reasons that the reader is invited to confirm for himself. Regarding the distribution of wealth, nothing very definite can be said on the basis of the bare model. A market economy with the institutions of private property and inheritance creates the conditions for amassing wealth and retaining it within families over generations. In our model this tendency remains (by assumption) unchecked by any deliberate action to redistribute wealth or income on the part of the state. On the other hand (also by assumption), monopoly is absent and economic opportunities are unconstrained by government, so that there are no artificial barriers to the replacement of old wealth by new.

56

[2]We defined static efficiency on p. 7.

We must distinguish clearly between the "real" result, the efficient alloca-tion of resources, and the particular *institutions* which tend to bring it about, which in this case are those of Anglia. It is possible that another set of institu-tions—that is, another model of an economic system—will bring about the same result, static efficiency. (Though not necessarily the same bill of goods. As we have just seen, the bill of goods depends on the pattern of final demand, which in turn depends on the distribution of income and wealth among households, which may well be different under a different set of institutions.) Thus, in Chap-ter 8 we shall look at a model of a *socialist* market economy, which in theory also yields full static efficiency. Moreover, it is conceivable, though in the near future not very likely, that all resource-allocating decisions in the economy will be entrusted to a battery of electronic computers properly programmed to achieve static efficiency and holding the requisite data in their "memories." The computers would presumably issue detailed production orders to individual firms, though households may still retain both sovereignty and freedom of con-sumer choice. In this case we would have a kind of command economy with what has been called "perfect computation,"[3] achieving the same resource-allocating—though probably not social and political—result as does the auto-matic but nonautomated market mechanism under perfect competition. In this imaginary case the electronic computing center—machines, mathematicians, and (hopefully) economists—is the functional equivalent of a social process.

On the other hand, the market mechanism as such must not be thought of as always producing static efficiency. It will do so, theoretically speaking, only under very special conditions, such as Anglia's, which are not satisfied in real economies, sometimes not even remotely. For instance, as we shall see in a moment, perfect competition is hardly the rule in advanced capitalist countries. We must therefore conclude that real—especially, advanced—economies op-erate at levels of static efficiency that are considerably short of perfect. This is regrettable but not necessarily tragic. Full static efficiency is only one of several desiderata that we expect of the economy, and to a significant extent we have to sacrifice the former in order to do better on other scores, such as higher growth, stability, higher overall productivity, equity in income distribution, and so forth, as we saw in Chapter 1. Ours would be an unhappy world if society's only purpose in the economic domain were the attainment of perfect allocative efficiency.

THE ADVANCED
CAPITALIST ECONOMY

We are now ready to turn to the modern, advanced capitalist (or mixed) economy. In the remainder of this chapter we shall enumerate some of

[3]The phrase is Wiles's; see P. J. D. Wiles, *The Political Economy of Communism* (Cambridge: Harvard University Press, 1962), Chap. 10. This is an imaginative and stimulating book on alternative institutions and systems, capitalist as well as communist.

the ways in which it contrasts with the uncomplicated world of Anglia, as well as the sources and nature of some of its major problems. The next chapter will be devoted to a discussion of the ways in which the modern, advanced, industrial, capitalist (or mixed) economy is subjected to conscious social regulation and control.[4]

How, then, does such an economy differ from Anglia? Perhaps the most fundamental difference is that firms are often big, not uniformly small as in Anglia, or tend to band together into large associations of various kinds to advance their common interests by economic or political means. This bigness in the production sector is the result of an historical process, conditioned as it was by nineteenth- and twentieth-century technological advances that at times entailed larger economies of scale, by the natural tendency of private firms to grow as large as is profitable (and sometimes even larger), and the desire to limit competition through merger or some looser sellers' association. To be sure, even in the United States, there is still a great deal of small business, but it is the giant corporation that dominates the economic scene.[5] Other economic interests, faced with big business and big government, have tended to band together to form labor unions, farmers' associations, and even consumer organizations to enhance their own bargaining power vis-à-vis the giants. And government at all its levels, faced with (or acting for) the many agglomerated economic problems of industrialized society, has long since abandoned any professions of *laissez faire* even in those countries (United Kingdom, Netherlands) where it can be said to have been entertained in the earlier, capitalist era. In France, Italy, the United Kingdom, and several other advanced industrial countries of Western Europe, the national government participates importantly in the production sector by means of nationalized enterprises.[6] Along with bigness, and because of it, modern society in the West, let alone in the Communist East, tends to be bureaucratized—in large corporations, government departments, labor unions, educational institutions, and other sizeable organizations. And bureaucratization means hierarchical relations, managers and the managed, and a "web of rules" in society as a whole and within every organization.

[4]In addition to the United States, Canada, and most countries of Western Europe—all of these falling into the North Atlantic group—the advanced capitalist (or mixed) countries are usually deemed to include Australia, New Zealand, Japan, and the Union of South Africa, the last with reference to its white minority. Any such classification is somewhat arbitrary.

[5]In the United States, in 1972, the 500 largest (by sales) industrial corporations accounted for about 65 percent of the aggregate sales and about three-quarters of the profits and of the total employment in manufacturing and mining. The largest, General Motors, had sales of $30.4 billion, held assets of $18.3 billion, earned net profits after taxes of $2.1 billion, and employed 760,000 persons in this country. Of the 500, 142 had sales of over $1 billion. The 500th had sales of 204 million. (*Fortune*, May 1972, pp. 184 ff.) Note, however, that many of the largest corporations are "conglomerates," that is, they are in many lines of production. For this and other reasons the relative importance of the 500 is not a direct indication of the degree of competition in the economy; cf. Lee E. Preston, "The Industry and Enterprise Structure of the U.S. Economy" (New York: General Learning Press, 1971), pp. 10 ff. Preston's essay is a very useful summary account of its topic.

[6]More on nationalized enterprises below, pp. 79–82.

Its Institutions

1. Private property, ownership, and management. In the millions of small businesses, ownership and management still either reside in the same person(s) or are in any case closely connected, but this is not so in large "private" corporations. In the latter, the nominal ownership rests with thousands—sometimes hundreds of thousands—of dispersed shareholders, while management is in the hands of a small group which may own only a very tiny proportion of the corporation's outstanding shares of stock. Thus, in the large corporation, the business form that dominates our economic landscape, ownership and control are separated. Ownership does not carry with it managerial responsibility, while those who bear such responsibility are not significant beneficiaries of the firm's successes or do not take much pecuniary risk in its failures. Often, management is virtually self-perpetuating, since no group of outsiders, even if stockholders, can hope to dislodge it easily. This independence of corporate management is bolstered by the tendency of corporations to finance the expansion of their assets primarily from internal sources, i.e., depreciation reserves and retained profits.[7] Under these circumstances, what motivates managers to hold down costs, operate efficiently, earn high profits for the firm, innovate, expand the business in response to favorable expectations, or for that matter even to prevent dissipation and undermaintenance of capital assets? How much of a difference is there between such management in private corporations and its counterpart in nationalized companies? In fact, in nationalized companies management may be much more amenable to control on the part of the nominal owner, the state. All in all, we might expect big business to be sluggish, unenterprising, undynamic, inefficient. Yet we know that, by and large, even in the giant private corporations, this is not so. Management in advanced capitalist countries does the things that are expected of it by society and on the whole does them fairly well. As we have already pointed out, capitalism on both sides of the North Atlantic has been unusually dynamic during the post World War II era.

These and related problems have been studied a good deal since the problem of separation of ownership of control was first systematically posed in the early thirties,[8] yet there is no convincing, simple explanation for the "proper" behavior of corporate management. Many factors seem to be at play, such as the incentive effect of the bonuses that executives derive from successful operation (but to what extent are these bonuses in effect self-awarded?), the general understanding by managers that profits are a yardstick by which the rest of the

---

[7]During the sixties, in the United States, the share of internal sources fluctuated between 50 and 70 percent.

[8]The pioneering classic work was Adolf A. Berle, Jr. and Gardner C. Means, *The Modern Corporation and Private Property* (New York: Macmillan, 1933). For a latterday return to the same subject by one of its authors, see Adolf A. Berle, *Power Without Property* (New York: Harcourt, Brace and World paperback, 1959). On this related issue, see also Edward S. Mason, ed., *The Corporation in Modern Society* (Cambridge: Harvard University Press, 1959).

business community takes their measure, the cultural forces in an advanced industrial society that place high value on such things as efficiency and growth, and the feeling of professionalism among managerial personnel, which carries with it a sense of social responsibility and of pride in a job well done. But wouldn't all or most of these factors be operative under public ownership ("socialism") as well? They probably would, provided managers were given a high degree of autonomy (which is not the case in Soviet-type economies, so that these do not provide a fair answer to our question). Indeed, the experience of nationalized enterprises in Western Europe suggests that, under comparable conditions, management is approximately equally effective and efficient in both sectors.

2. Profit and other goals. However, it would be naive of us to assume that the exclusive goal of firms in advanced capitalist countries is profit maximization. To be sure, the large private corporation, like any private firm, must avoid consistent losses or it will go out of business. It may, however, merely aim at some "satisfactory" rate of profit—it may be "satisficing" rather than maximizing. Or it may strive to maintain some "traditional" share of the industry's market; or it may attempt to maximize the rate of growth of its sales, because this rather than profits may be the chief "success indicator" in the business community.[9] Withal, it may still be trying for higher profits, though how hard it tries may depend on many things, such as whether the firm is young and aggressive or the opposite; what the norms of behavior in this regard in the given country or industry are; how pressing are the immediate or anticipated needs for financial liquidity, and whether management is not apprehensive that high profits will invite pressure from labor unions for higher wages or the attention of the Antitrust Division of the U.S. Department of Justice. Lastly, the large corporation may feel a sense of responsibility to all with whom it deals directly and to the public at large.[10]

In sum, profit-*making* still seems to be a very important goal for the large capitalist firm. But it is not the same as simple profit-maximizing, the standard assumption of economic theory; hence the theoretical conclusions that we may draw regarding efficiency and the like in the advanced economy must also be surrounded with appropriate qualifications.

3. There is no reason to assume that the behavior of *households* or the freedom of choice available to them is significantly different in an advanced capitalist economy than in Anglia, apart from enjoying a higher standard of living and partaking more or less of the welfare state.

4. Competition. Clearly, with all its big business and government intervention (not always to promote competition), the advanced capitalist economy

---

[9]This thesis has been forcefully argued and explored by Robin Marris in *The Economic Theory of "Managerial" Capitalism* (London: Macmillan, 1964).

[10]The late A. A. Berle has done much to popularize this view; see for instance, his *The 20th Century Capitalist Revolution* (New York: Harcourt, Brace and World paperback, 1954). We shall return to the question of "social responsibility" of business; see pp. 174–76.

is hardly *perfectly* competitive. Indeed, the preservation of at least a "workable" degree of competition in industries and sectors dominated by big business—or the regulation or nationalization of those industries in which competition would be unlikely or uneconomical—is one of its major politico-economic problems. For *some* significant degree of competition—not necessarily perfect—is essential in a market economy to limit market power (which is translatable into political power as well), to safeguard reasonable efficiency of operation, and to ensure that the profit-making is a socially beneficial motive force and not merely a charge on the national income.

Altogether, the economy as we know it seems to be quite competitive, even if far from perfectly so. Often the competition focuses not on price but on product quality, terms of sale, delivery conditions, and other nonprice dimensions. There seems to be considerable agreement among specialists that the American economy (to mention one) has not on the whole suffered any substantial reduction in competitiveness, at least in the product markets, over the past forty years.[11] Two developments that have contributed to maintaining the intensity of competition since World War II are: (1) rapid technical progress, which may create patent-protected monopolies, but also increases the range of mutually substitutable products and thus enhances competition among them; and (2) the reduction in scope and "height" of barriers to international trade, which has tended to intensify competition across national frontiers.

5. *Prices* perform the same two functions as in Anglia: They supply information on which economic decisions are based, and they are a direct or indirect source of individual and corporate net income. However, in industries that are not perfectly competitive, sellers (or buyers) have power to affect prices. In these cases, which are important, covering, for instance, a large part of manufacturing, prices are also often not very flexible; they do not respond quickly to changes in demand or supply. In the regulated industries prices are usually set by governmental commissions and are therefore quite inflexible in the short run. In some respects price inflexibility is a good thing. It helps general price stability, makes economic decisions based on these prices less uncertain, and may cause less fluctuation in the incomes of certain groups than if prices were very flexible. But since price flexibility is also an important factor in the adjustment process that reallocates resources in response to changing demand and supply conditions, the lack of it in a modern market economy may interfere with reasonably speedy adjustment to disturbances or to changes in social objectives.

This problem becomes especially pronounced when prices are held at certain minimum or maximum levels by government action. Examples are, respectively, the farm price supports in the United States (and, in some form or other, many other countries) and general price controls at times of serious inflationary

---

[11]Cf. Joe S. Bain, *Industrial Organization*, 2nd ed. (New York: John Wiley & Sons, Inc., 1968), Chap. 6.

pressure (often in wartime, but also at other times, as recently imposed in the United States in 1971 and again in 1973). The common purpose behind this and similar measures is a perfectly legitimate—and often socially and politically desirable—one of protecting (or raising) the incomes of certain groups within the country that would be adversely affected by the unhampered operation of the market mechanism. But in doing so, these measures may also impair the performance of the other major function of prices, that of facilitating resource reallocation in the economy.

When the price of a good is supported by government action above the equilibrium level, the big problem is additional supply that cannot be sold at the given (high) price. The government may have to step in to buy up the surpluses and/or to limit production by administrative action, as the experience with U.S. farm-price supports illustrates. Both means of coping with the surplus are costly and politically difficult to administer. When prices are held by government decree at maximum (ceiling) levels, the price:cost ratio may become in some cases so unfavorable, while at the same time, owing to the inflationary pressure, there may be such an excess of money in the public's hands, that production and work incentives may be seriously damaged. Whether the sociopolitical effects of tampering with prices outweigh the economic costs to society as a whole and to individual groups is of course in itself a political question.[12]

An interesting problem arises when the price is paid not by the consumer of the good but by a third party. The best known instance in the United States is the sponsoring of radio and television programs. The consumer enjoys the programs free—though he may be paying a price in terms of having to listen to or watch advertising ("commercials") that he may rather forgo, and possibly in terms of the quality and nature of the programs made available to him. The sponsor pays for the program and therefore usually at least influences the content; he is obviously interested in maximizing the number of listeners or viewers so as to maximize exposure to his commercials. This situation, it has been often charged, leads to pitching the programs' appeal to a mass level, ignoring minority interests and tastes, and deleting controversial material. On the other hand, a way (for instance, "pay-TV") that would sell the service directly to the individual consumer, who may be willing to pay for the less conventional and more controversial programs, would presumably create the demand for such programs and would elicit their supply. An analogy can be drawn with books and journals. Since the consumers pay for them directly, they tend to be available in the greatest variety, though even here pressure from advertisers may seriously affect the content of journals heavily dependent on advertising, as mass-circulation journals are. Note that the problem discussed in this paragraph is attributable not so much to the market mechanism as such, as to the perversion of the role of prices where the final consumer does not pay for the good himself.

[12]This situation—price control and excess of money in circulation—is known as "repressed inflation."

STRENGTHS AND DEFECTS OF THE MARKET MECHANISM

This brings us to a broader appraisal of the strengths and weaknesses of the market mechanism in an advanced economy. It behooves us to proceed with some care, for there is a great deal of misunderstanding on this score, the nature of which often depends on the vantage point from which the problem is viewed. Thus, in the capitalist West, the "market" is blamed for most of our socioeconomic ills, and in the process the very important positive role of the market mechanism is often overlooked. In Eastern Europe and the USSR, where the market mechanism has indeed been banned for decades, a fashionable opinion is that most of *their* ills will be cured if only the market mechanism is introduced into the socialist economy. And in the process, the market mechanism's serious weaknesses and limitations are frequently ignored.

The market mechanism is essentially just that—a mechanism for the carrying on of the work of the economy. Its role is, first, to bring about the adjustment to disturbances as they arise in the system, and to do so more or less automatically, without the active participation of some superior authority in every case. The disturbances may be on the demand side or on the supply side, as we saw in Chapter 2. The market mechanism tends to bring the amount of a good demanded and the amount supplied into equality with one another, thus permitting an orderly (and, under certain special conditions, reasonably efficient) use of resources for the satisfaction of wants.

Second, the market mechanism carries out adjustment in yet another way: by bringing about innovation. The innovation may be in the form of new products, or of new production processes (for example, new technology); it may also be in the form of new institutions—what we have called "adaptation" in Chapter 2.

These processes of adjustment and adaptation depend on a feedback flow of information to those who take the decisions. The information is mostly in the form of prices, and these are generated by the market itself (though they are also often seriously affected by deliberate government policy). But the prices are not only messages or signals; they are also actual dollar-and-cents prices paid by somebody to somebody. Thus, by generating prices—of which wages are one variety—the market also brings about a certain distribution of income and wealth in society. Of course, this distribution of income and wealth can be and is directly modified by deliberate government policy as well.

Setting aside its distributive function for the time being and focusing on its resource-allocating function (adjustment, innovation, adaptation) we can say that, by and large, the market mechanism in the advanced countries operates remarkably well, though within certain limits. It brings about adjustment of demand and supply, and does so reasonably quickly. It promotes innovation at

63

a fairly rapid pace. It permits the adaptation of institutions to new needs and conditions. All this we generally take for granted—which is in a way a silent tribute to the mechanism's efficacy on these scores. But these are no mean accomplishments, something we can best ascertain by understanding the particular problems of nonmarket economies, specifically the Soviet and other communist economies, which we shall take up in later chapters. In sum, the market mechanism is a powerful social instrument for some purposes, not so good for other purposes.

It also has some broader, social functions. Since it is a decentralized process, it may help disperse economic power—though it may at the same time have the offsetting effect of helping to agglomerate power through the promotion of monopoly and the accumulation of private wealth. As we have already seen, the intensity of competition and freedom of economic opportunity play an important role in this connection. The market economy disperses not only power but also decision-making, responsibility, and initiative—which is desirable from the standpoint of the viability of democratic institutions. The market is, further, a social mechanism for the resolution of conflicts at a relatively "low" level, also perhaps desirable.

It localizes ordinary economic business conflicts, settles them in the market place, and keeps them from migrating up to the higher levels of the political structure, as would be inevitable in a hierarchically organized economy. On the other hand, it also encourages the formation of pressure groups to bargain for economic advantages in the political arena where it cannot be obtained in the marketplace.

The market mechanism's very impersonality, often and at times justly criticized, has its positive side. The market respects economic worth and purchasing power whatever direction it may come, and thereby tends to provide economic opportunities where they might otherwise be barred by social or political prejudice.

Yet with all its advantages and virtues, the market economy has a good number of faults and gives rise to enough problems to keep thousands of economists, lawyers, politicians, and legislators, as well as cranks and crackpots, busy trying to solve them. Which failures are caused by the fact that the advanced capitalist economy is a decentralized (market) economy? that its producers are primarily after pecuniary profit? that the means of production are typically privately owned? Analyzing the problem this way we may, at times, arrive at surprising answers.

The Market and Equity

Being impersonal, even blind to nonpecuniary considerations, the market mechanism pays little heed to distributive justice. It lavishes favors on the movie star and the professional athlete, allows the lucky property owner to reap windfall gains, but deprives of opportunities or suddenly impoverishes others through

64

no fault of their own. Clearly, no modern society can leave income distribution to the market alone, not only out of feelings of solidarity with and compassion for the poor and the unfortunate, but also because in a democracy (and even to some extent in a dictatorship) the adversely affected groups—not necessarily poor—are likely to bring political pressure on the government at some level to redress the social balance[13] in their favor. It is more difficult to do justice to groups of underprivileged citizens who, for various reasons, are politically powerless to command the attention of society, as we have learned in connection with the "War on Poverty" in the U.S.A.—though it is not entirely impossible, as the same fact testifies.

Faults of Decentralization

Effective as a market economy is in balancing demand and supply in individual product markets, it is much less dependable with regard to macroeconomic balance. In other words, it has a pronounced tendency toward fluctuation in the overall level of economic activity and in the general level of prices. It also has a tendency toward imbalance in one specific market, the market for labor; thus, in the United States between 1954 and 1972 despite relatively prosperous times otherwise, unemployment as a proportion of the civilian labor force (annual figures) fell below 4 percent in only four years, 1966–1969. In short, unless vigorously counteracted, the market economy has a definite bias toward instability and less than full employment.[14]

The fundamental reason is its decentralized nature. The many millions of economic units—firms, households, governmental entities on all levels—make their spending and saving decisions autonomously and without direct coordination. However, in the aggregate the separate decisions tend to have cumulative effects and to generate waves of favorable or unfavorable expectations regarding the future. The result can be, and often has been, boom or bust, prosperity or depression, inflation or deflation—unless appropriate stabilizing measures are successfully taken by the government (of which more in the next chapter).

A closely related cause of malfunctioning of the market economy arises from uncertainty regarding the future as it is seen by the individual firm. What will future prices and costs be? What technological advances will occur? What will be the state of business one, two or five years hence? Should one risk a large investment in a new plant or in promoting a product? Each firm acting on its own may wish to observe a margin of safety, yet the cumulative effect is to hold back innovation and investment, dampen technical progress, reduce the rate of growth, and increase unemployment in the whole economy. Thus, not only is each firm justified in its caution, but the tone is set for further pessimism.

---

[13]As a politician once put it: "Those farms may be marginal, but the voters on them aren't."

[14]These aspects of the market economy are investigated in Charles L. Schultze, *National Income Analysis*, this series, (Englewood Cliffs, N.J.: Prentice-Hall, Inc., 1967).

Depressions, unemployment, inflation, sluggish growth—these are obviously among the most serious problems an advanced economy has to face. They have been at the center of the socialist critique of private enterprise. Fundamentally, they stem from the decentralized nature of decision-making in the market economy rather than from private ownership of means of production. They are hazards as well in a *socialist* market economy, as the experience of market-socialist Yugoslavia testifies. There is need for social intervention in order to ensure reasonable macroeconomic stability—and perhaps growth—in the market economy, capitalist or socialist.[15] The crux therefore lies in the sociopolitical and ideological climate. Would such a climate permit or, on the contrary, resist and prevent public authorities from taking adequate stabilizing and confidence-inducing measures? The socialist argument has traditionally been that powerful private-property interests in a capitalist society would prevent government intervention even for stabilizing purposes, and historically there has been much evidence to support this view. But, as we have already noticed in preceding chapters, lately there has been a considerable shift toward greater pragmatism in the prevailing ideology of modern capitalism on this score. Once hostile to resolute stabilizing measures by the government, the climate of opinion in the North Atlantic countries now tends to accept and even expect them.

Another very important type of problem that is attributable primarily to the decentralization of decisions is the problem of so-called externalities, of external economies and external diseconomies. As we saw in Chapter 2, both are bad in the sense that both lead to decisions that may be rational for the given firm but undesirable from the standpoint of the community or society. Let us remind ourselves that in the case of external economies some of the value of the benefit from a given activity that would accrue to society cannot be appropriated by the firm. Hence, the firm may well forgo or restrict the activity—with the community or society as the loser. Previously, we cited the example of the dam. Another and more common instance is the training of labor by individual firms. Since the workers so trained can easily leave the firm's employ, and even go to work for its competitors, the firm may well refrain from spending much on training, though society would clearly benefit thereby.

In the case of external diseconomies, as we have seen, the firm does something that throws no burden on it but inflicts harm on either specific individuals or the larger community. Here, there is little *private* cost (to the firm) and significant *social* cost. The social cost, however, does not enter significantly into the firm's calculations; hence, the firm has no reason to refrain from the activity. The examples are familiar to all of us: pollution, damage to the landscape, "uglification" of cities.

Note that in both cases the market fails to lead to a socially desirable re-

[15]By this we do not mean to imply that the nonmarket (command) economy does not require government intervention for purposes of stability and growth. Rather, there the question does not arise because nearly everything that happens in the command economy happens because of deliberate government action.

sult not because there is something wrong with the mechanism per se. The market works when those who use scarce resources pay for them, and therefore take the corresponding prices into account in their decisions. (Of course, the prices should be more or less "correct".) But in the case of external economies, those who gain—owners of properties downstream from the dam, the workers who receive the training, the competitors who hire away such workers—do not pay anything (or enough) for the benefit that accrues to them. In the contrary case of external diseconomies, those who use up valuable resources—clear water or air, natural beauty, urban convenience—pay little or nothing for the privilege, usually because the resources are owned by no one (or by everyone, which is the same thing) and no prices are charged for them. In both cases, the most effective solution is likely to be some kind of centralizing within the context of the community or polity. Either some level of government should take over the authority to make relevant decisions: to build the dam, to train workers at public expense, or to prohibit the damage to the environment. Alternatively government should centralize the information, and then offer subsidies for training programs or levy taxes for the discharge of pollutants, leaving the decisions still to the individual firms. In the latter case, firms "internalize" the benefits and costs, and then decide the proper course of action themselves.[16]

Popular opinion often blames damage to the environment on the "profit system"; that is to say, on the fact that business is after profits. This is an incorrect—or at least, an incomplete—view of the problem. Environmental disruption occurs because the economic unit pursues some specific objective of its own, and because the socially harmful activities are not costly enough to the unit in terms of its objective. In a capitalist society the objective is usually profit. But the problem would not be much different if the objective were something other than profit; say, maximizing production or providing a given service. Thus, nonprofit entities in our society such as schools, government bureaus, military establishments, and even households also contribute to pollution and inflict other social costs. Moreover, as we shall later see, enterprises in the Soviet economy are also guilty of environmental disruption, although they are neither privately owned nor primarily profit-oriented (nor, ironically, enjoy much decentralized power, except to disregard the usual external economies and diseconomies).

Faults of Profit-Making

Indeed, a firm under any economic system must have a fairly clear-cut objective in order to take reasonably rational decisions and to be evaluated by its

---

[16]It has been shown that the "internalizing" alternative—for instance, levying taxes or fees for the discharge of pollutants—may be a more efficient way of controlling environmental disruption than outright prohibition of the offending activities. Brief and readable economic analyses of environmental disruption will be found in: Sanford Rose, "The Economics of Environmental Quality", Fortune, January 1970; and Edwin G. Dolan, TANSTAAFL: The Economic Strategy for Environmental Crisis (New York: Holt, Rinehart & Winston, Inc., 1971, paperback).

owner(s) or superior authority. And although the firm is not thereby absolved from acting responsibly vis-à-vis society in all other respects, it also cannot be expected to take into account all the effects of its actions on all third parties, lest it either be paralyzed by the enormity of the task or be completely directed by some superior authority, thus losing all its independence or autonomy. (Of course, there is no assurance that the superior authority itself can take everything into account.) The most common such objective in a market economy is *profit*, although, as we have already seen, this need not always mean simple profit-maximizing.

In a moment we will turn to the faults of profit-making in a market economy. But first we should be aware of the fact that it is difficult to devise a generalized objective for the individual firm that would be socially superior to profit-making. (Note: profit-*making*, not necessarily profit-*taking*. What is in question here is the firm's objective, not who pockets the profit.) With appropriate prices, profit—the difference between gross value produced and cost incurred—is the best measure of the firm's net contribution to the national income, whether under capitalism or under socialism, and therefore the best social criterion for its autonomous action.[17] This much has been realized even by many Soviet and East European economists after decades of painful experience with other "success indicators" for firms, as we shall see further on.[18]

A major social rationale of profit as an automatic regulating instrument is that its simultaneous pursuit by all firms will be largely self-defeating—that competition will prevent excessive profits while pushing production of individual goods to levels consistent with (or at least approximating) overall allocative efficiency. Needless to say, the individual producer takes a different view. He *likes* "excessive" profits and regards competition within his own industry with less than joy. There is nothing wrong with this. On the contrary, the very strength of the capitalist market economy lies in that it harnesses for social ends such a powerful motive force as the universal desire for economic self-betterment. It is therefore as illogical as it is unrealistic to expect people to eschew profits out of social consciousness, so long as they do not transgress the limits of law and accepted ethical standards. But it is society's function to ensure that profits serve a constructive function and that the profit motive propels activity into socially desirable directions rather than the opposite. In the American tradition this has meant that competition—an automatic and effective profit-restraining social

[17]The theoretically sophisticated will immediately realize that, externalities apart, "appropriate prices" are those that (a) define the demand-supply equilibrium, and (b) are equal to marginal cost, and that this is the situation with perfect competition at equilibrium.

[18]The old saw "production for use and not for profit" is a fallacy. To be sure, not everything that is in fact profitable need be produced from a social standpoint. But profit is the most important single signal in the system that tells producers what is useful and how much by way of resources may be committed for its production. In other words, "use" refers only to the good's utility; profit links utility with cost, which is the more relevant if not the decisive consideration.

device—is encouraged where feasible; and industries in which it is not feasible because it would be too wasteful ("natural monopolies") or for other reasons, are publicly regulated or controlled.[19]

Nonetheless, even under reasonably competitive conditions some serious problems are caused or accentuated by profit-making. The most common of these is the defrauding or deception of the buyer by the seller. This is done in so many ways, crude or subtle, and takes so many forms, and is such a well-known phenomenon, that it requires no more than mere mention here. Deception or fraud can be checked by competition among sellers if there is a good chance of the buyer's discovering it and shifting his patronage to a more honest seller; indeed, this is the main reason why there is not much more of it than there is. Otherwise, competition only forces the more scrupulous to follow the lead of the less scrupulous sellers in order to survive the competitive struggle. Because of his economic weakness and relative ignorance, the individual consumer is a more likely victim of deception and fraud than the buying firm. Government action—in the form of requirements to disclose package contents or product ingredients, standardizing nomenclature and product specifications (for example, the U.S. Pharmacopoeia), enforcement of quality and purity standards, disclosure of true terms of sale, such as financing charges, and so forth—is called for, though it rarely reaches far enough because of producers' opposition. Other ways of combating deception and fraud are through "consumer unions," which test products and publicize their findings, or through consumer cooperatives,[20] which attempt to safeguard consumers' interests at the distributing and producing stages.

Another but related problem is that of excessive expenditure on advertising and other means of attracting consumer demand to a given product. There is no space in this context to discuss this complex matter in any detail.[21] We may mention, however, that (strictly speaking) neither excessive advertising nor consumer deception is as much a phenomenon of capitalism as of the profit-oriented market economy in general. There is no reason to believe that profit-oriented *socialist* firms would desist from these practices much more readily than do capitalist firms, in the absence of restraints on the part of public authorities or of countervailing pressure on the part of organized consumers. The seller wants to increase profits (or, possibly, just sales); it does not seem to matter whether

---

[19] See Richard Caves, *American Industry; Structure, Conduct, Performance* (Englewood Cliffs, N.J.: Prentice-Hall, Inc., 1967), this series; and Bain, *Industrial Organization.* Note also the saying that the best check on a capitalist is another capitalist.

[20] Consumer cooperatives may have various rationales: ideological (mainly anticapitalist, as with the important European consumer-cooperative movements), consumer education, enhancement of bargaining power vis-à-vis suppliers, and compensation for inadequate resource mobility. On the last point, if resources were mobile enough, private enterprise would presumably provide the economically justified services that cooperatives supply to their members.

[21] Again the reader is referred to Caves, *American Industry.*

the profits benefit the owner-manager, or the corporation as such but not directly its executive, or even the socialist state.[22]

Yet this is not to absolve private ownership as such from certain important faults of its own. One of them is that the unit of ownership may be too small. A classic example is the oil and gas industry. Here, the fact that a single underground deposit of oil or gas is owned by many owners of surface lots of land, each of whom fears that his share in the deposit may be lost to a neighbor unless he acts swiftly to extract it, leads to an uneconomically large number of wells, excessively rapid extraction, and perhaps the loss of some of the fuel underground. Another example pertains to the fragmentation of urban landholding among very many owners with the result that it may be difficult to assemble a sufficiently large unit of land for an otherwise economical project, say, a large apartment house. There are of course ways of bypassing these obstacles for some purposes. In the petroleum industry, the rate of extraction from a given well is regulated by law in many states (though the same device may be used to protect the interests of the resource owners at the expense of consumers), which, however, does not restrain the drilling of too many wells and may even encourage it.[23] In cities, large projects are undertaken by public authorities which resort to the privilege of eminent domain to assemble ample land areas.

Another defect is that the private owner may have too short a "time horizon"—he may discount the distant future more heavily than society as a whole would. This "after-me-the-deluge" attitude has caused much predatory exploitation of land, mineral resources, forests, and the like, especially in the earlier period of this country's westward expansion and industrialization when natural resources seemed to be inexhaustible. At times, the result was literally the deluge, as when deforestation impaired surface water retention and increased flood hazard. As a result, very costly soil reclamation, reforestation, and flood-control measures have to be undertaken by society, not to mention the irreparable losses of natural resources that have to be endured.

In a capitalist economy, private enrichment has a social function; it is the incentive for productive activity. To discourage it unduly is to undermine the economic order. But because it is difficult to distinguish in practice between

---

[22]Deception and defrauding of the consumer are widespread in the Soviet economy, where firms are not profit-oriented but are production-maximizers.

[23]A good, brief statement and analysis of the petroleum problem will be found in Bain, *Industrial Organization*, pp. 626–33. See also K. William Kapp, *Social Costs of Private Enterprise* (New York: Schocken, 1971), Chap. 8. Kapp's book contains a wealth of rather nontechnical data on many kinds of social loss through externality and other failures of the market. The first edition (1963) was entitled *Social Costs of Business Enterprise*. The substitution of the word "business" by "private" in the title is not an improvement, since much of the social loss in question is not caused by *private* ownership as such but by dispersion of decision-making.

enrichment that is the result of productive activity and that which is not, the latter tends to get the same legal protection and social sanction as does the former. From the social standpoint this is wasteful; some consider it unjust as well. For instance, the value of urban land appreciates as the city grows; landowners thus reap windfall gains without any productive contribution on their part.[24] Many other examples could be cited.

But perhaps the main difficulties that ensue from private ownership in the capitalist economy are of a different order. Thus, it creates powerful vested interests that are at times hard to control and regulate by democratic processes even if the general welfare would seem so to require; for example, the tribute collected by the domestic silver-mining interests from the U.S. Treasury for the better part of a century, or the opposition of local propertied interests to purely local improvements for fear of raising the property-tax rate. Perhaps as important but more elusive is the impact of the prevalance of private ownership on outlooks and attitudes. One result may be a subtle confusion of ends and means. Calvin Coolidge is reputed to have said: "The business of America is business." It is not, of course, in any ultimate sense. Private business is mainly a means to a more fundamental end, the material well-being and the general welfare of this and future generations. Private property, private enterprise, the profit motive —these are powerful social instruments for the achievement of society's goals. They are delicate instruments in that their effectiveness rests on confidence and trust. But they are still primarily means, not ends.

Furthermore, a private enterprise economy tends to bias production in favor of goods sold in the market ("private goods") and against public services, as has been forcefully argued by John Kenneth Galbraith, among others.[25] To begin with, public services are provided by government, and government tends to be suspect. Second, such services have to be financed by taxes, which are a burden to bear. Third, private goods are aggressively promoted by their producers; public services are more often than not apologetically defended.

---

[24]We are referring here to the value of the land as such, not to man-made improvements. Of course, land can fall in value as well as appreciate. The most eloquent condemnation of "unearned" income from the appreciation of urban land is Henry George's *Progress and Poverty*, first published in 1879 and still a classic. His proposal for the socialization of land ownership, the income from which would constitute the only form of government revenue (the "single tax"), at one time received much attention but is not regarded by economists as the panacea for social ills that George and his zealous followers assumed it to be.

[25]*The Affluent Society* (Cambridge: Houghton Mifflin Co., 1958), pp. 132 ff. and 309 ff. The book is an eloquent critique of thinking and policies on the problems of the contemporary American economy. These ideas were further developed in his *The New Industrial State* (Cambridge: Houghton Mifflin Co., 1967), a work that has received much attention for its vivid—but much disputed—account of the control of demand for its products by the modern large corporation.

Planning and Control

in Capitalist Market Economies

CHAPTER FIVE

PLANNING AND CONTROL

Attempts by the state to shape or guide the economy through the prohibition or encouragement of trade, by means of public works, and with the help of price and wage controls go back to the dawn of history and have continued through the ages.[1] But it has been in the last generation—owing to the Great Depression of the thirties, the Second World War, and the many pressing problems of the postwar world—that the role of government in economic life increased greatly everywhere in the world and growing attention came to be given, even outside the communist countries, to systematic and coordinated control over the national economy and its growth. Concurrently with these developments and closely related to them, there has been a marked advance in economics, which has brought a better understanding of the causes of business fluctuations, new insights into the growth process, new tools of analysis (especially mathematical), and a large body of writings on the planning, controlling, and "steering" of the economy. Of the greatest importance in this connection has been the development of the electronic computer after the Second World War, which has made it possible to handle rapidly large amounts of data for research, the testing of economic theories, and for actual planning.

By control we mean the purposeful, deliberate shaping of eco-

[1] With regard to the nineteenth and twentieth centuries see, for instance, Hugh G. J. Aitken, ed., *The State and Economic Growth* (New York: Social Science Research Council, 1959).

nomic phenomena by public authority in the most general sense. It includes the concept of *planning*. The difference between the two is that planning carries a greater connotation of being rational (in the sense of being strictly subordinated to some definite goals), systematic, and of operating largely with quantitative variables. It is also the more accepted term when a longer period is in question.

Planning should not be confused with socialism, if by the latter term we mean widespread ownership of the means of production by the state or other public authorities. Although a socialist economy almost certainly is also likely to be a planned one, planning in the broad sense in which we understand it does not necessarily call for nationalization of industry. Nor does it necessarily call for interference with freedom of enterprise or the freedom of the household. There can be and are very different kinds of planning with very different implications for democratic values. Some kinds, such as the Soviet variety, are clearly opposed to democratic values and to freedom of enterprise. Other kinds are quite compatible with them.[2] Regulation of aggregate demand by means of monetary and fiscal policy in order to maintain economic stability at high employment levels ("macroeconomic planning"; see below, this chapter); promotion of certain socially desirable programs (for example, urban renewal, area redevelopment, education); protection against some kinds of economic insecurity— all such measures, rather than restricting economic freedom, go a long way toward enlarging the opportunities for private business and for consumers. This is the kind of planning that has been pursued by the recent national administrations in the United States, even if in this country we usually avoid the word because of its negative ideological and semantic connotations when applied to the federal government.[3]

Essential Elements of Planning

All planning worthy of the name displays the following elements or aspects.[4]

1. Purpose. By definition, planning must be directed toward the attainment of some objective or goal, though the objective may be quite general, such as full employment.

2. Authority. Since planning is deliberate activity, someone must initiate and undertake it. And since it operates by affecting the behavior of economic agents, its measures must be backed up by authority. In the case of governmen-

---

[2]Thus, Eugene V. Rostow, *Planning for Freedom* (New Haven: Yale University Press paperback, 1959), speaks of "liberal planning" for this reason.

[3]But even in the United States the word "planning" carries a pejorative connotation only in reference to the federal level of activity. Business corporations, cities, counties, and even states freely admit that they engage in "planning" without fear of opprobrium. Because "planning" carries a pejorative sense in some contexts, the word "programming" is occasionally preferred.

[4]For a brief treatment of the formal aspects of planning see Jan Tinbergen, *Central Planning* (New Haven: Yale University Press paperback, 1964). A helpful introduction to planning in a broad sense is Neil W. Chamberlain, *Private and Public Planning* (New York, McGraw-Hill Book Co., 1965).

tal planning, the authority is of course political. Moreover, a distinction typically is made between the authority that sets the goals, approves the plan or control measures, and enforces them, and the technical and administrative staff(s) that draw up the plans and observe their execution. The latter generally act only in an advisory capacity to the authorities, although in practice they may wield a great deal of influence because of their technical expertise and control of information.

3. Level and scope. The aims of planning and the authority behind it to a large extent determine the level of the planning activity—local, state, national, international—and its scope; that is, whether it embraces all or nearly all of the given political unit's economy, a particular industry, a certain region, or an individual firm.

4. Time period. During which period will the plan be in operation? Often there is a hierarchy of time periods—say, a general ten-year plan and detailed annual plans deriving from it.

5. Estimate of the present and forecast. The very intention to plan implies the perception of some existing or anticipated problem and is therefore to some extent always preceded by an estimate of the present situation and a forecast of future conditions that will obtain in the absence of a plan. The decision to plan may be followed by a much more thorough appraisal of the present or prospects for the future. Plans should be distinguished from forecasts or projections. While they necessarily rest on some estimate of the future, plans aim to affect deliberately the course of events and not merely to foresee them.

6. Economic model. All planning presupposes some idea of the relations among the relevant economic variables, some kind of economic model in the planner's minds. For instance, if the purpose of the plan is to eliminate a deficit in the balance of payments and so to stop an outflow of gold, it is essential to know the significant factors that affect the balance of payments directly and indirectly before corrective measures can be effectively taken. Often, the model is only implicit in the planner's actions. But the more sophisticated economic plans are based on explicit models, which in turn rest on economic theories.

Both the theories and the models may be couched in mathematical terms. Thus, a planning model may consist of a matrix (table) depicting the flows of goods and factors of production among the economy's sectors and industries. An input-output model would be an example; it could tell us what changes in flows and production will be called for by anticipated or desired changes in other outputs. Alternatively, the mathematical model might be an *econometric* one consisting of a set, perhaps several dozen, equations, linking a large number of variables (the price level, the wage level, rate of investment, level of consumption, level of income, for example) and certain constants.[5]

[5]A recent step is the attempt by an international group of econometricians to link together into a single world economic model the mathematical models for some eighteen economies or groups of economies. See C. Moriguchi, "Forecasting and Simulation Analysis of the World Economy," *The American Economic Review,* 63:2 (May 1973), pp. 402–9.

7. *Variables and instruments.* Any economic model that explicitly or implicitly underlies planning contains at least two kinds of variables. There are first those variables that planning seeks to bring to certain desired (target) levels or magnitudes, often called *target variables.* For instance, it may be desired to bring the outflow of gold down to zero or to maintain prices at a given level or to achieve a certain annual average rate of growth of national product. Sometimes the targets can be attained by a direct order; for instance, the conversion of the domestic currency into gold may be stopped by decree and thus the gold outflow may be halted, or price controls may be enacted to keep prices at the existing level. However, these are extraordinary measures. More commonly, the government will manipulate some other variables, often called *instrument variables,* in order to affect the target variables indirectly. Thus, in order to stem the outflow of gold, the authorities may raise the domestic structure of interest rates, which will tend to keep domestic capital at home and attract foreign capital. The instrument variable is the structure of interest rates, and the explicit or implicit economic model is one that relates international capital movements to changes in interest rates. The range of instrument variables available to the authorities depends on the constitutional legal provisions, the nature of economy, custom, and so forth. We shall return to consider instrument variables presently.

8. *Methodology and procedure.* The drawing up of an economic plan at whatever level is a complicated and time-consuming procedure. The timing of the work, the methodology employed, the procedures for putting together the plan document—these can vary widely. They will depend in large part on the aims of the plan, the nature of the underlying model, the available instruments, and of course many political and cultural variables.

9. *Enforcement and execution.* Some instruments are easy to handle, such as those that give away something for nothing (welfare payments, production subsidies, above-equilibrium prices, tax rebates). Others—taxes, price and wage controls, exchange controls—require much more elaborate enforcement because they may seek to compel people to act against their wishes or interests. Sound planning requires that the course of plan execution be closely watched for possible revision of policies if the effects diverge from the expected ones.

Types of Planning

A distinction often is made between *macroeconomic and microeconomic* planning or control. As the name suggests (*macro* means "long" in Greek), macroeconomic control or planning concerns itself with the economy as a whole and its major components or sectors. Its goals (target variables) are such as full employment, a certain rate of overall growth, stability of both production and prices, and equilibrium in the balance of payments. Macroeconomic planning does not concern itself, as a rule, with what happens to individual prices so long as the general price level remains constant, nor at what rates individual industries are growing so long as overall growth is satisfactory. Being unconcerned with detail, macroeconomic planning tends not to affect individual firms or even industries *directly*, though it very much affects them indirectly. Hence, it enlists less intense attention on the part of individual interest groups, which may be both an advantage and a disadvantage for its launching and success.

Microeconomic control or planning (*micro* means "small") aims at affecting an individual industry, sector, distinct region, or even firm (if it is large and important enough). In the United States, not only the federal government but all levels of government engage in microeconomic control. The purposes are many; the examples are innumerable. Among its purposes one may mention preservation or enhancement of defense potential (by protecting the watchmaking industry against foreign competition, and by subsidizing such industries as shipbuilding and shipping) and natural resource conservation (as in the discussed case of petroleum, see p. 70). While most of us will agree that there arise quite a few situations when microeconomic planning is desirable in the public interest, there is inevitable controversy regarding individual policies and their instruments. And since in specific instances it is likely to be advocated by those who are to gain most from it, it constantly tests the distinction between public welfare and the mere furtherance of private interests.[6]

Instruments

Control or planning represent a centralization of decisions and activities in the market economy.[7] In seeking to accomplish its aims, public policy in a market economy may either work through and with the market mechanism, or it may work against it, thwart its operation, or substitute something else for it. Instruments that work with and through the market mechanism are sometimes called *indirect controls* because they reach at their targets indirectly. Those that ignore or thwart the market by reaching for their targets directly are known as *direct controls*.

Direct Controls

Direct controls either prohibit specific economic acts or attempt to force them. Instances are many even in the United States, where the general ideological opposition to them is stronger than in most other advanced, democratic countries. *Negative direct controls*, those that are prohibitive, include such measures as an embargo on trade with some countries, acreage limitations in the case of price-supported agricultural commodities, proscription of trade in narcotics or of importation of sugar above the annual quota, and so forth. The historical arch-example on the national scale is, of course, Prohibition in the twenties. Negative direct controls are especially numerous on the state and local levels in connection with zoning regulations (which forbid various kinds of construction or business activity in given urban districts), safety and sanitary codes, licensing, and so forth. To this category also belong (maximum) price and wage

[6]Gerhard Colm, "Economic Planning in the United States," *Weltwirtschaftliches Archiv* 92, no. 1 (1964), pp. 31–56, is a convenient survey. For another basic distinction—between indicative and imperative planning—see p. 87 *infra*.

[7]For advantages and disadvantages of centralization see pp. 32ff.

controls. Price control is often accompanied by rationing so that the limited supply of the given good(s) is distributed in accord with equity or social priorities.

The common economic feature of negative direct controls is that they cause disequilibrium in particular markets by restraining the adjustment of either supply or prices in the face of excess demand. This causes problems, not so much because some of the demand remains unsatisfied, which after all is usually one of the purposes, but because it invites evasion, black markets, contempt for the law, and costly enforcement. Moreover, price control causes wrong signals to be communicated to both sellers and buyers regarding the true scarcity of the good(s), thus distorting the operation of the market mechanism and reducing the economy's efficiency.

Instances of *positive direct controls*, which require certain economic acts (other than taxpaying) of otherwise independent or autonomous entities, are also quite numerous, even in the United States. They range from the requirement that public utilities serve all legitimate customers, through federal and state antidiscrimination and industrial relations legislation, to the various local safety and health codes. Two major instances are compulsory education and compulsory military service. All these examples (with the exception of public utilities), however, tend to affect production as such only marginally, because in a market economy, and a democratic one at that, forcing firms by means of the government's police power into lines of production against their will tends to be both ineffective and politically unpopular. It is economically and politically often wiser to "bribe" them instead—to use indirect controls.

Indirect Controls

As we have indicated, indirect controls work with and through the market mechanism. They do so generally in one of two ways: by enlarging or contracting overall purchasing power, or by making particular activities more profitable or less profitable. Often, both effects occur simultaneously, as when more favorable terms on government-financed housing at once stimulate the construction industry and, by expanding the volume of loans for the purpose, also enlarge the total purchasing power within the economy.

Stabilization policy, the major part of macroeconomic planning, naturally depends heavily on instruments that influence overall purchasing power. This is not the place to discuss either the policy or the instruments. Suffice it to remind ourselves that the most important instruments are (a) fiscal—the size of the government budget and the net budget surplus (or deficit), which directly affect private incomes; and (b) monetary policy, which manipulates the cost and availability of credit and thereby influences the actual volume of credit (and, hence, money) in the economy.[8] Macroeconomic planning also can utilize *selec-*

---

[8]Yet another significant, though as yet not commonly used, stabilization instrument was developed in Sweden (see p. 86). This is the freezing and unfreezing of firms internal liquid funds, the so-called investment reserves, in order to utilize private investment better for countercyclical purposes. With internal sources playing the dominant role in corporation finance in many advanced countries, this instrument is likely to receive more attention in the future.

tive credit controls, as in the housing example mentioned in the preceding paragraph.

Selective indirect controls are of course the main tools of microeconomic planning, and the toolbox available to government is large indeed: tariffs; taxes of all kinds; subsidies,[9] the terms and repayment provisions of credit for special purposes; matching or outright grants; support (above-equilibrium) prices, of which the U.S. farm price support program is among the most famous (or infamous, depending on one's view); and so forth.

Indirect controls have the important advantages of impersonality on the economic plane and compatibility with the market mechanism. In effect, often they announce the rules of the game and let the market take over from there. (In the case of support prices, the government must of course be prepared to absorb the surpluses that the high prices bring forth.) The fact that indirect controls "distort" resource allocation or income distribution is not necessarily a convincing objection. Their purpose, after all, *is* to alter these things in order to achieve goals that the uncontrolled market will presumably not achieve by itself. Nonetheless, indirect controls *may be* objectionable for one of these reasons: The goal may be objectionable (we may not wish to stimulate family farming or private home ownership); the goal may be acceptable but the means may be regarded as inferior (it may be better to pay each farmer a capital lump sum in government bonds in exchange for terminating farm price supports); the indirect control is only a byproduct of a measure imposed for another purpose, such as fiscal revenue, which nevertheless may be inhibiting some economic activity.

A major disadvantage of all selective controls, direct and indirect, is that they invite the pressure of special interests on all levels and against all branches of government. But in a market economy indirect controls are preferable to direct ones because they work through and not against the market mechanism, generally do not create disequilibria in individual markets, and are often more impersonal. Psychologically and politically, they have the great virtue of preserving the economic agent's freedom of choice while affecting the data on which alternatives are appraised. By contrast, direct controls are a form of coercion. Why then are direct controls used at all? Two answers suggest themselves: (a) when public interest calls for the complete cessation or unexceptionable pursuit of an activity that may not be stopped by taxing (trading with the enemy, distribution of narcotics) or sufficiently encouraged by "bribing" (compulsory education); (b) when resources have to be mobilized and redeployed so rapidly and in such a volume that "bribing" would not only create income inequities but would start or aggravate an inflationary spiral. The obvious example is the wartime economy, but .many developing countries trying to advance as rapidly as possible find themselves in a similar situation. What makes the resort to direct controls in this case even more likely is that the main resource is likely to be labor, and it is very difficult for political and psychological reasons to *reduce*

78

[9] A useful compendium is U.S. Congress, Joint Economic Committee, *Subsidy and Subsidy-Effect Programs of the U.S. Government* (Washington, D.C.: Government Printing Office, 1965).

money wages where labor is not wanted under the emergency conditions. This leaves money wage increases as the indirect instrument for redeploying labor to where it is wanted; hence, the inflationary potential of such a policy. Wage controls and (at times) direct limitations of labor mobility may therefore be indicated.

Other Instruments

One of the most powerful instruments in the government's hands inheres in its roles as consumer, producer, and investor. In the United States, since the mid-fifties, all levels of government have been purchasing about one-fifth of the gross national product[10] and have been accounting for about the same proportion of gross fixed investment. In Western Europe, these proportions have been the same or higher—the government's share in investment being sometimes twice as high as here—while government-owned enterprises in the production sector are much more important than here. All this gives government considerable leverage in regard to promoting economic activity, stimulating depressed or backward areas (such as the South in Italy), influencing wage and labor standards, and so forth.

We have already had occasion to mention government's regulation of monopolistic industries and promotion (sometimes, restriction) of competition. This has been the American approach to monopoly: Regulate it if it is a "natural" one; otherwise, don't permit it to develop except in a number of specifically sanctioned exceptions. The European approach has been nationalization of the natural monopolies and of other concentrated industries and a more tolerant attitude toward private monopolies and cartels. In the final analysis, there is probably not much to choose between regulation of nominally private "public utilities" and their nationalized operation (see next section). As for antitrust policies in the United States, their purposes and effects have been debated vigorously. Some feel that the policy's effects have been economically beneficial not only through its direct impact on some industries but also by way of example and deterrent for others. Others are more skeptical. Others feel that the chief benefits have been political—preventing undue concentrations of private power.[11]

NATIONALIZATION
AND PUBLIC ENTERPRISE

In the United States, the climate of opinion has been generally hostile to government—at any level, and especially at the federal—engaging in produc-

[10]This ratio has remained quite stable since the middle fifties, but within total government purchases of goods and services the share of state and local government has been rising and by 1973 was one and one-half times as large as the federal share.

[11]Again the reader is referred to Richard Caves, *American Industry: Structure, Conduct, Performance* (Englewood Cliffs, N.J.: Prentice-Hall, 1964), this series; Joe S. Bain, *Industrial Organization* (New York: John Wiley & Sons, Inc., 1968); and Edward S. Mason, *Economic Concentration and the Monopoly Problem* (New York: Atheneum, 1964).

tion. As a result, there is relatively little public enterprise in this country. Even such industries as the telegraph and telephone services, radio and television broadcasting, airlines, railroads, and central banking, which are nearly always or at least frequently state-owned in other advanced countries, are privately owned here—though in all the mentioned cases, subject to close regulation by public authorities. Nonetheless, quite a few of the activities that compete with or replace actual or potential private enterprise are publicly owned and operated in the United States, ranging from the Post Office, through federal arsenals, power-[12] and water-distribution projects, various institutions in the fields of credit and insurance, to locally owned public housing and urban transportation. Though rarely thought to be such, the provision of education is a major "industry" where public operation predominates. And a very important publicly owned resource is forest lands,[13] together with the associated mineral, water, and recreational resources.

We saw in Chapter 3 that nationalization of major industries, once a cornerstone of the socialist program, has been largely abandoned as a goal by the present-day democratic socialist parties of Europe. Here we pause briefly to discuss nationalization[14] and public ownership as control instruments and to take a glimpse at some of their problems.

Retreat from Nationalization

Nationalization has been traditionally advocated for two kinds of reasons: general and particular. In the socialists' view—by now greatly attenuated—the general reasons for extensive nationalization were to minimize private ownership of the means of production and thereby to reduce the alleged evils of capitalism, including economic instability, labor strife, and maldistribution of wealth, income, and power. With time, however, it has become increasingly evident that on one hand, the inflated power of the state is also an evil, and that, on the other hand, capitalist firms are not unamenable to restraint in the social interest.

Furthermore, it has been realized that nationalization as such contributes relatively little to economic stability and that instruments of macroeconomic planning would have to be invoked in a market economy however much or little nationalized. (However, it is true that a large public enterprise sector helps the government to pursue a contracyclical or a growth-generating investment policy.) As for redistribution, here too, the various tax and welfare instruments can

[12]In 1970, of the total electric power production in the United States (including production by industrial plants) 21.2 percent was generated by publicly owned installations.

[13]As of 1970, the federal government owned 21 percent and state and local governments owned 5.8 percent, of commercial forest land. *Statistical Abstract of the United States*, 1972, p. 626.

[14]Strictly speaking, nationalization is to be distinguished from *socialization*, the latter referring to ownership (or takeover) by any public authority; the former, to the national (federal) government. *Municipalization*, a form of socialization, and ownership by other levels of government below the national are frequently preferred over nationalization by advocates of public ownership as a way of avoiding undue concentration of power.

accomplish much more than nationalization. As for power, it has come to be appreciated that in an industrial society a great deal of power resides with managers and labor leaders, regardless of who the nominal owner(s) of the firms might be. Nor, it has been discovered, is labor strife eliminated by nationalization. It is quite possible for conflicts to arise between a socialist government and labor unions in nationalized industries, as the British Labor Party found out while in power during the postwar years, for example.

The particular reasons pertain to individual industries. They may be nationalized because they are unprofitable and inefficient and have little prospect of improving under private ownership. Such was the case, for example, with the British coal industry and railroads when they were nationalized by the Labor government immediately after World War II. By consolidating operations and pouring in large funds for reequipment and research, the state can bring about improvement that was beyond the means of former owners. Alternatively, nationalization may be advocated not because the industry is sick but because, on the contrary, it is too strong and healthy for the public good—that it is a successful monopoly or exercises potential control over a vital area of the economy. It is for reasons such as these that electric power, transport, steel, munitions, and other industries are frequently nationalized. (In the U.S., the processing of fissionable materials is restricted to federally owned installations in order to maintain public control over this strategically important activity, though these may be operated by private firms under contract.) In such cases, an alternative to nationalization is government regulation, which is the preferred solution in the United States. It is difficult to say which is generally the better arrangement from the public's standpoint. More correctly, nationalization may not do away with the need for regulation, since those in control over state-owned industry still have to be made amenable to the general interest and accountable to political authority. These last problems are among the thorniest relating to public enterprise.[15]

The legal form that is widely regarded as most suitable for public enterprise is the *public corporation*, an autonomous entity, accountable to a ministry of the government and through the ministry to the legislature for general policy but not for detailed activity. Many examples are to be found in Western Europe, especially in the United Kingdom. In this country, on the federal level, the autonomous public corporation has been less common. Historically, an important example is the Tennessee Valley Authority (TVA); established in 1933 as a

---

[15]Three other very important reasons for nationalization must be mentioned. First, the government may assume ownership or control of private firms as a way of rescuing them in a severe depression. Thus, a large part of Italian nationalized enterprises came into the hands of the state in the thirties in this fashion. Second, nationalization may be primarily political—for example, to take over, with or without compensation, the property for foreign nationals, especially of citizens of unfriendly countries. Such for instance, was the case with extensive nationalization in Egypt and Cuba in the early sixties. Third, the state may retain the monopoly of certain economic activities for fiscal purposes, such as state ownership of tobacco, salt, and match industries in some European countries.

public corporation, it later lost some of its autonomy. More recently, a number of important public corporations were created by the federal government. Among them are the U.S. Postal Service (1970), successor to the U.S. Post Office, a federal department; the National Railroad Passenger Corporation (Amtrak), which took over the operation of passenger trains on the still private railroads; and—as an interesting institutional innovation—the mixed public-private Communications Satellite Corporation (Comsat) to develop and operate communications space satellites as a monopoly. The public corporation form of nationalized (or mixed) enterprise combines flexibility, businesslike management, and freedom from undue political interference, as well as ultimate public responsibility. Naturally, whether it in fact functions with efficiency and initiative is not a matter of certainty.[16]

PLANNING AND CONTROL
IN SEVERAL COUNTRIES

The United States

The positive concern of the federal government with the promotion of economic activity is as old as the Republic. Alexander Hamilton's *Report on the Subject of Manufactures* (1791) has remained a classic argument for the promotion of industry with the aid of such indirect instruments as tariffs and subsidies. And from George Washington's first administration until 1934, with the exception of some thirty years immediately before the Civil War, the protective tariff was a major instrument of American "planning" for industrialization. Another important tool for the pursuit of positive economic policy by the federal government was, for a long time, the vast amount of public land in its possession. The land was used successfully to encourage family farming (as with the Homestead Act of 1862), to stimulate the construction of railroads, and even to induce states to set up schools of higher learning (Land Grant College Act of 1862).[17] The Great Depression turned attention to stabilization,[18] and

[16]A brief survey of public enterprise in the United States may be found in Merle Fainsod, Lincoln Gordon, and Joseph C. Palamountain, Jr., *Government and the American Economy*, 3rd ed. (New York: W. W. Norton & Co., Inc., 1959), pp. 737–51. See also Clair Wilcox, *Public Policies Towards Business* (Homewood, Ill.: Richard D. Irwin, Inc., 1960). A voluminous inquiry into the public corporation and other aspects of nationalization in Great Britain is William A. Robson, *Nationalized Industry and Public Ownership* (London: Allen & Unwin, 1960). An interesting collection of essays analyzing the experience of Italian nationalized enterprise and its applicability elsewhere is Stuart Holland, ed., *The State as Entrepreneur* (London: Weidenfeld & Nicolson, 1972).

[17]A useful historical sketch of the promotion of business by the federal government will be found in Fainsod et al., *Government and the American Economy*, Chap. 5.

[18]This is not to say that the objective of stabilization did not prompt important federal measures even before the thirties. Thus, the establishment of the Federal Reserve System in 1913 was a consequence of the serious financial panic of 1907.

after World War II Congress passed the Employment Act of 1946, which for the first time explicitly recognized the federal government's responsibility for the country's economic well being. The government was charged with using "all practicable means . . . to foster and promote free competitive enterprise and the general welfare . . . and to promote maximum employment, production, and purchasing power."

The act created a *Council of Economic Advisers* to the President which analyzes economic trends and prospects and advises him on policy.[19] The strategy that all administrations of both parties have since followed, though in different degree, has been that of macroeconomic planning of the "liberal" variety[20] and of promoting specific programs. The pursuit of both positive guidance and stabilization of the economy, and especially the bolder use of budget deficits to stimulate higher levels of business activity and employment and faster growth, was particularly vigorous under the Kennedy and Johnson administrations. A new departure was taken by President Nixon in August 1971 when he suddenly imposed a price and wage freeze (later relaxed and then reimposed for prices in a series of "phases") and let the U.S. dollar float in terms of other currencies (eventually leading to two formal devaluations, in 1972 and 1973), to try to stop simultaneously an accelerating inflation and a rapid drain of the gold reserve.[21]

Although one cannot speak of national planning in the strict sense in the United States—no national plans as such are produced—and although it is not obvious that there is need for such planning, at least in a rigorous and comprehensive way, nonetheless for some decades now the federal government has been deeply committed to "liberal planning" for stabilization and promotion of the general welfare. The resort to direct controls in peacetime by President Nixon, a Republican president at that, has been declared to be a temporary expedient and not a fundamental rejection of reliance on macroeconomic policies for stabilization. Whether it is such or not is still too early to tell at this writing.

The Netherlands

Both the Netherlands and Sweden share with the United States democratic political structures, a preponderance of private enterprise, and emphasis by the national government on short-term stabilization as against long-term planning. But they differ considerably from one another and from the United States regarding the methods and instruments of economic control. The case of the

---

[19]At the beginning of each year, in pursuance of the Employment Act, the President submits an *Economic Report* to the Congress. This *Report*, together with a much more detailed report to the President from the Council and with a substantial statistical appendix, is published early in the year and constitutes a valuable source of information on the state of the economy and on the administration's policies.

[20]That is, paying respect to economic freedoms.

[21]Cf. Leonard Silk, *Nixonomics*, 2nd ed., (New York: Frederick A. Praeger, Inc., 1973, paperback).

Netherlands is noteworthy because of the consistent use made of an elaborate econometric model for purposes of year-to-year stabilization planning. The model consists of thirty-six equations and as many variables. The chief target variables are the surplus (deficit) of the balance of payments, employment, level of investment, the proportion of wages in the national income, and the price level. The main instrument variables are levels of direct and indirect taxes, government expenditures, the wage level, and credit. (Note that these are all indirect controls available to other democratic governments—except for the wage level, a form of direct control which the Dutch authorities, unlike the United States government, have the power to set.)[22]

The model was constructed by the Central Planning Bureau, an advisory government agency. By means of the model, the Bureau prepares an annual set of projections indicating expected values of target variables on alternative assumptions with regard to values of the instrument variables, and submits it, first to a Central Planning Commission, consisting of representatives of government departments and the public, and then to the Social and Economic Council. The latter, composed equally of representatives of employers, representatives of labor unions, and experts serving in their private capacities, is only an advisory body but in fact wields great power, including that of wage-setting. Its recommendations for the use of the various instruments then in fact constitute the annual plan, though they have no legal force.

Apart from the econometric model, the most distinctive feature of Dutch planning has been the central role of governmental wage and price controls as key instrument variables. Annual wage increases have been negotiated on the national level between representatives of employers and employees, as for example also in Sweden, but in the Netherlands, in contrast to Sweden, the government has had statutory power to enforce a settlement of its choosing. The Dutch government has also had relatively little hesitation to use price control as means of bringing about compliance by the business sector. In this it has been helped by the high concentration in Dutch industry. The high degree of cooperation that the authorities were able to elicit from both labor and business, at least until the mid-sixties, may be explained by the sense of national solidarity flowing from the wartime experience, and by the crucial importance of the balance of payments in a country where the share of exports (or imports) is around one half of the GNP.

The orderly determination of wage increases, however, broke down in 1963–64, at the same time as the ever-greater integration of the country into the European Economic Community (Common Market) increased its dependence on the outside world. For these reasons the task facing Dutch planners in the short run, that of staving off unemployment, inflation, and balance of payments difficulties, has been considerably more complicated since the middle sixties.

[22]Reference here is to the so-called 1961 model; see James G. Abert, *Economic Policy and Planning in the Netherlands, 1950–1965* (New Haven: Yale University Press, 1969), pp. 190–229.

It was also in the mid-sixties that the first attempts toward long-term (five-year) planning have been made in the Netherlands. A different mathematical model has been used for this purpose. As yet, long-term planning has been of only limited importance, however.[23]

Sweden

Although Sweden has had a social-democratic government since 1932, private enterprise is almost as prevalent in that country as in the United States. There is hardly any public enterprise other than public utilities, railroads, and mining. The private sector accounts for about 95 percent of the employment in manufacturing, and for about 90 percent of employment in business enterprises in general. Private investment is stimulated by government policies, although since the late sixties there has also been a tendency for the state to acquire shares in companies in some particular lines of activity. Cooperatives are important, though not dominant, in retailing, wholesaling, food processing, and a few other areas in what is the classic country of consumer cooperation. Welfare measures are highly developed in what is also a classic example of the welfare state.

Lately, Sweden has had the highest per capita national income in Europe and the second highest in the world, after the United States. At the same time, it has had one of the very highest ratios of tax revenue to GNP—over 40 percent, as against about 30 percent in the United States. The high tax burden and heavy reliance on progressive income taxes together mean that many families, even with relatively modest incomes, find themselves in a very high income-tax bracket. This situation, plus a general egalitarian attitude of the trade-union and social-democratic movements, may have significantly weakened material incentives among the Swedish population, in the opinion of some competent observers.

Sweden has pioneered in the shaping of instruments for contracyclical policy and stabilization. A major step in this direction was the budget reform of 1937, which divided the government's budget into two parts, the current and capital budgets, in order to bring out the distinction between current consumption and investment by the state, and began the deliberate utilization of budgetary deficits and surpluses for stabilization purposes. Along with a number of

---

[23]A comprehensive study of Dutch planning in several of its aspects is Abert's monograph, cited in note 22. An authoritative, brief review is Pieter deWolff, "Central Planning in the Netherlands," in Yngve Larsson et al., *Governmental Planning and Political Economy* (Berkeley: Institute of Business and Economic Research, University of California, 1967), pp. 25–52 (and pp. 89–114 for deWolff's discussion of the econometric model). Of great interest are the observations on Dutch planning and policy by Andrew Shonfield in his *Modern Capitalism: The Changing Balance of Public and Private Power* (New York: Oxford University Press, 1965, paperback), pp. 211–20 and throughout. (Shonfield's book, though of course not uncontroversial, is one of the most thorough analyses of the evolution of capitalism in the advanced countries since World War II, and as such is strongly recommended to the reader.) On Dutch incomes policy and the breakdown of wage control in the mid-sixties see Lloyd Ulman and Robert J. Flanagan, *Wage Restraint: A Study of Incomes Policies in Western Europe* (Berkeley: University of California Press, 1971), pp. 48–87.

more or less standard tools—general fiscal and monetary policy, public works, a standby emergency public works budget, loans for housing construction (90 percent being financed by government credit), and extensive measures to promote labor mobility—Sweden has developed a distinctive instrument, the investment reserve. No mathematical model is used in this connection.

The key organization in the investment reserve system is the National Labor Market Board (NLMB)—like the Dutch Social and Economic Council, not a government bureau but a tripartite entity consisting of representatives of labor, employers, and government. The NLMB, together with twenty-five local Labor Market Boards and many regional offices, is responsible for the full employment program, collects information, prepares forecasts, stimulates labor mobility, and advises firms on location.

The investment reserve system is complex in detail but simple enough in principle. Firms receive tax incentives to set aside up to 40 percent of their pretax profit in any year as an investment reserve. Of the amount so set aside, 46 percent is deposited with the Central Bank and remains frozen there until officially released. The remaining 54 percent is retained by the firm. When business conditions decline and increased investment activity becomes desirable, the Ministry of Finance decides how much of the investment reserves may be used and under what conditions and so informs the NLMB, which in turn gives permission to individual companies. The reserves must be used for approved types of investment projects, the two portions of the reserve being utilized in the same 46–54 ratio. Further incentives by way of accelerated depreciation write-offs and taxes are extended at this time in order to stimulate the actual use of the reserves for investment. Since 1963, the device has also been used to promote business in depressed areas regardless of general economic conditions.

The investment reserve system finds its rationale in the importance of internal funds for company financing and the instability of unregulated investment outlays over the business cycle. It is flexible regarding timing, amount released, and sector or region of impact. It works through the market and does not discourage efficiency.

Sweden presents an interesting amalgam of capitalist and socialist institutions and ideologies. The social-democratic government's policy has been, on one hand, strongly in favor of private enterprise in the economy ("liberal" in the European sense), while carrying welfare and egalitarian measures to a very high degree, on the other hand.[24]

[24]A convenient account of Swedish stabilization policies and instruments is U.S. Congress, Joint Economic Committee, *Economic Policies and Practices: Paper No. 5, Unemployment Programs in Sweden* (Washington, D.C.: Government Printing Office, 1964). Specifically on the investment reserve see also Martin Schnitzer, *The Swedish Investment Reserve: A Device for Economic Stabilization?* (Washington: American Enterprise Institute for Public Policy Research, 1967). An excellent discussion of the economics underlying the Swedish policies is to be found in Assar Lindbeck, "Theories and Problems in Swedish Economic Policy in the Postwar Period," *American Economic Review*, 58:3:2 (June 1968), pp. 1–87. See especially Lindbeck's discussion of "liberalism or socialism" on pp. 78–79. There has also been since 1948 some long-range planning of a very loose sort in Sweden, the plans never being formally adopted as such by the government (Lindbeck, *American Economic Review*, pp. 58 ff.).

If the Netherlands and Sweden have stressed short-run stabilization, France has developed in the postwar period and continues to practice the most elaborate and detailed planning system among the advanced Western countries, one that emphasizes the longer term and is more oriented toward growth than stabilization. The central institution in French planning is the General Commissariat (Commission) for Planning (G.C.P.), but many other bodies, governmental and multipartite, are also involved. Established as early as 1946 in order to plan the postwar reconstruction of the French economy, the G.C.P. soon became concerned with planning for the utilization of the European Recovery Program ("Marshall Plan") funds supplied by the United States.

Two phrases frequently used in connection with French planning by its partisans are *économie concertée*, which may be translated as "a preconcerted economy," and "indicative planning." The former denotes that the plan emerges as a broad consensus among various major groups in the society, while the term "indicative" is meant to stress that the planning provides only the framework and guidelines for future economic activity and does not attempt to force or coerce anyone to comply (as is the case with Soviet-style planning, which is accordingly termed "imperative"). Indicative planning, however, does not preclude the use of rather strong instruments by the government to carry out the plan, as we shall see.

The fundamental purposes of the plan are (1) to stimulate overall economic growth, (2) to promote the modernization of the economy, (3) to shape the sectoral, industrial, and regional pattern of production in more desirable directions, while (4) preserving full employment, stability, and balance of payments equilibrium, and (5) to carry out "social investment" by the state, investment in facilities to produce public goods of various kinds. The Fourth Plan (1962–65) explicitly aimed to steer consumption in the "Galbraithian" direction; in other words, toward public goods as against personal consumption ("gadgets" was the expression used). The Fifth Plan (1966–70) took the politically difficult direction of projecting an incomes policy by setting targets for wages, prices, and profits. The Sixth Plan (1971–75) again emphasizes industrial development.

Short-term stabilization, however, has generally functioned apart from the plan, and has tended at times to be at odds with the realization of the plan.

Drawing up the plan is a complex process that intentionally seeks to involve a large number of interested parties and professional experts. The process begins with the G.C.P. and the I.N.S.E.E. (National Institute for Statistics and Economic Studies) preparing studies of the current situation and of medium-term and longer-term possibilities. Several alternative sketches of the plan are produced for consideration by the Investment and Planning Section of the Economic and Social Council, a multipartite body, and then by the executive branch of the government. After the government has laid down the directives for the plan, stipulated its main purposes and goals, and has drawn up a balanced ac-

87

count for the plan's target year, the so-called Modernization Committees take over. These committees, about two dozen in number and multipartite in structure, concern themselves with individual sectors, industries, or problem areas. Their proposals are coordinated by the G.C.P. until a consistent plan emerges, leading eventually to approval by the government, consultation with the Economic and Social Council, and final approval in toto by Parliament. The operative document that finally emerges in this fashion consists primarily of a series of growth targets for the economy as a whole, its main sectors by use of product (consumption, investment, and so forth), and the various production sectors and industries. No production targets for individual firms are given (except for some of the larger nationalized public utilities), for doing so would transform the plan from an "indicative" to an "imperative" one.

It is clear even from this summary sketch that great emphasis is placed on consensus among government representatives, experts, and spokesmen for various interest groups. This in itself is an important instrument of plan execution in that it tends to maximize the acceptance of the plan's objectives by the public and to give the targets greater credibility. And in fact, for a country as politically diverse as France, the degree of consensus achieved around the plan has been notable, though there is no assurance that it will continue indefinitely.

But in addition, the authorities dispose of an impressive arsenal of tools for executing the plan. First, some 40 percent of all gross fixed investment involves either the "general government" sector or public enterprises, and together with the private investment financed by the state, the government has direct leverage over more than half of all investment in the country. Beyond this, the government has control over the larger loans and over stock issues and uses this power to ensure that priority in financing is given to economic activity conforming to the plan and its sectoral divisions. Tax exemptions of various kinds, depreciation write-off privileges, loan guarantees, and even subsidies are employed to the same end. Lastly, the government retains price controls over a number of key commodities and uses this power to increase compliance with the plan.

Many observers have stressed that French planning is thus deeply rooted in French history and tradition. It can be seen as a manifestation of the centuries-old *dirigisme*—the philosophy and policy of active intervention in the economy by the French state. It also rests on the traditional authority and power of the upper reaches of the civil service, and the close ties between it and the leading private firms.

But to return to the methods: For the first quarter century French planning (unlike, say, the Dutch variety) eschewed any mathematical formalization of the methodology. But beginning with the Sixth Plan (1971–75), an elaborate mathematical model has been employed, engagingly named the FIFI Model (for "physical and financial"). It is a very large model—1,500 equations—that is based on some rather original conceptions of the economic structure. It is, however, not a "dynamic" model (like the Dutch), in the sense that one period's variables are not made to depend on the values of previous periods' variables. The experience with this model is yet too brief to allow of conclusion regarding its utility.

The FIFI Model incorporates an explicit and important distinction between those industries that are subject to foreign competition and those that are not. The distinction is indeed an important one also in a historical perspective, in that the French economy has been increasingly integrated into the European Economic Community, and has therefore been also more and more subject to external influence. As with Dutch planning, this trend has rendered French planning more difficult to undertake and carry out.

The French experience with planning after the war has engendered some very strong opinions and a great deal of controversy both at home and abroad. Some of its leading practitioners and partisans have been imbued with almost messianic zeal, arguing (at their more modest) that it is a democratic method of strengthening and reinvigorating a free economy by decreasing uncertainty about the future, while at the same time solving some socioeconomic problems. Its opponents, naturally, disagree.

Arising as it did almost immediately after the war, French planning was at once an expression of deep disappointment with the stagnation of the economy during the interwar decades, and of the social optimism that flowed from the wartime Resistance and the victory of 1945. The earliest plans thus had a considerable reformist content. By the middle fifties this aspect of the plans tended to disappear for various reasons, and the general tenor has been a rather conservative one, at least in the sense of strengthening the private sector.[25]

Indeed, the close connection between the state and large-scale private enterprise in the French planning process has been one of the chief criticisms leveled from the side of both the moderate and not-so-moderate left. It is a fact that labor has played a rather minor role in the planning process, its representatives having been considerably outnumbered by those of business and other groups on the various commissions. At the same time, it has been charged, the process of "concertation" has afforded ample opportunity for business firms to coordinate their interests and actions with one another and with those of the state. The government's intervention in the economy as part of the plan's execution, it is alleged, serves to strengthen private industry. Both need one another, since the state needs economic growth, and both have developed a convenient symbiosis. "The important and innovative development was the conversion of the protective cartel system into a modernizing, expansionist cartel system."[26]

[25]Cf. Richard B. DuBoff, "The Decline of Economic Planning in France," *Western Political Science Quarterly*, 21:1 (March 1968), pp. 98–109.

[26]Stephen S. Cohen, "From Causation to Decision: Planning as Politics," *American Economic Review*, 60:2 (May 1970), p. 181. Professor Cohen is a leading academic proponent of the view that French planning has had the effect of strengthening private power. See also his *Modern Capitalist Planning: The French Model* (Cambridge: Harvard University Press, 1969).

From the free-enterprise ("liberal") side the criticism has been not entirely dissimilar, except that in its view the chief victims have been the free market and enterprise. The close cooperation between the state and some of the leading firms, it is charged, has amounted to favoritism and has led to a diminution of competitiveness in the economy; and, further, that the state's means of intervention, far from being simply "indicative," have in fact enhanced *dirigisme* and have tended to impair the market mechanism.[27]

Another major point of contention is whether French planning has made a positive contribution toward economic growth. Proponents point to the very high rate of growth of the French economy in the postwar period—one of the highest in Western Europe—as proof of success, recalling that in the interwar period the French economy was notoriously stagnant. Skeptics reply that some Western European countries with no national planning at all, especially West Germany and Italy, have experienced even higher rates of growth during the postwar period. They also point out that the attainment of sectoral goals under the plans has not been uniformly close.

There is little dispute, though, that the imperatives of short-term stabilization have severely interfered with the carrying out of the plan time and again. Restraining inflationary pressures, defending the balance of payments, adjusting to sharp wage increases brought on by political upheaval (as immediately after the strikes and disturbances of May 1968)—all such emergency policies quite understandably took priority over the execution of a medium-term plan at the given moment.[28]

French Planning for the U.S.?

Is the French planning experience exportable? In view of France's relatively high growth and virtual absence of unemployment during the fifties and sixties, this question has often been asked in such countries as the United States and Canada, which have had substantial unemployment and much lower growth rates, and the United Kingdom and Belgium, also with relatively low growth though without significant unemployment.

So far as the United States is concerned, the case for borrowing French planning methods is not at all obvious, even if we grant for the moment (which

[27]Cf. Vera Lutz, *Central Planning for the Market Economy: An Analysis of the French Theory and Experience* (London: Longmans, 1969).

[28]French planning has prompted the publication of many books and articles in English, let alone in French. A standard treatise is John and Anne-Marie Hackett, *Economic Planning in France* (London: Allen & Unwin, 1963). A translation of a 1962 French work is Pierre Bauchet, *Economic Planning: The French Experience* (New York: Frederick A. Praeger, Inc., 1964). See also the references in the preceding footnotes. A less critical appreciation than some others is A. S. Vasconcellos and B. F. Kiker, "An Evaluation of French National Planning: 1949–1964," *Journal of Common Market Studies* (Oxford), March 1970, pp. 216–35. Andrew Shonfield's *Modern Capitalism* (Chaps. 5, 7, and throughout) is full of insights on this subject, while Ulman and Flanagan, *Wage Restraint*, has a good chapter on French incomes policy, including a section (pp. 164 ff.) on the Gaullist policies regarding stockholding, profit sharing, and participation in management by workers.

is in fact questioned, as we just saw) that national planning has made a considerable contribution to the very good performance of the French economy in the postwar years.

First, it is not clear that much is to be gained in the United States by setting a precise target for overall economic growth some four to five years in advance. The duration of a presidential administration in this country is only four years; besides, any such definite commitment would be politically unwise if taken seriously by the public, and ineffectual, if not. To instill confidence and encourage capital formation, it is probably quite sufficient for the administration to convince the public that it will resolutely pursue measures within its powers to attain and maintain high employment, keep prices relatively stable, and stimulate growth. And while growth targets for specific industries and sectors may reduce some uncertainty regarding the future, they would not seem to be so desirable as to be set up in the face of very likely opposition of business and at the risk of the targets' being discredited through uneven attainment.

Equally important is the fact that some of the most effective enforcement instruments are not available—or not to the same degree—to the U.S. government. Public investment at *all* levels of government accounts in this country for about one-fifth of total fixed investment, or about half its relative importance in France, and attempts by an administration to establish tight control over it all would run counter to our federal political structure. Nor does the United States generally exercise direct control over important prices in peacetime. Perhaps most significant, the very rigorous control over credit and stock issues that is exercised by the French government would hardly be voted by Congress or accepted by the financial and business communities in this country in normal times. Finally, attempts to reach consensus within industries in the French manner would tend to clash with our tradition of keeping business as competitive as possible wherever feasible.

SUMMARY

In its broadest meaning, public planning is the purposeful, deliberate, systematic shaping of economic phenomena by some public authority. It should not be confused with socialism or with nationalization; it exists in market economies as well as in command economies; some forms of it are quite compatible with economic freedoms and political democracy. Macroeconomic planning aims at maintaining such conditions as full employment, price stability, and a desirable growth rate. Microeconomic planning deals with individual sectors, regions, and industries. The instruments of control or planning in a market economy include, among others, indirect controls (which work through the market mechanism) and direct controls (which attempt to thwart its operation) to achieve certain social goals. In the United States, national economic policy (not usually called "planning") works primarily through macroeconomic planning, indirect controls, and specific programs. The Netherlands and Sweden have developed elaborate methods and institutions of short-term stabilization. France is the outstanding example of an advanced western country resorting to longer-term planning to control the direction and pace of its economic growth, using some distinctive procedures and instruments. The effects and successes of French planning are subject to much dispute.

The Command Economy:

The USSR

CHAPTER SIX

Considerable as the differences in institutional arrangements, ideology, and economic performance among the advanced Western countries may be, they are relatively minor compared to the differences between them and the countries we generally call "communist." What is more, the communist countries themselves, once strikingly uniform in their governing ideologies and institutions, have in many cases so diverged from one another over the past two decades that today they represent a striking variety of economic systems. Some of the most interesting insights in the field of comparative economic systems are therefore to be obtained by inquiring into the internal arrangements of the various communist economies, and by comparing them with the Western economies on one hand and among themselves on the other. This is what we briefly do in this and the ensuing two chapters. This chapter takes a look at the Soviet economy—the first communist economy historically, still the most important communist economy, and at one time or another the model for nearly all the other countries that embarked on the communist road. The next chapter deals with several communist countries—among them China and Cuba—that have in some respects significantly deviated from the Soviet model, though without embracing the market mechanism. Lastly, Chapter 8 will deal with those communist countries that have been "marketized."

The First World War gave Lenin his chance. Capitalizing on the country's war-weariness and the peasants' hunger for land, he and his Bolshevik (later, Communist) party seized power in Russia in November[1] 1917 and retained it through a prolonged, bloody civil war. Their ultimate aim was to redo not only Russia but the whole world in the image of Marxian socialism and full communism—a world without want, classes, exploitation, injustice, and war. But first there were two paradoxes to be resolved. The Communists were a tiny minority in the population, some four-fifths of which consisted of backward and poor peasants who did not share communist values or goals. Thus, dictatorship and at least some coercion were unavoidable internally if the Communists were to remain in power and to pursue their own goals resolutely, which they fully intended to do. Second, the outside world, especially the advanced countries, did not oblige by following revolutionary suit, as the Communists had expected. Instead, the Soviet Union found itself isolated in an ideologically unfriendly world, angry at the expropriation of the large amount of foreign capital within Russia, and resentful of Moscow's unceasing attempts to export its revolution. These two facts—continuous struggle with an uncooperative population, particularly peasantry, at home and an antagonistic relationship with most of the outside world—have profoundly affected Soviet economics as well as politics ever since.[2]

The Soviet economy at the time of the communist takeover presented a mixed picture. On one hand, it was predominantly agricultural, backward, and very poor on a per capita basis. On the other hand, thanks to very rapid industrialization since the 1880s and its large population, by 1917 Russia already had the fifth biggest industrial complex in the world, a relatively large heavy industry, and an appreciable nucleus of scientists and engineers. On the basis of this modern sector, and with the aid of millions of laborers to be drawn from the villages, rapid industrialization was to resume under the Soviets, according to the plans that were being drawn up and hotly debated[3] during the twenties. When Stalin took power at the end of that decade, he was determined to build up as quickly as possible the country's industrial and military might to ensure security from external attack and "the victory of socialism" within the USSR. To do so he proceeded in three main directions: (1) He put extreme pressure on the country, and especially on the peasants, to mobilize all resources and to devote as large a share of them as possible to capital formation (and, later, defense), almost heedless of the consumers' well being. (2) He launched a series of Five-Year Plans, the first in 1928, and replaced the market economy and

[1]It was still October by the Julian calendar then in effect in Russia; hence the name "October Revolution." The Tsarist regime had been overthrown the previous March (February Revolution); in the meantime, the country was ruled by a democratic Provisional Government.

[2]A good, brief historical survey of the Soviet economy is Alec Nove's *An Economic History of the USSR* (London: Allan Lane, 1969). For much fuller descriptions and analyses of the present-day Soviet economy the reader is referred to Abram Bergson, *The Economics of Soviet Planning* (New Haven: Yale University Press paperback, 1964); Robert W. Campbell, *Soviet Economic Power* (Cambridge: Houghton Mifflin Co., 2nd ed., 1966); and Alec Nove, *The Soviet Economy—An Introduction* (New York: Frederick A. Praeger, Inc., 2nd rev. ed., 1969).

[3]On these debates, see Nicolas Spulber, *Soviet Strategy for Economic Growth* (Bloomington: Indiana University Press, 1964), and Alexander Erlich, *The Soviet Industrialization Debate, 1924–1928* (Cambridge: Harvard University Press, 1960).

whatever then still remained of private enterprise (mostly in agriculture and small-scale production elsewhere) with a highly centralized command economy and almost complete state ownership of means of production. (3) He soon began a ruthless police terror that was to send millions into concentration camps and untold numbers to death. Whatever its real reasons, the terror served to enforce the public's often severe privations, the constraints on personal economic freedom, and the high degree of centralization of the economy.

Ever since then, the Soviet economy has always been in a hurry to raise itself, with relatively little outside help, from a position of comparative backwardness to one of preeminent industrial and military power. The Soviet leaders' ideology, though couched in Marxist and revolutionary terms, has been one of the prime instances of an industrializing ideology in modern times.[4] The haste with which Soviet industrialization has been conducted goes far to explain many of the characteristic features of the Soviet economy, such as the very high share of investment in the national product (high "investment rate") and the highest priority accorded to the development of the "heavy" industries. It also helps explain the rapid growth, the ambitiousness of the national plans, the constant pressure on the country's resources, and the chronic shortages of materials, equipment, and skilled labor. These in turn help explain the extreme centralization of the organizational structure in the form of the command economy, although the authoritarian nature of the political faith and the ideological bias against the market mechanism doubtless also played a role in this regard. Finally, these consequences of haste help explain many of the Soviet economy's inefficiencies. How to get rid of the inefficiencies has been a major concern of the Soviet leadership for some time; hence, the problem of "reform."

Although the Soviet economy has grown tremendously in both size of output and technological sophistication since the Five-Year Plans were launched and the present institutions were implanted in the late twenties and early thirties, and despite the much-publicized economic reforms (especially that of 1965), the Soviet economic system has changed relatively little in its essential and characteristic features in the meantime. Its strengths and weaknesses have also remained the same—though, if anything, the changing circumstances have made its strength less apposite and its weaknesses more conspicuous than before.

ORGANIZATION
OF THE SOVIET ECONOMY

Ownership

The Soviet economy is officially designated as "socialist" because of the predominance of public ownership of production assets. Note that it is never referred to by Soviet spokesmen as "communist"—the term is reserved ex-

95

---

[4]On industrializing ideologies, see p. 36.

clusively for the Marxist ultimate society of the future[5] that the USSR is now said to be in the process of "constructing."

The direct employment of one person by another is not permitted (except for the very few domestic servants). Households own their personal possessions; they may also own deposits in savings banks, state bonds, and insurance policies. But all natural resources, including all land, are owned by the state, as is the bulk of reproducible capital goods. Yet in three sectors—agriculture, retail trade, and housing—there is also substantial nonstate ownership, including private ownership. The situation in agriculture shall be taken up presently. As for retail trade, in 1971, state-owned stores accounted for 68.8 percent of the value of retail sales, cooperative stores (under close government control, mostly rural), 28.8 percent, and the *kolkhoz market*, 2.4 percent. The last consists of a series of "farmers' markets," mostly in cities, to which peasants and collective farms may sell their own produce freely at unregulated prices. In housing, at the end of 1971, 69 percent of all *urban* dwelling space was state-owned and (to a small degree) cooperative; the rest was privately owned for supposedly personal use. Most rural housing is privately owned.

A few other, and mostly quite minor, instances of private economic activity may be mentioned. Professionals—doctors, dentists, lawyers, teachers—are permitted to engage in private practice and often do. More numerous are various artisans and craftsmen working on their own account: tailors and seamstresses, cobblers, carpenters, and the like. There is a great deal of "moonlighting" by state employees. Last but not least, there seems to be a large amount of illegal trading and even manufacturing for private profit. The extremely severe penalties, up to death, meted out for "economic crimes"—such as embezzling and pilfering from the state, bribe-taking and bribe-giving—suggest that Soviet man may not be much less self-serving or much more civic-minded than Western man despite decades of education in socialist morality.

The Organizational Pyramid[6]

The whole Soviet economy—with the exception of the household sector—can be depicted as an enormous bureaucratic pyramid, or a series of pyramids with a common apex. All the significant decisions are made at the top. Indeed, all the most important ones and a surprising number of detailed ones are made by the the dictator himself, as was the case under Stalin and Khrushchev, or by a very few men in the brief periods (such as the present) when there seems to have been no single boss. These men are (or were) at once leaders of the Communist party of the Soviet Union and of the Soviet government. This is one of the senses in which the party rules the country. The bottom tier of this pyramid consists of hundreds of thousands of individual firms (including farms)

---

[5]For the Marxist distinction between "socialism" and "communism" see p. 45.

[6]All description of the Soviet economy in this chapter pertains to the situation following the 1965 reorganization, except as otherwise noted.

whose main task is to carry out directives from above. Between the bottom tier and the top of the pyramid there is a welter of planning, administrative, financial, statistical, and other bureaucratic hierarchies, not the least important of which is that of the Communist party itself and closely related organizations.

The most important planning agency of the Soviet government is the State Planning Commission of the USSR, usually known by its Russian abbreviation *Gosplan USSR*. The "USSR" in the title indicates that this is the commission on the national level; there is a Gosplan for each of the constituent republics,[7] as well as province and district planning offices. Gosplan USSR prepares both the long-term and the short-term plans and in fact decides many other issues of economic policy, although in theory it is only an advisory body within the government. A most powerful institution, it does not, however, have complete monopoly of planning even at the highest level. Other high-level bodies concern themselves with planning construction (a very important sector in a rapidly growing economy) and many other specialized areas and activities, such as research and development. The State Commission for the Supply of Materials and Equipment (*Gossnab USSR*) is in charge of distributing most of those materials and Equipment that are centrally allocated; but since almost every important producer good is centrally allocated—there have been in recent years fifteen to twenty thousand such commodities—this is a very powerful organization indeed. Like Gosplan, the other planning agencies usually constitute large hierarchical organizations on a territorial basis. Still other planning bodies concern themselves with the problems of individual republics or large regions, cutting across sectors, industries, and functional areas.

But the planning and day-to-day management of individual sectors of industries of the economy is done by so-called *ministries*, of which there are several dozen.[8] Each ministry is in charge of a hierarchical organization, at the bottom tier of which are the individual enterprises. There are many other government departments with authority in economic affairs, but they must remain unmentioned here for lack of space. There is a great deal of jurisdictional overlap and friction within the overall organizational pyramid, and confusion (enhanced by frequent reorganizations) is as much the rule as order.

Within the pyramid there is relatively little communication horizontally,

[7]The Union of Soviet Socialist Republics (USSR) is formally a federation of fifteen republics, which are in fact much less autonomous than the American states, however. By far the largest and most important of them is the Russian Socialist Federated Soviet Republic (RSFSR), which accounts for over three-fourths of the area and some 53 percent of the population of the USSR. The second most populous, the Ukrainian Soviet Socialist Republic, has 19 percent of the USSR's population, while the least populous (and economically one of the most advanced), the Estonian SSR, has only one-half of one percent. Readers interested in the political structure and processes of the Soviet Union are referred to Merle Fainsod's very thorough *How Russia Is Ruled* (Cambridge: Harvard University Press, rev. ed., 1963) or the concise account in Gwendolyn M. Carter, *The Government of the Soviet Union* (New York: Harcourt, Brace and World, 1962).

[8]This is so since October 1965, and was so before July 1957. From 1957 to 1965, industrial enterprises were mostly subordinated to regional authorities (sovnarkhozes), of which there were at first just over 100 and later somewhat under 50.

even among firms, but there is a large flow of messages vertically. The upward-flowing messages carry, in great volume and detail, data about the state of the economy and particularly about the execution of past directives, and requests for permission to act—information that is essential for the top authorities on which to base plans and other decisions. The equally detailed information flowing downward consists of specific directives, instructions, and permissions (or denials thereof). Communication lines tend to be long, causing delays in adjustment to errors in planning and changing conditions. The *Central Statistical Administration USSR* and its many regional and local offices collect an enormous number of periodic and occasional reports, process them, and channel the data upward to the many planning, financial, and administrative authorities. It and the *USSR Ministry of Finance* set reporting and statistical standards for all economic units. The accuracy of the information reported up presents a major problem, since there is strong temptation at all levels to distort the data in one's own favor. This prompts innumerable audits and inspections by a great variety of authorities, ranging from banking and fiscal offices to the Party and the police.

Harking back to Chapter 2, we note that there is almost no adaptation by self-organization in the Soviet economy. In other words, new institutions are created not "on the spot" but by the highest economic and political authorities, though, of course, not without suggestions from below. Thus, institutional change may be decisive and far-reaching (though there is a strong conservative bias in the Soviet leadership against fundamental changes), but many less dramatic institutional innovations may be very slow in coming.

The Industrial Firm

In industry, the basic production unit—called the "enterprise" in Soviet usage even though it has relatively little scope to be enterprising—usually consists of a single factory.[9] The manager ("director") of a Soviet enterprise does not have to contend with any independent labor union and therefore has great authority with regard to the work force as compared with his Western counterpart. But in most other matters the Soviet manager and the enterprise as such have relatively little freedom of action.

The chief task of the enterprise is to carry out directives from above. These directives, usually formalized as the enterprise's plan for the year (or quarter, or month), pertain primarily to sales, outputs, inputs, finances, profit, and invest-

---

[9]Since the middle of the sixties there has been some effort to merge enterprises with similar or complementary lines of production into superenterprises, so-called *production associations*. By April 1973 some 12 percent of total industrial output (by value) was accounted for by the associations, a relatively small fraction compared to some other East European countries with the same tendency. But in that month it was decreed to step up the process of formation of production associations, and in some cases to merge them further into super-super-enterprises, the so-called *industrial associations*. At this writing it is still impossible to say how far the merger process might go and what its effects might be, but it does look as though the average size of the Soviet industrial enterprise—already very large by even American standards—may increase a good deal yet. In the discussion that follows the terms "firm" and "enterprise" must be understood accordingly.

ment, and in toto govern the firm's activities in great detail. The industrial enterprise's plan typically includes two kinds of directive with regard to the results of its activity. The first is a global target, by which the enterprise's performance is primarily judged. This is its chief "success indicator." Since the economic reform of 1965 the global target is usually one of the following: total sales at officially set prices, total sum of profit, or profitability, that is, the ratio of profit to total assets.[10] Second, the firm receives output targets for individual commodities. The number of such targets varies with the character of the output and is often quite large. They are usually expressed in physical units (tons, meters, units, and so forth), unless the commodities are heterogeneous, in which case the targets may be expressed in value.

Although the 1965 reform enhanced the importance of profit and profitability as objectives of the firm's activity, in point of fact the main success indicators continued to be those relating to production as such: the volume of sales and the physical output of individual commodities. Management is strongly induced by means of monetary bonuses and other rewards, and is pressured in other ways, to meet and to exceed sales and output targets—in Soviet parlance, "to fulfill and overfulfill the production plan"—and it tends to respond, often at the expense of other desiderata, such as cost or quality.

With regard to inputs, the enterprise is typically assigned a maximum limit for the amount it may spend on wages per month. It is allowed to consume no more than certain amounts of individual important materials and fuel per unit of output. But as we have already mentioned, most important materials and fuel are allocated (rationed) to the enterprise in predetermined quantities, anyway.

Soviet enterprises use money and pay or receive prices and wages. Since the prices (wages) of all inputs and outputs are fixed and known at the time that the directives (plans) are drawn up, it is a relatively simple matter also to establish targets for unit cost of production and for aggregate profits (or losses). The chief importance of profits from the standpoint of the firm is that they are the main financial source of incentive funds, the exact amount of which is determined by meeting the above-mentioned targets. There are three incentive funds financed from profits: (a) the fund from which bonuses are paid to managerial personnel and to other employees of the firm: (b) that from which expenditures are made for the welfare of the staff (housing, recreation, and so on); and (c) the fund from which management may spend for investment purposes. The last, so-called decentralized investment, accounts for only a very small part of total investment in the economy or in industry. Also out of profits the firm makes the so-called payment for assets—a kind of interest charge (usually at 6 percent per

---

[10]Before the reform of 1965 the global target for the industrial firm was the value of *output*, rather than sales, expressed in so-called constant prices. This was a very unsatisfactory target, in part because it induced enterprises to produce "for the plan," regardless of the demand for the goods or their quality. The changeover to sales as the global target is an improvement, although under conditions of the sellers' market producers can still pay too little heed to demand.

annum) that the firm pays to the state for the investment in its assets.[11] Any profit left over is recaptured by the state, an unfortunate provision in that it reduces the firm's incentive to earn greater profit through greater efficiency.

The plans (directives) cannot possibly cover every detail of the enterprise's operation, so it is necessary to provide guidance to management for whatever decisions it may have to take on its own. Collectively known by the Russian abbreviation *khozraschet*, these rules enjoin the enterprise to manage its own finances, to keep books, to be solvent (unless otherwise instructed by its superiors), and to maximize its profits or minimize its losses within its very limited range of choice. But "the plan" always comes first, and the enterprise's range of choice pertains to little more than control over obvious waste. It is in this very narrow sense that one must understand the Soviet notion—at least as held hitherto—of profits (losses) as a "synthetic indicator" of managerial efficiency.

Agriculture

More varied is the organizational structure in agriculture, where there are three sectors in terms of ownership. The *state farm* (*sovkhoz*) is state owned, like the industrial enterprise, and is run somewhat like the latter. Its labor force is hired for wages and it is subject to rather rigid production plans (although also at the mercy of the elements). The *collective farm* (*kolkhoz*) is nominally cooperative, that is, owned by its members (except for the land, which is completely nationalized). More on this peculiarly Soviet and historically very important type of institution presently. Thirdly, there is also a substantial private sector, which in turn consists of some distinct subsectors. The relative importance of the three sectors in Soviet agriculture in 1970 is shown in the following table:

	State Farms	Collective Farms	Private Plots	All Sectors
			P e r c e n t	
1. Gross output	28	40	32	100
2. Marketed output	40	48	12	100
3. Cultivated land	49	48	3	100
4. Labor input (annual average)	24	45	30	100

Source: Lines 1, 2, 3—official Soviet statistics; line 4—Murray Feshbach, "Manpower Trends in the USSR, 1950 to 1980" (U.S. Department of Commerce, Foreign Demographic Analysis Division, May 1971, mimeographed), Table 18.

The kolkhoz, then, is still the most important organizational form, although its relative importance has declined considerably since the late fifties. Nominally a producers' cooperative whose members are peasant households (households, not individuals) in a given village or a group of neighboring villages, the institution was in fact forced on the peasants and has been since very

[11]The capital value of the state's investment in the firm is not repayable by the latter. However, the depreciation of physical assets is recognized as a proper charge against the cost of production and is accounted for.

closely managed and controlled by the government. To understand the kolkhoz's role in the Soviet economy—especially in the process of early forced industrialization—and its problems we must glance back to the late twenties once again.

As Stalin prepared to begin the great industrialization drive, he realized that its success would depend on a sharp increase in the state's acquisition of farm products in order to feed the cities that were soon to grow rapidly and to provide increasing surpluses for export to buy machinery abroad. But there was no assurance that the peasants, then farming in traditional ways, would comply, especially since Stalin was not prepared to devote large resources to "bribe" them. So, at the end of 1929, he launched a feverish collectivization drive. In the course of a few years virtually all the country's peasants were forced, mostly against their will and sometimes with considerable violence, to join collective farms, surrendering their livestock and other major assets in the process. In the long run, these large farms were intended to become highly mechanized and efficient producers. But from the very beginning their main function was to deliver produce (chiefly, grain) to the state at minimal cost to the latter, thereby providing a large part of the economic resources for industrialization. At the same time, he compelled the peasants to work for the kolkhozes, which they did reluctantly and carelessly because of the very low remuneration, faulty connection between effort and pay, and because they preferred to work their private plots (on which more presently).

The results were in part successful and in part disastrous. The state was indeed able to obtain greatly increased amounts of produce at very little direct cost to itself. But the collectivization drive precipitated an immediate drop in output and widespread slaughter of livestock by the peasants. There was a sharp initial decline in the peasants' consumption level, at times leading to famines in the countryside as the government relentlessly claimed and collected its share of produce. The stagnation of agricultural production and the peasants' economic misery continued until the end of Stalin's rule (1953). Since then peasant incomes have been repeatedly and markedly raised as part of a determined effort to increase incentives. Agricultural production has responded positively.

The collective farm is a very large production unit, containing on the average some 15,000 acres of agricultural land, of which 7,500 acres are sown to crops, and over 400 peasant households—as well as about 3,000 animals (excluding fowl) and numerous structures and machines. The kolkhozes are still required to make deliveries to the state at fixed prices, though not nearly so low as in Stalin's day. They are told when, and how, to sow, cultivate, and harvest. These and many other forms of incessant pressure and interference from the local authorities have been among the chief reasons for the kolkhozes' lack of incentive, drive, and efficiency.

The peasants have been—and still are—obligated to put in certain minimum amounts of labor per year at their kolkhozes, and formally cannot freely leave them. The obligation to work used to be a very onerous one when the return for the work for the kolkhoz used to be very small indeed, and at times next to nothing. The response was understandably as little effort as possible and very low productivity on the job. For their work the members of the kolkhoz used to receive points of sorts. When the results of the year's farming were known, and after the obligatory deliveries to the state had been made and the required addition to the farm's capital had been set aside, most of the remainder was distributed, in kind and in cash, among the peasants in proportion to their accumulated points. Before the mid-sixties, only in the wealthier kolkhozes were the peasants paid in cash at guaranteed rates and without waiting for the end of the year.

Beginning with the mid-fifties, in order to raise agricultural output from its disastrously low level, higher prices and other advantages have been continually extended to the kolkhozes, which has permitted them to raise the pay to their members markedly. Since the mid-sixties, kolkhoz peasants are no longer residual beneficiaries of the operation of their respective farms, but are guaranteed certain minimum rates of pay and have been eligible for the benefits of state social security. However, there is still a good deal of poverty among kolkhoz peasants, considerable inequality of incomes, and still very low productivity (though the last is due not only to poor pay and low morale, but also to much mismanagement by the higher authorities).

There is yet another side to the kolkhozes, however. Each peasant household is permitted to work a tiny plot (up to one acre), to raise what it wishes on it (though it is allowed to keep no draft animals and only one milk cow), and freely to dispose of the produce, including selling it on the "kolkhoz market." Because they are relatively so profitable, these tiny plots attract much of the peasants' time and effort, often at the expense of working for the kolkhoz. These tiny garden plots in the aggregate form the larger part of the third sector of Soviet agriculture, the private sector. Also in the private sector are the garden plots of sovkhoz workers, and those of the nonagricultural population. As the reader may have already noticed in the table, there is a remarkable feature to the private sector as a whole: Although using only 3 percent of the total cultivated land, it accounts for almost one-third of the output of agriculture and 12 percent of the marketed output, while claiming 30 percent of the labor input. The explanation is that: (1) private plots are much more intensively cultivated, in part because they are *private* and directly benefit the cultivator, and in part because of the nature of the products raised on them; (2) there is accordingly much higher productivity of both land and animals on the private plots; and (3) they concentrate on the production of high-value products, such as meat, milk, eggs, fruit, and some vegetables, obtaining the feed for the animals in large measure from outside the private sector (especially from the kolkhoz itself).

The Communist Party

No description of the Soviet economy (or any other communist economy) is complete without mention of the Communist party. The Communist party of the Soviet Union (CPSU) is not only the sole legal political party in the country, but it is also very different from the major political parties as we know them in the West. It is in charge of nearly everything in the country and the society. Indeed, the only important institution that the party has not been able to penetrate significantly is the family. The party controls the state, the economy, police and the military, everything that is published, and of course, all official ideology. But while exercising full dictatorship *over* the country, the party is itself dictatorially organized and governed by a small group of leaders at the top. Until his death in 1953, Stalin was as close to being an absolute dictator as has been any man in modern times. Since then dictatorial power has not been concentrated in one man to the same extent, and there seems to have been a good deal of jockeying for power and influence among various groups in the party's upper reaches.

The top party leaders are usually also the highest government officials. The provincial and district party secretaries are the local bosses, though they are watched closely by *their* party superiors. There is a party cell in every enterprise or institution of any size. Although party members comprise only 6 percent of the population, they include within their ranks the vast majority of the important and the influential. The ambitious join the party for the sake of advancement, for party members have preference in appointment to responsible posts. But the rank and file of the party do not hold much power; rather, it is held by a relatively small fraction of the members, the secretaries and other professional party functionaries.

It would be quite incorrect to think of the CPSU as a legion of revolutionary zealots. There seems to be little ideological fervor left within its ranks. Instead, the party is primarily preoccupied with running the country on a day-to-day basis, protecting its monopoly of power, and preserving such benefits and privileges as accrue to the ruling group. In this sense, the CPSU—and most of the other ruling communist parties—are conservative parties within their own setting.

In the economic domain, the party runs things in various ways. All major decisions are made by the top leaders (although they may often hold different views on the issues). Nearly all the important and influential planners, managers, trade-union leaders, and so on, are party members and are ultimately subject to party discipline. Most importantly, local party authorities pass on all important personnel appointments. Local party cells are expected to lead enterprises to ever-higher successes, to ensure ideological purity and political reliability, and to maintain continuous watch for slackness and transgressions of all sorts. Regional party bosses act as economic troubleshooters, coordinators, and arbiters in their domains, and as champions of "their" enterprises against outsiders. Note that much of the party's role in the economy stems from the absence of a market mechanism that would otherwise resolve conflicts, coordinate economic activities, and enforce priorities through the exercise of effective demand. It follows that in this sense the party—and especially its corps of professional functionaries—would be among the chief "losers" in the event that a market mechanism were installed in the Soviet economy.

Important as it is, the party is only one agency of supervision, surveillance, and control in the Soviet Union. There are innumerable others ranging from the secret police to the local bank that inspect the enterprise's affairs for adherence to plan and compliance with the law.

The Household; Labor

The households, at once consumers and providers of labor services, are tied to the production sector via markets for consumer goods and labor. The state decides what consumer goods and in what quantities will be produced[12] and places them on sale, under normal conditions without rationing and at more or less equilibrium prices. The consumer can "take it or leave it" at the quoted prices, though he is naturally limited to what the authorities choose to make available in the official stores in the given locality. Thus, generally speaking, there is freedom of consumer choice even if not consumer sovereignty. Similarly, the individual in his capacity as worker can usually select and change his job, being guided by the wages or salaries offered in other jobs.[13] And accordingly, wages and salaries are so set by the planners in the long run as to help deploy labor among occupations, levels of skill, industries, and regions in conformance with the planners' intentions. In sum, there is freedom of household choice in a broad sense, though not household sovereignty.[14]

There are good reasons for freedom of household choice in the USSR (as elsewhere). It is simpler for the state and preferable for the household if consumer goods are distributed in orderly markets with the exercise of free consumer choice and with the aid of money rather than by means of rationing. And it is much more satisfactory for the individual if he is free to choose and change jobs by means of direct assignment of individuals to jobs. There have been, however, very important exceptions to the principle of household choice in Soviet history. Consumer goods were rationed from 1929 to 1935 and from 1941 to 1947. Urban housing, very scarce throughout most of the Soviet period, has been rationed throughout and continues to be. As for labor, we have already seen that peasants may not leave collective farms without official permission, and that many millions were sentenced to forced labor (especially between 1930 and 1956). Even "free" workers were, between 1940 and 1956, formally— though not necessarily de facto—frozen in their jobs.

Thus, insofar as freedom of choice obtains, the economics of the Soviet worker's household is essentially the same as that of one in any other system,

---

[12]Except the goods traded in the kolkhoz market.

[13]In fact, a major problem of the Soviet economy in the seventies, as in the thirties, is excessive labor turnover as workers move from job to job in search of better pay, working conditions, housing, and availability of consumer goods.

[14]For the meaning of these terms, see pp. 9–11.

keeping in mind that it may acquire virtually no capital goods (nor, of course, shares of stock). It may, however, save any portion of its income and may invest its savings in state-owned savings banks, in state-issued bonds, and in private or cooperative housing for its own occupancy.

Nearly all workers and employees belong to labor unions, but these are very different from what we know in the West. Not independent in any real sense, the Soviet labor unions are just another of the regime's many arms. Their main purpose is to spur labor productivity and to do their part in indoctrination and propaganda. Their influence on wages is minimal. The right to strike exists in name but not in fact. Yet, at the factory level the union local may perform an important function in supporting the grievances of individual workers against management.

Soviet workers and employees are eligible for paid vacations, sickness and maternity leaves, (relatively modest) old-age pensions, and other fringe benefits. Many college-level students receive scholarships, while tuition is free. Old-age pensions were extended to cover all collectivized peasants only in 1964. The whole population is eligible for free medical care and hospitalization. There is no unemployment insurance on the premise that there is no unemployment—though there is a fair amount of frictional unemployment as people change jobs.

Incentives

As we have just noted, wages, salaries, and other forms of labor remuneration tend to be such as to deploy labor where it is needed in relation to the economic plans (though the plans themselves obviously are adapted to the availability of labor by skills and locales). This is another way of saying that rewards to labor roughly tend toward levels that equate the specific supply of labor with the corresponding demand. This is accomplished in part by the continual adjustment of the official wage and salary scales, and in part by "wage drift"—the unofficial adjustment of remuneration by open or tacit bargaining between employers and employees in response to the forces of demand and supply, despite the authorities' efforts to contain it. In the terminology of Chapter 2, the Soviets now rely primarily on remunerative controls (material incentives) to deploy labor where it is needed, rather than on coercion, normative controls, or moral incentives.[15]

Of equal significance are material incentives designed to maximize the individual's performance on the *given* job. These take the form of widespread piecework pay, innumerable specific rewards ("premia") for such things as economizing on inputs or raising the quality of output, large bonuses to managerial personnel for fulfilling the production plan and meeting other targets, one-time rewards for inventions and constructive suggestions.

---

[15]In 1973, possibly in consequence of the economic difficulties of the time, a new set of measures was adopted with the general purpose of heightening material incentives.

One consequence of the heavy reliance on material incentives is considerable inequality of earnings. The Soviets have published almost no systematic information on income distribution since the policy of accentuating the differentiation of rewards was adopted in the early thirties, and, of course, this official reticence is in itself suggestive of considerable inequality. Such partial evidence as can be garnered suggests that: (a) among workers and employees (nonpeasants) incomes are distributed approximately as unequally as are *labor* incomes in Western countries at similar levels of economic development;[16] (b) the inequality of income distribution among peasants is quite great; and (c) peasant incomes are on the average substantially below those of nonpeasants, though the two are difficult to compare owing to differences in modes of life. Property incomes, which heavily contribute toward income inequality in capitalist countries, are, of course, quite insignificant in the USSR (except perhaps in the recesses of illegality in the economy). However, it must be borne in mind that those in the Soviet economy who hold positions of power, though without formal property ownership, have access to many material benefits that may not be available to others.[17]

Lastly, the emphasis on material incentives and the unequal distribution of income and other benefits place in question the moral and ethical transformation of the Soviet man into a nonacquisitive, socially responsible, and committed person, as the official ideology wants him to become in the relatively near future. This is the essence of the Chinese and Cuban critique of Soviet reliance on material incentives as a betrayal of socialist principles, as we shall see later on. The Soviet reply, however, is that given the human material at their disposal after the Revolution, there was no way to involve people fully in production and economic growth except by appealing to their self-interest through material incentives. The outside observer might conclude that both sides are right to some degree.

Money

Money is used in the Soviet economy very much as in any other economy. It is a means of payment, a unit of account, and a store of value. The monetary unit is the ruble, divided into 100 kopeks. There are in effect two kinds of means of payment in domestic use, though both are denominated in rubles and are converted (but not freely) into one another at par. They are *currency*, which circulates almost exclusively within the household sector and in transactions between households and the state, and *bank money*, which circulates almost

---

[16]Cf. Frederick L. Pryor, "The Distribution of Nonagricultural Labor Incomes in Communist and Capitalist Nations," *Slavic Review*, 31:3 (September 1972), pp. 639–50, though, unfortunately, the Soviet data in this comparative statistical study are very skimpy.

[17]See the stimulating little book by David Lane, *The End of Inequality: Stratification under State Socialism* (Penguin Books, Inc., 1971) for a broad sociological inquiry into inequality in the USSR. It includes a useful bibliography.

exclusively within the state sector, between state enterprises and agencies. Of course, currency and bank money are constantly converted into each other—to allow enterprises to pay wages, or by way of depositing the receipts of retail stores in banks—but only under strict controls. The reasons for this distinction between and careful segregation of the two kinds of money are (1) to prevent the overissue of currency that might lead to inflationary pressures in the household sector, and (2) to maintain strict control over the activity of enterprises and state agencies.

Indeed, such control is a main function of the USSR State Bank (*Gosbank*) with its thousands of branches; it is the bank of currency issue and has a virtual monopoly of all commercial banking. The savings banks serve the household sector by holding savings deposits and performing other services.

Currency can usually be spent freely by households, though many types of transactions that are legal in the West are not so in the USSR. On the other hand, bank money can be spent by enterprises much less freely; often some form of administrative permission is required before a purchase can be made legally (for example, in the case of nearly all producer goods). In this sense, Soviet bank money has less "moneyness" than the money we know in the West.

Prices

Being a money-using economy, the Soviet economy has prices; but since it is not a market economy, the prices (understood here in the broadest sense, including wages, interest, rents, and exchange rates) clearly do not always have the same functions as in a market economy, whether capitalist or socialist. In this section we consider only *established* prices, those that are actually paid or received by somebody.

To begin with, some things in the Soviet economy carry no price, usually for the doctrinaire Marxist reason that only objects created by human labor have "value." Examples: land, both rural and urban, which commands neither price nor rent; most other natural resources before entering production (though there are important exceptions now).

But as a rule goods carry prices, and perhaps the best way to understand how the prices are formed is to invoke the concept of freedom of choice, on both the buyer's and the seller's side. The seller either may be free to sell or not to sell, or he may be under some compulsion to sell at a given price. Similarly, the buyer may be free to buy or not to buy at the quoted price, or he may in effect have little choice in the matter. With two alternatives for the buyer and two for the seller, there are altogether four kinds of transaction in this sense. These are represented schematically by the four quadrants of the diagram in Figure 6.1.

Quadrant I represents the situation in which both the seller and the buyer are free to transact or not to transact. This is the situation of the free market, where prices are formed by the interaction of demand and supply with a tend-

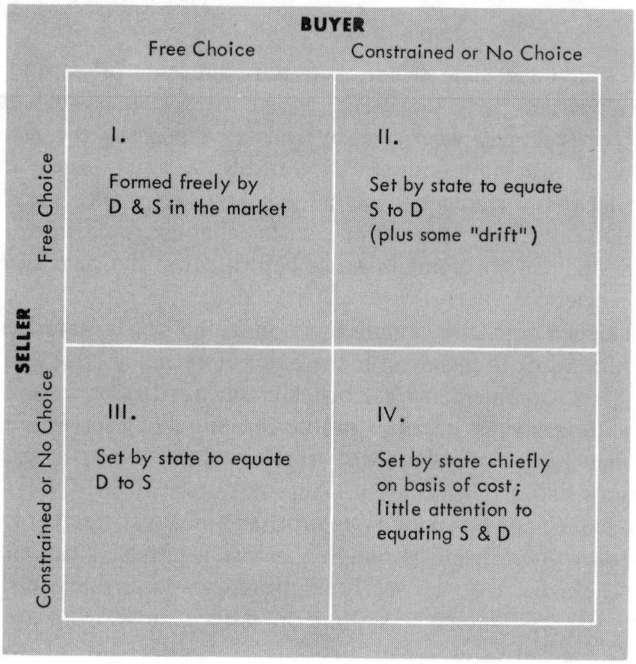

	BUYER	
	Free Choice	Constrained or No Choice
SELLER Free Choice	I. Formed freely by D & S in the market	II. Set by state to equate S to D (plus some "drift")
SELLER Constrained or No Choice	III. Set by state to equate D to S	IV. Set by state chiefly on basis of cost; little attention to equating S & D

FIG. 6—1 Price Formation in the Soviet Economy.

ency toward equilibrium levels (prices at which the demand and the supply of the given good in the given place at the given time are approximately equal). The most important (legal) example is the kolkhoz market, in which the buyers are primarily households and the sellers are either kolkhozes or peasants selling on their own account. Although occasionally the authorities try to control kolkhoz-market prices, as a rule they are left to move freely in response to demand and supply. Some transactions between state entities may also fall into this category as, of course, do all illegal transactions.

Quadrant II depicts the case where the seller has free choice, but the buyer, typically a state entity, is constrained in some major way, as for instance when he must meet a quantitative target. The most important example is the hiring of labor by state enterprises. The employers are bound by their production plans and frequently have insufficient incentive to economize on cost. In part for this reason, the central authorities prescribe to the employers the particular wage and salary rates that they may (and must) pay; otherwise there would be danger of wage inflation. But as we have seen, the fact that workers are generally free to choose their jobs means that these centrally determined wages cannot ignore the interrelation of demand and supply in particular cases. Consequently, they are administratively reset from time to time so as to bring them closer to equilibrium levels. In addition, there may be uncontrolled "wage

108

drift." (Insofar as the wage drift is decisive, we revert to Quadrant I.) Also in the second quadrant are farm prices in those cases where there is no significant compulsion on the peasants or kolkhozes to sell—in other words, where they sell freely in response to prices "posted" by the state.

In Quadrant III the situation is reversed; here it is the buyer who has the effective freedom of choice in the individual transaction and the selling unit does not. Prices are centrally fixed. The typical case is that of consumer goods sold in state stores to households. As a rule, the store has no choice whether or not to sell at the prices set by proper authorities. But since the state wishes to avoid both disorderly distribution of goods and formal rationing, the fixed prices are generally so set as to approximate equilibrium levels.[18] Yet this happens quite imperfectly, so that general and local shortages and excesses of consumer goods are common.

The value of consumer goods at retail contains a large tax component— about one-quarter in recent years. This is the famous Soviet *turnover tax*, an indirect tax that is usually paid at the manufacturing or wholesale-distribution stage and is an integral part of the price paid by the consumer. It has two important functions. Macroeconomically, it sops up a part of the households' income and thus reduces inflationary pressure in an economy in which both investment and general government expenditure are very large. Microeconomically, it fills a large part of the gap between the average cost of production and the equilibrium price of each good. The proportion of turnover tax in price varies greatly, depending on the relation between demand and supply, and the policy that may lie behind the supply (encouragement or discouragement of the consumption of individual goods, limitation of imports, and so forth). Some goods carry subsidies that might be thought of as negative taxes, in order to keep the price to the consumer below the cost to the state for social or political reasons. Major examples are meat and housing. (The situation of a consumer good with a turnover tax is depicted in Figure 6.2.)

The most complex case is that of Quadrant IV, wherein the typical instance is that of producer goods transferred (sold) within the state sector. Since most of the important producer goods cannot be freely purchased but are allocated (rationed) or otherwise controlled, there is little freedom of choice on the buyer's part, nor is the seller typically free to dispose of them without proper directives. Prices are centrally fixed, but (in contrast to the situation in Quadrants II and III) with little attention to equilibrating demand and supply. Rather, the objectives are: preventing the prices from rising (given the strong inflationary pressures), limiting the profits of the producers-sellers, and facilitating compliance with various directives and plans. Here, the situation is primarily one of *price control* rather than price policy, and as with all price control, capitalist or socialist, there is a strong bias toward relating prices to average cost

---

[18]A major exception is state-owned housing (which accounts for some 70 percent of urban housing), where rents are very low and strict rationing is in force.

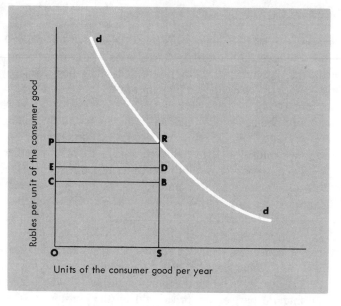

FIG. 6—2

dd   — demand curve for a given consumer good
OS   — planned supply
OP=SR   — equilibrium price at retail
OC=SB   — planned average unit cost of production and distribution
CE=BD   — planned profit per unit
EP=DR   — turnover tax per unit of the good
    OSRP   — expected total revenue from retail sales
    OSBC   — expected total cost of production and distribution
    CBDE   — planned total profit from the given good
    EDRP   — planned turnover tax revenue for the good.

(since average cost is a relatively easy standard to compute and follow). Average-cost pricing also happens to correspond to Marxian theories of price—capitalist price, to be sure—and can therefore be doctrinally justified. Since 1966–67, industrial prices have been, therefore, set as follows: *average* cost[19] of the given good in the whole industry plus a margin of profit equal to 15 percent of the *average* capital investment per unit of the good in the industry. Thus, if the given firm has lower average cost or lower capital/output ratio than the industry, which the authorities wish to encourage, it will make larger profit per unit than the average for the industry.

[19]This cost does not include any interest on invested capital or rent on natural resources; see next paragraph.

Out of this profit the firm pays a levy on the value of assets that it uses—in effect an interest charge, though not so called for ideological reasons—in order to induce it to economize on capital. In industries in which costs of production are strongly affected by natural conditions, the more fortunately situated firms also pay so-called "fixed payments" per unit of product—a kind of rent on the better natural resources. The remaining profit in part goes to form various incentive funds within the firm, and in part is captured by the treasury.

It is important to note that producer-good prices are neither equilibrium prices (balancing demand and supply) nor scarcity prices (representing the scarcity of the given goods from a social standpoint). Thus, they are not very suitable either to ensure orderly distribution of goods without administrative intervention, or to guide production in desirable directions. Instead, they are part and parcel of the system of plans and administrative controls.

Lastly, also in Quadrant IV, belong the fixed prices paid to kolkhozes for the produce that they are obligated to deliver to the state. That these prices are in some sense low is implied in the existence of coercion (obligation to deliver). However, they are no longer nearly as low as in the thirties, forties, and first half of the fifties, when such prices were nearly confiscatory, the obligation to deliver was single-mindedly enforced, and a large part of the financial resources for industrialization and other needs of the state came from the state's "profit" on farm produce.

SHORT-TERM PLANNING AND OPERATION

The purpose of Soviet short-term plans is primarily to coordinate the activities of the many thousands of economic units—to substitute for the market mechanism's short-term functions. In this it differs sharply from the medium- and long-term plans, five and more years in duration, whose object is to lay down the directions and time-rates of economic development.

One-Year Plans

The drawing-up of a one-year plan is an extremely laborious process that extends over nearly the whole of the preceding year and is not really completed until well into the plan year (if at all). But in essence the procedure and method are simple enough. To begin with, the regime's leaders indicate to the planners (and with advice from the latter) the main outlines of the economy for the coming year: the desired increase of the national product and of the outputs of the main sectors and industries; distribution of the national product between consumption, investment, defense, and other major uses; distribution of investment by main industries; average consumption level of households; locational trends;

111

and, last, but not least, the production targets for a series of the most important commodities. These *political goals* for the coming year in part derive from the targets of the longer-term plan then in effect, and in part from the wishes and policies of the leaders at the given moment. Even the initial political goals must have some economic basis. Thus, the indicated rate of growth must be attainable; the volume of investment must be adequate to bring it about; the share of the national product going into consumption must be consistent with the planned average consumption level; and so forth.

It is the planners' job to translate these political goals into precise, detailed, and consistent production targets and directives for thousands of individual commodities and many tens of thousands of enterprises for the coming year. The result of their efforts is a hierarchy of one-year plans for individual enterprises, ministries, republics, and the national economy as a whole. The planners also draw up a parallel hierarchy of *supply plans* that determine the physical allocation of most important materials and items of equipment among potential users. Incidentally, one of the chief and rarely fully solved problems of Soviet planning is that of coordinating these two plans, as they clearly must be if the economy is to function smoothly. Our sketch will concentrate on the production plan, however.

In addition to the political goals for the year, the central planners have two other kinds of information that permit them to proceed with their work. First, they know, though not always accurately, the economy's resources and productive capacity for the year. Second, they have many thousands of input-output ratios—in Soviet parlance, *norms*—that state the quantities of certain materials, labor, and equipment required to produce a unit of a certain product. Some of the norms stem from past experience; others, from engineering calculations. Finally, what greatly facilitates their job of drawing up the plan is the fact that the *changes* in production from year to year are not likely to be great.

The actual procedure involves, among other things, the sending down of a draft or sketch of a plan to lower levels in the hierarchy and receiving countersuggestions from below. This is accompanied by a great deal of bargaining vertically between adjoining levels, as subordinates aim to exact relatively "easy" plans for themselves, while pressure for the opposite is brought to bear from the top down. By far the most laborious task faced in formulating the one-year plan at all levels is that of achieving *internal consistency*—that is to say, ensuring that all requirements for individual factors or commodities are matched by anticipated availabilities (from current production, inventories, or imports)—the job that in the market economy is performed by the market mechanism. In performing this task, the planners do not refer to relative prices or profitabilities. Rather, they utilize in physical terms an essentially very simple form of account, the so-called *material balance*, which lists on one side all the anticipated availabilities of a given good and on the other, all the expected requirements. In turn, the requirements and availabilities of the given good are linked to those of other individual goods by means of the norms, so that all the material balances are supposedly mutually consistent. If the two sides of a given material balance match, all is fine. But they rarely do at first, and typically the sum of the requirements exceeds the sum of the availabilities.

The process of "balancing" the material balances takes up much time and effort, especially since the adjustment of one balance often calls for numerous adjustments in many others. For example, if the requirements for copper initially exceed its expected availability, the amounts of copper to be allotted to various copper users may be cut back. In this case, the relative priority ratings of the users from the standpoint of national importance are involved. Alternatively, more resources may be shifted into copper production, or additional goods may be earmarked for export in order to purchase more copper abroad. These and other likely adjustments will affect material balances for goods other than copper, which in turn will affect yet others (perhaps also copper again), and so on indefinitely.[20]

In practice, only a limited number of "rounds" of adjustments can be undertaken. Considering that in recent years the central planners and supply allocators have been operating with nearly 20,000 material balances, one can imagine the enormity of the job and the imperfect internal coordination of the final plan. Moreover, even if a reasonably *consistent* plan should be produced, there is nothing in the method to suggest that it will also be a statically or dynamically efficient one—that the available resources will be so deployed as to maximize the achievement of the plan's goals or obtain the most growth from resources devoted to growth. Eventually, at times considerably after the beginning of the plan year, the individual firm receives *its* plan, its set of targets and directives for the year.

Operating Problems

Whatever its appearance on paper, in practice this system of short-term planning and management operates very poorly in many respects. This is not only the conclusion of outside observers; it is also the opinion of many economists in the USSR and other East European countries, whose criticisms have been persistent and often extremely sharp. This is, of course, the main reason that all the Soviet-type economies have undergone reforms of their economic institutions since the mid-sixties, though—as we shall see—the reforms have had little effect on the operation of the system in most cases. What are the main faults?

To begin with, the internal coordination of the plans, and between the

[20]Those familiar with input-output methods will recognize that the problem of adjustment can be solved mathematically with the aid of an "inverse matrix" of coefficients. However, in practice this would not be easy because of the great detail of Soviet planning and because it may be desirable to introduce judgment at some points. So far, input-output methods have not been extensively used for "balancing."

production and the supply plans, is often quite imperfect. This leads to bottle-necks, much idle capacity, unwanted inventories, and other waste of resources. Not infrequently, firms are ordered to produce goods for which there is no demand. Yet because of the tight centralization of decisions and the complexity of the system, corrections can be made only very slowly and with much difficulty. And if made, they tend to disrupt the smooth working of the enterprises. Thus, a common complaint of directors is that their plans are constantly revised, which would be bad enough in any case, but is particularly unsettling under Soviet conditions, where materials are very hard to obtain.

Second, since management's bonuses induce it to maximize physical output at the expense of other desiderata, cost tends to be overlooked and quality tends to be depressed. Also, the enterprise tends to produce that product mix that maximizes its output in planned units rather than that which is highest in demand by customers. For example, ordered to produce as many pairs of skis as possible, Soviet enterprises have been prone to produce too many children's skis and too few skis for adults. This is inconvenient enough for the consumer. But when the good is a producer good, its low quality and incorrect specifications can have an adverse chain effect on several subsequent stages of production.

These faults have been aggravated by a closely related phenomenon, the *sellers' market* for most producer goods. This phrase denotes a situation in which it is generally easier and cheaper to dispose of (sell) goods than to procure (buy) them. In the Soviet case the sellers' market for producer goods—a chronic condition since at least the appearance of the command economy—owes it existence to the high production targets under the plans (in relation to resources) and to the great pressure to meet the targets with little regard for cost. At the same time, every producer or seller knows that he will have little difficulty in disposing of his products though they be of poor quality or obsolete design.[21]

The emphasis on maximum current production has another damaging effect. It causes the enterprises to resist innovations that may disrupt the flow of output or endanger plan fulfillment. The firm has little to gain from an innovation because the positive results—say, profits—will be taken by the state, while the risk of losing bonuses if something goes wrong remains with the management. Even worse, the next plan will only raise the targets accordingly, thus depriving the enterprise of the innovation's benefits. If the Soviet economy has nevertheless been experiencing rapid technological progress, this fact is to be credited, first, to the building of many new plants where there is yet no management to resist innovation and, second, to continuous pressure on management from the top for modernization of production processes and products.

These defects have been with the Soviet economy since its inception, but

[21]There are exceptions. In recent years, in contrast to the earlier situation, there has been much consumer resistance to shoddy and unattractive goods.

only after the relaxation of political controls in the mid-fifties did there appear open and widespread proposals for the system's improvement.

ECONOMIC GROWTH

In its concentrated drive to attain technological leadership and industrial primacy in the world, the USSR has employed comprehensive medium- and long-term plans, tools in whose development the USSR pioneered decades before they became a standard feature of most countries' development program. True, the long-term ("general") plans—ten, fifteen, or twenty years in duration—have been little but gross projections and guidelines for development, and in most cases were quickly rendered obsolete by the course of events. The medium-term plans have been five-year plans (FYPs), except for one seven-year plan.[22]

Medium-term Planning

The FYPs have represented the formal expression of the major goals and priorities of the Soviet leadership, such as:

—very high overall rates of growth in order to reduce and eventually eliminate the gap in per capita productivity between the Soviet Union and the advanced capitalist countries, particularly the United States;

—high priority for industrial development, and within industry, to heavy industry, and within heavy industry, to those branches such as fuel, steel, machine-building that contribute most to further industrialization and military power;

—emphasis on rapid increase in military power, including of course nuclear weapons and rocketry;

—universal primary education and large-scale training in technical, scientific, and vocational skills, especially those that would further the just-mentioned goals;

—the attainment of economic self-sufficiency vis-à-vis the outside world, both for defensive and for ideological reasons (though this goal was perforce modified in regard to the other communist countries after World War II).

For a long time, consumption held a low priority in this scheme of things, while agriculture, as we have seen, was relied upon to supply resources for industrialization. This occasioned such a low standard of living for the population and such stagnation in agriculture that these two sectors and supporting branches of industry have had to be accorded considerably more attention since Stalin's death.

[22]First FYP—October 1928–32, 2nd FYP—1933–37, 3rd FYP—1938–42 (cut short by war in 1941), 4th FYP—1946–50, 5th FYP—1951–55, 6th FYP—1956–60 (abandoned by 1957). Seven-Year Plan—1959–65; 8th FYP—1966–70; 9th FYP—1971–75.

The core of the FYP is the investment plan, which specifies the volume of capital formation over the five years, its distribution by industries and regions, and many of the larger individual construction projects. Much attention is devoted to the lines of technical advance.

The following differences between medium-term and short-term planning should be noted. (1) Over five (or seven) years there is considerably more opportunity to shuffle resources, let alone to expand total resources significantly, than over one year. Hence, the element of political choice of goals is much more important in regard to the medium-term plan. (2) The FYP needs to be drawn up in considerably less detail than the one-year plan; especially since (3) the targets of the FYP do not constitute directives to any producers in the economy —such directives are later elaborated in the one-year plans. (4) Since the sixties, long-term planning has been in part conducted with the aid of formal input-output models and other mathematical techniques. As yet, however, the mathematical techniques occupy only a subordinate role in the planning process.

The Five-Year Plans have occupied a central place in Soviet economic development, especially industrialization, since the end of the twenties. In addition to spelling out the strategy of development and specifying the means of carrying it out, they have been widely used to mobilize public support for the government's programs and policies at home, and to present a favorable image of a rational and successful process of growth for foreign consumption. The FYPs have, of course, been incorporated into the other Soviet-type economies, and have served as a major example of long-term planning even for many noncommunist countries. Nevertheless, it would be incorrect to assume that Soviet (and East European) industrialization and economic development have strictly and closely followed the FYPs.

To begin with, for over thirty years, from the end of the thirties to the beginning of the seventies, (between the third and ninth FYP), no FYP as such was published in the USSR. For this long period all we have to go on are relatively brief "directives" from the party to the planners as to what the FYP should be like; and it seems likely that none in fact were produced even for internal use. It is therefore difficult to speak in reference to this period of the Soviet economy developing according to FYPs, or of the fulfillment or nonfulfillment of FYPs (other than the above-mentioned "directives").

That it was often very difficult to draw up a FYP pursuant to the party's "directives" is understandable if one bears in mind its highly detailed nature. The very laborious process of the Plan's preparation is easily overtaken by the flow of events, such as changes in domestic political leadership or in the priorities held by the given leadership, major natural events (such as crop failure), less-than-expected growth of labor productivity, or significant shifts in the world situation. Or, if the FYP is drawn up after all, its relevance and feasibility are frequently undermined by the same set of domestic and external forces. Thus, when the summary of a FYP—the Ninth FYP—was finally published in the spring of 1972, the document became obsolete almost before its printing was finished, owing to major international developments and the severe crop failure of the following weeks and months. In sum, the Soviet experience is not very encouraging regarding the wisdom of attempting to draw up *detailed and rigid* economic plans with *ambitious targets* (little slack) for the medium term, let alone for periods longer than five years in duration. Still, whether as completed plans or in the form of initial "directives," the Soviet five-year plans have acted as important guidelines for economic development.

The Record Since 1928

What, then, has been the record of Soviet growth since 1928, the year in which the economy had already fully recovered from the effects of the Civil War and the accompanying disastrous economic policies, and in which the first FYP officially began? The country is bigger now, having added about 2 percent to its vast territory as well as 12 percent to its population in the course of annexations between 1939 and 1945 (mostly in Eastern Europe). From 1928 to 1973, the Soviet Union's population increased by two-thirds, from 150 million to 250 million (beginning-of-year figures). Actually, this increase over forty-five years is much smaller than what one would expect from the annexations and the high rates of natural increase during most of the period. The explanation lies with two demographic disasters. Taking into account both an increase in deaths and births below the expected "normal" level, we find that the collectivization crisis of the early thirties set the Soviet population back by some ten million, and the Second World War and its immediate aftermath, by forty to fifty million. The latter figures, on the order of the population of France at the present time, is also an indication of the enormous damage inflicted by the war on the Soviet economy. But economic recovery was rapid; the war set Soviet economic growth back by perhaps as little as six years (and population growth by some fifteen years).[23]

The composition of the population has changed greatly. In 1928, it was some 80 percent agricultural and rural; by the sixties, it had become more urban than rural and more nonagricultural than agricultural. In absolute numbers, the urban population increased more than fivefold to 1973, from 27.6 million to 145 million. The educational level of the population rose sharply.

Even apart from wartime and postwar reconstruction, the Soviet economy grew far from smoothly under the FYPs;[24] more irregular was the growth of

---

[23]It took eight years for production in most respects to return to the prewar (1940) level. But for the next two years (1948–50) production grew at approximately double the "normal" rate, thanks to the continuance of physical reconstruction. Hence, we consider the setback in production associated with the war to have been six years.

[24]Cf. Naum Jasny, *Soviet Industrialization, 1928–1952* (Chicago: University of Chicago Press, 1961), and Abram Bergson, *The Real National Income of Soviet Russia Since 1928* (Cambridge: Harvard University Press, 1961).

individual sectors, especially those with lower priority (such as agriculture). But it is not always easy to tell just how fast the growth was. The official Soviet series for national income, industrial production, and other "aggregates" are more often than not unreliable, sometimes very greatly exaggerating the actual growth, insofar as Western observers have been able to determine. The recomputations of aggregative series for the Soviet economy that various Western economists have consequently undertaken have given us a fairly clear picture of its growth, except that these estimates are sometimes very sensitive to particular methods employed and to "weights" utilized in their computation.[25]

The most thorough estimates of the Soviet real gross national product (GNP) have been made by Professor Abram Bergson, who finds that it increased at the following average annual rates (in percentages): during the first two FYPs, from 1927 to 1937—4.8–11.9; 1950–60—7.0; and for the entire period 1928–60—4.5–6.3.[26] If we eliminate the six years by which, at the least, Soviet growth was set back by the war, the average annual rate for 1928–1960 was 5.5 to 7.7 percent.[27] During the sixties, the rate of overall Soviet economic growth held up rather well. Using a method similar to Bergson's, Professor Stanley H. Cohn estimates that between 1960 and 1971 the Soviet GNP grew at an average annual rate of 5.2 percent.[28] These are, of course, very high rates of GNP growth to be sustained over decades, even if they have been equalled and surpassed in noncommunist as well as some other communist countries. The outlook for the seventies, however, is one of likely retardation in overall Soviet growth, owing to the significant decline in rates of increase of the non-agricultural labor force expected for the near future and the poor performance of agriculture in 1971 and 1972 (especially the latter year).

As we might expect from our knowledge of Soviet priorities, industrial output grew more rapidly than GNP. By Western recomputation it increased at an average annual rate of just about 10 percent between 1950 and 1960; and considerably more slowly—though still quite fast—since then, namely, at 6.7 percent between 1960 and 1972.[29] Within industry, the main emphasis has been on its "heavy" branches, as perhaps well represented by the thirty-fold increase

[25]Cf. Campbell, *Soviet Economic Power*, Chap. 6.

[26]Bergson, *The Economics of Soviet Planning*, p. 306. Where a range is given, the lower figure weights production increases by Soviet 1937 prices, the higher figure, by 1928 prices. The methodology of these estimates is rather complicated.

[27]Bergson deducts only the four war years and obtains 5.2–7.3 percent.

[28]See his contributions to the following two compendia of the Joint Economic Committee of the U.S. Congress: *Economic Performance and the Military Burden in the Soviet Union* (Washington: U.S. Government Printing Office, 1970), and *Soviet Economic Prospects for the Seventies* (Washington: U.S. Government Printing Office, 1973). Cf. also his *Economic Development in the Soviet Union* (Lexington, Mass.: D. C. Heath and Co., 1970, paperback).

[29]See the relevant contributions to the two compendia cited in the preceding note. Industrial production here is limited to civilian output for reasons of data availability.

in steel output between 1928 and 1972.[30] Even faster has been the growth of machine-building output, thus permitting the very rapid expansion of the capital stock as well as the extremely large buildup of military capability.

A contrasting picture is presented by agriculture. Following the severe setback during the collectivization drive, and another during World War II, and being continuously squeezed to provide resources for industrialization, agriculture barely recovered its 1928 level of output by the time of Stalin's death, and was still below the 1928 level per capita of the total population. And although a considerable injection of resources into this sector after 1953 succeeded in raising total output by about 50 percent over the next five years, the growth since the end of the fifties has been both much slower and rather uneven. Thus, between 1960 and 1971 (both "average" years in terms of natural conditions), by Western estimate, net agricultural output increased by 45 percent, or by 3.4 percent per year (which still amounted to a respectable 2.2 percent per person per year).[31] But by the early seventies agriculture became, once again, a serious drag on the economy.

As for average consumption levels, they, too, suffered severe setbacks during the early thirties and again during the forties, then rose rapidly from abysmally low levels just after the war, and again for about five years after Stalin's death. Since then they have advanced more slowly but still quite rapidly. Thus, by Western estimate, per capita consumption grew between 1960 and 1971 (or 1972) by about 4 percent. Especially marked since 1928—or 1938 or 1958—has been the increase in consumption of durable goods, education, medical services, recreation, and the like. The per capita supply of traditional goods—foodstuffs, clothing, housing—has risen much more slowly, in part because of the difficulties in agriculture.

However, changing consumption patterns, and especially the intervening large-scale urbanization of the population, make it difficult to determine just how much higher consumption levels are now than in 1928. When a peasant moves to the city, his whole mode of life changes; he ceases to supply himself with many things and buys them in the shops and develops new needs. Under such conditions, monetary yardsticks become quite unreliable. Nonetheless, it is quite clear that the Soviet consumer has so far partaken of only a small part of the increased productivity of the Soviet economy. It has been his prolonged privation—and, at times, starvation—that has helped transform the country from a relatively backward one into the second largest industrial power in the world. In the meantime, the Soviet consumer's expectations have risen very

---

[30]This averages to 9.4 percent per annum for thirty-eight years (the forty-four calendar years less the six years for wartime setback, as above). However, from 1960 to 1972 the rate of growth of steel output was much lower: 5.6 percent per annum. In 1971 the USSR attained one of its long-sought goals: to produce more crude steel than the United States.

[31]See the relevant contributions to the two compendia cited in note 28.

greatly, and the regime now assigns a much higher priority to raising consumption levels than ever before. This new emphasis represents a considerable challenge to the Soviet economy, whose institutions and operating methods so far have been much better adapted to producing capital goods and munitions than consumer goods and services.

FACTORS
BEHIND RAPID GROWTH

The most fundamental factor underlying the rapid growth of the Soviet economy has been undoubtedly the regime's determination to industrialize and amass military power as fast as possible, not hesitating to impose severe sacrifices on the population and to enforce its will through ruthless police control and terror. True, since Stalin's death police terror has been less in evidence and more attention has been paid to the consumer; but the determination to continue rapid industrialization remains.

More specifically, the Soviet Union has been devoting a large share of its resources to growth, year in, year out. Thus, the rate of investment (the ratio of gross investment to gross national product) has been around 25 percent in "normal" times, rising to over 30 percent by the 1960s, very high rates for a none-too-rich country that is simultaneously spending heavily on military needs. In addition, large outlays on training, research, and similar activities have been made. (Official statistics claim that the number of professionals and trained technicians increased 3.5-fold between 1928 and 1972.) Second, these resources have been purposefully, if not always efficiently, directed into the high-priority industries, those industries that underpin national power and produce the capital goods for further growth. By contrast, those industries that serve primarily private consumption, including housing, were for a long time relatively neglected.

Third, technology has been taken over from the advanced countries in the largest and most highly organized operation of this sort ever undertaken anywhere. Very large amounts of machinery and equipment have been imported from the West, and since World War II also from the more advanced communist countries as a way of speeding capital formation and importing advanced know-how. Thousands of foreign technicians were brought to work in the Soviet Union in the twenties and thirties. As for foreign capital, there has been no direct investment (apart from the minor experience of the so-called "concessions" in the twenties). But the First FYP was partly financed by considerable short- and medium-term borrowing abroad, and the inflow of Western capital on a significant scale—now usually jointly with Western technology and know-how—resumed in the later sixties. As this is being written, the USSR is seeking Western capital in the billions of dollars, also jointly with technology, to develop whole regions and industries, as a way of counteracting the relative backwardness of the country and the retardation in the growth of production and of consumption levels.

While these measures have served to enlarge rapidly the stocks of physical capital, human skills, and technological knowledge, there has simultaneously been a rapid expansion in the nonagricultural labor force. The main sources of this expansion have been the increment in the total working-age population, an absolute decline in the agricultural labor force, and the entry of many women into gainful employment outside agriculture. We should mention also that unemployment (not counting disguised unemployment among the peasants) disappeared soon after the FYPs began and the opposite problem, excessive hiring and hoarding of labor, made its appearance.

There is no mystery about the high growth rates of the USSR and other countries with Soviet-type economies. They are explainable by the factors just listed, and particularly by rapid increases in capital stock and in the nonagricultural labor force. The "dynamic efficiency" of Soviet growth apparently has not been especially high.[32] The most distinctive element in this record is the determined application of all the power of a totalitarian state to maximize its industrial might. Even so, the process was greatly facilitated by the country's relatively highly favorable population-resource ratio and by the considerable industrialization that had already taken place before the Revolution. With at least as much determination but lacking these two factors, Communist China has found it much more difficult to industrialize on the Soviet model, relying primarily on her own resources more than did Russia thirty years earlier, as we will see in the next chapter.

SUMMARY

The Soviet economy is a socialist command economy with money, considerable freedom of household choice (but not household sovereignty), and detailed centralized planning. Much of the planning is coordinative, substituting for the absent market mechanism. Individual material incentives are widely used to elicit compliance with plans and to spur productivity. The system is so organized—including the collectivization of agriculture—as to mobilize resources to the utmost, maintain a high rate of investment, and utilize modern technology in order to maximize the rate of growth. Preference in development has been going to heavy industry so as to enlarge rapidly the capacity for further capital formation and to maximize national power. After decades of neglect, agriculture and consumer goods are now receiving considerably more attention than before.

[32]Cf. Bela Balassa, "The Dynamic Efficiency of the Soviet Economy," *American Economic Review* 54, no. 3 (May 1964), pp. 490–505; Abram Bergson, *Planning and Productivity under Soviet Socialism* (New York: Columbia University Press, 1968); Cohn, *Economic Development in the Soviet Union*, Chap. 6.

This system succeeded in rapidly increasing industry production—often with much waste and at the expense of variety, quality, and service—but has been lately showing signs of being too centralized and crude for the growing sophistication of the economy and the consumers' mounting aspirations. Improvement of the system, including the introduction of some elements of the market mechanism, was widely and intensely discussed for a while, but the economic reform that followed in 1965 introduced only minor changes, which have now been partly reversed.

The Command Economy:

Reform—Cuba—China

CHAPTER SEVEN

INTRODUCTION

The fourteen countries ruled by communist governments represent a considerable variety of economic systems and institutions.[1] But for nearly thirty years, from 1917 until the end of the Second World War, the USSR had been the only communist country of any significance.[2] This fact, together with the country's size and general importance, its domination of the world communist movement at the time, its military power, and its impressive industrialization before the war, virtually predetermined that the communist regimes that came into power shortly after the war would closely follow the Soviet economic model. And they did. But the uniformity did not last long. The differentiation of the communist economies, their deviation from the Soviet model, at times so far as to explicitly reject it, and the development of a variety of communist economic systems and institutional patterns is then the main theme of this and the next chapters. Why and how did it happen? Are there any regularities underlying this process of evolution and differentiation? What are the trends for the future? What light do these

---

[1]They are: in Europe—Albania, Bulgaria, Czechoslovakia, East Germany (the German Democratic Republic), Hungary, Poland, Rumania, the USSR, and Yugoslavia; in Asia—China (the Chinese People's Republic). North Korea, Mongolia, and North Vietnam; and Cuba.

[2]Mongolia is the other communist country to come into existence before the war, having been ruled since July 1921 by a Soviet-dominated communist regime. Area: 604,000 square miles, population: 1.3 million (1971). This large, sparsely populated land in the heart of Asia had virtually no relations with any country other than the USSR before the War, or other than communist countries since the war.

123

questions shed on the broader study of comparative economic systems? These are some of the problems that will concern us now.

First, a crucial political fact. The above-mentioned thirteen communist countries, other than the USSR, fall into two groups: those in which the communist regime came to power thanks primarily to Soviet military force; and those where power had been seized by local communists by dint of their own efforts, with no or little direct help from the Soviets. The latter group comprises Albania, Yugoslavia, China, North Vietnam, and Cuba. In these countries, the communist regimes have been relatively free of Soviet domination from the start. It is noteworthy from our standpoint that all of these five countries have sooner or later gone their ways in regard to economic institutions. Of the first group of countries, those where the communist regime owed its establishment to Soviet force, only Hungary has now an economic system that is markedly different from the Soviet (to be discussed in the next chapter).

The remarkable fact is perhaps not that about half the communist countries have deviated considerably from the Soviet model, but that about as many still adhere to it. For although they all officially share a Marxist-Leninist ideology—with widely different interpretations—and many similarities in internal political style,[3] they differ greatly from one another and from the Soviet Union on many important scores. They range in population size from the giant, China, with about three-quarters of a billion people, to Mongolia (over one million) and Albania (two million). In their cultural heritages they are as diverse as Czechoslovakia and China, Cuba and North Korea. Ethnically, some are highly homogeneous (for instance, Hungary, Bulgaria, Korea); others are multinational states (Yugoslavia, the USSR itself). Geographically, they range from the tropics to the arctic. Some are very sparsely settled, as is Mongolia; others are densely populated, like East Germany. Some were among the world's least-developed, least-industrialized, least-modernized countries when the communist regimes took over; others were already highly industrialized and modern, with educated and highly skilled populations (for example, Czechoslovakia and Germany). Some had had virtually no first-hand experience with capitalism or with socialist movements; others had experienced both to high degrees. And to mention a point to which we shall soon return: Some of the communist countries are extremely poor in natural resources and are therefore highly dependent on imports of fuel and raw materials, while others are very well endowed in these respects. It is thus hardly surprising that an economic system designed for the purpose of rapidly industrializing a country with such specific characteristics as the Soviet Union would not necessarily be well suited to all of the other thirteen lands. In addition, as we have seen, the system has displayed some major weaknesses even in its country of origin. Indeed, one of the interesting observations to be made about the transplantation of the Soviet system is that while its strengths mani-

[3]The chief exception to this generalization is Yugoslavia, which considers itself to be Marxist but not Leninist, and which is much more pluralistic in internal political structure than the others.

fested themselves to quite unequal degrees in the other countries, its weaknesses reappeared everywhere in full force.

In the rest of this chapter we will look at the adaptation and transformation of the Soviet economic system in three different parts of the world, Eastern Europe, Cuba, and China.

REFORM IN EASTERN EUROPE

When the Soviet economic system was extended to them at the end of the Second World War or shortly thereafter, the countries of Eastern Europe were in a parlous and in some cases desperate economic condition. Ravaged by the war (though to a very unequal degree), exploited for years by Nazi Germany, in several cases subjected to wholesale dismantling of production capacity and to the payment of heavy reparations by the Soviets who drove the Germans out, exhausted by the Great Depression even before the war, and soon to be drawn into the economic warfare and military preparedness of the Cold War— the East European countries had to *mobilize* all their resources for the execution of a relatively small number of high-priority tasks, of which sheer reconstruction of wartime damage was the most urgent. This the Soviet-type command economy—coupled with the quickly imposed political dictatorship—was able to do. The East European economies rebuilt themselves quite rapidly and then proceeded to industrialize further on the Soviet pattern, with emphasis on the heavy industries and at a rapid pace. Table 7.1 shows the growth of industrial output and gross national product in six East European countries between 1960 and 1967, as estimated by a Western authority. Note that the growth indexes roughly vary inversely with the countries' levels of development. It should be noted that in one important respect they deviated significantly from the Soviet example. Whereas Stalin undertook his mass collectivization drive in the countryside almost at the same time as he started the rapid buildup of industrial capacity, that is, during the first years of the Five-Year Plan era, the East European regimes generally proceeded much more slowly with collectivization, thus minimizing the clash with the peasantry and the damage to agriculture that were traumatic in the Soviet case.

The rapid economic growth of the early postwar period was of the kind that later came to be known to East European economists as *extensive* growth. By this they mean that the growth—mainly industrial expansion—was fed primarily by a rapid growth in the supply of production factors within each economy, rather than by more efficient ways of utilizing the combined factors. In other words, both physical production capacity and the employed labor force grew rapidly. The production capacity (physical capital) did so thanks to a very high rate of investment out of the national product (which naturally required at least temporary sacrifices in terms of current consumption), while the nonfarm

125

Table 7–1   **GROWTH OF INDUSTRIAL OUTPUT AND GNP IN SIX**

EAST EUROPEAN COUNTRIES, 1950–67

	Industry and Handicrafts	Gross National Product	
	Index, 1950 = 100	Index, 1950 = 100	Average Annual Increase per Capita, Percent per Year
Bulgaria	712	304	5.9
Rumania	467	271	5.0
Poland	360	217	3.1
Hungary	300	215	4.0
East Germany[1]	305	212	5.2
Czechoslovakia	256	199	3.3

[1]The growth of the East German economy shows up rather well in this table because in the base year, 1950, postwar reconstruction had progressed less far than in the other countries. If this fact were allowed for, the indicators for East Germany would be quite close to those for Czechoslovakia.

Source: Adopted from tabular data in Thad P. Alton, "Economic Structure and Growth in Eastern Europe," in U.S. Congress, Joint Economic Committee, *Economic Developments in Countries of Eastern Europe* (Washington: U.S. Government Printing Office, 1970), pp. 41–67.

labor force also grew rapidly owing to large-scale absorption of the farm population into the modern sectors, the drawing-in of housewives into the labor force, and—last but not least—large-scale training of manpower at all levels of skill for purposes of industrialization. In the countries that are better endowed with natural resources such extensive growth also relied heavily on large increases in domestically mined fuels and materials; but for most East European countries the process of extensive growth chiefly meant greater dependence on imports of crude and raw materials, including in some cases larger and larger imports of crude foodstuffs, all of these primarily from the Soviet Union. Lastly, such growth has been accompanied by only moderate advances in technology as compared with the technological revolution simultaneously occurring in the West. (Soviet economic growth as described in the preceding chapter was thus eminently of the extensive kind.) By contrast, *intensive* growth, although still resting on a rather high rate of capital formation, would be characterized by a much smaller rate of increase of the nonagricultural labor force, and by a swifter pace of technological advance, probably associated with a more flexible organizational structure and a more supple adjustment of production to demand.

Because extensive growth depends so much on the large-scale transfer of labor from agricultural to nonagricultural employment, its success—and, hence, the possibility of continuing improvements in personal consumption and with it internal political stability—is predicated on the presence of a large pool of underemployed rural labor. As a country reaches certain levels of industrialization and urbanization and as this labor reserve becomes exhausted, the rates of growth tend to slacken, the economy's difficulties multiply, new internal political tensions appear, and the question of shifting to an intensive pattern of development—the question of *economic reform*—becomes increasingly pressing. Several other things tend to happen simultaneously that contribute to the search for new institutional and organizational solutions. One is that the very success of the industrialization policy makes the economy much more complex and thus harder to plan and manage in a highly centralized manner. Second, in those countries that are poorly endowed with natural resources, economic growth raises the need for importation of fuel, materials, and possibly foodstuffs, thus placing a burden on the already strained balance of payments. Third, the rising levels of consumption lead the public to demand not only larger quantities of the same old consumer goods, but also better quality and larger variety, which the Soviet-type system is not well suited to provide.

These dynamic tendencies must be seen against the background of the specific problems of the command economy, such as the poor articulation of supply with demand, the general neglect of quality and variety (not only of consumer goods but of producer goods as well), the inadequate attention to cost and the attendant technical inefficiency (waste), the frequently inappropriate price relationships leading to economic inefficiency, and so forth, as we have already seen in the preceding chapter.

Of special significance is the problem of the balance of payments. Although on the average some 60 to 65 percent of the foreign trade of the East European countries (including the USSR) has been, during most of the postwar period, with one another, the crucial problem in this regard has been chronically that of the balance of payments with the West. In a nutshell, none of the East European countries (including the USSR) has been able to earn nearly enough hard (Western) currencies to meet its import needs from the West. With time it also became increasingly evident that this is related to the nature of the system; namely, that the Soviet-type economy does not easily generate manufactured goods of sufficient quality, modernity, and technological sophistication that can find for themselves large markets in the West. What is more, attempts to alleviate the hard-currency shortage by each country's developing import-substituting industries (if at all possible), or by relying on supplies from other East European countries, may in the longer run be counterproductive. This is so because greater self-sufficiency—apart from its frequently high domestic cost —increasingly isolates each European country and the region as a whole from the West, thereby only widening the technological gap between East and West and militating against future exports to the West. Which brings us to the closely related question of technological advance and innovation.

We have noted the difficulties that the Soviet economy has had in promoting innovation at the lower and intermediate levels of the economy (where the payoff is, after all). These difficulties have been replicated, and for the same reasons, in the other East European countries after they adopted the Soviet model. But for most of them it has been a more pressing matter than for the Soviets because of their more critical need to promote exports to the West.

127

Thus, for reasons of both the more limited possibilities for extensive-type growth, the greater complexity of their economies, and the more severe pressure from the side of the balance of payments, it was the most advanced of the East European economies that felt the inadequacies of the Soviet-type system earliest. These were East Germany and Czechoslovakia, soon to be joined by Hungary. Even the USSR itself, although still with one-third of its labor force in agriculture, began to experience a sharp retardation in the growth of nonagricultural employment by the early seventies, and hence to intensify its concern with technological advance and rising labor productivity.

However, the first abandonment of the Soviet-type system in Eastern Europe came under quite different circumstances. It happened in Yugoslavia, a country that adopted the Soviet economic system as quickly and as fully as any other newly formed communist state, and in addition, because of its relative underdevelopment and good endowment with natural resources was also perhaps as suited as any of the others to emulate the Soviet method of industrialization. The break between its communist leadership, headed by Marshal Tito, and Stalin took place in mid-1948. The main issue was Soviet interference in Yugoslav internal affairs, and Tito could successfully defy Stalin because he owed nothing to the Soviets for his seizure of power in Yugoslavia during the war and had a strong domestic political organization of his own. Having broken with Moscow, the Yugoslav leaders were free to rethink their internal arrangements and to experiment on their own. In the very few years that they had followed the Soviet economic model they became profoundly disappointed with it. Although postwar reconstruction was proceeding quite swiftly (but with substantial help from the West through the United Nations Relief and Rehabilitation Administration), the economy had already begun to exhibit the usual inefficiencies characteristic of the command economy. What is more, it had also begun to display evidence of overbureaucratization and of worker alienation, a lack of a sense of belonging by the workers in the work process, two phenomena that the Marxist leadership of the country regarded as being profoundly unsocialist. They set out to basically overhaul the economic (and social) system; the result is treated at length in the next chapter of this book. Suffice to note further at this point that the Yugoslav example had a strong bearing on the subsequent thinking about economic reform in all of Eastern Europe.

As the Yugoslav abandonment of the Soviet-type system was made possible by an event that in itself was political rather than economic, so the several moderate modifications of the system that took place in East European countries during the fifties were also triggered by primarily political shocks. Most notable of these is the virtual disappearance of collective farms in Poland immediately after the political upheaval of October 1956 and the freedom for peasants to leave the collectives that followed the "Polish October." Although only a little more than one-tenth of the cultivated land had been collectivized, about 85 percent of the collective farms disintegrated almost overnight (and what remained were often cooperatives of the looser sort). The bulk of Polish agriculture has been privately owned and operated since;[4] even though the rest of the economy continues to adhere to the Soviet model, the imaginative and much debated plans for reform that followed October 1956 having come to naught.

Another important deviation from the Soviet example ought to be noted. Although most of the other East European countries have embraced the Soviet policy of stressing material incentives, still the degree of inequality of labor earning (outside of farming) has generally tended to be smaller than in the USSR. Indeed, Czechoslovakia has had a remarkably small spread of wages and salaries—one of the least unequal distributions of income anywhere in the world—and as a result, in the opinion of many specialists, a rather inadequate structure of material incentives.

The wave of reforms in the sixties. By the early sixties, sparked by the slowdown in the growth of several countries (USSR, Czechoslovakia, East Germany), there sprang up throughout Eastern Europe a lively debate on ways of improving the functioning of the socialist economy. Much of the discussion was behind the scenes, but a good deal of it broke out in print or came otherwise to the notice of the world at large. Few voices—even in the USSR—spoke out in favor of continuing the existing institutions without at least *some* modification, although at the same time nobody openly advocated the abandonment of socialist ownership on a large scale (though some extension of private activity was frequently favored). But broadly speaking, the enormous range and diversity of views between these extremes can be grouped into two basic approaches: that which advocated various improvements in the functioning of the system without, however, abandoning the fundamental structure of a centrally managed economy, and that which would abolish or sharply reduce the operation of the command principle and replace it with some kind of market mechanism.[5]

The actual reforms began with that in East Germany, which was decreed in 1963 and went into effect at the start of 1964. Within four years all the other East European countries, except Albania, but including the Soviet Union, had followed suit. By the time of the publication of this edition we thus dispose of a full ten years of experience with East European economic reforms—a rich lode of empirical information on the modification of institutions and the redesign of whole economies that yields some interesting lessons for the study of economic systems.

The reforms also can be divided into two groups on the same principle. Let us call *major reforms* those that dismantled much of the command structure, replacing it with a market mechanism. On the other hand, let us call *minor reforms* those that essentially retained the command economy while modifying some of its features and possibly even gave more scope to the market in isolated

[4] In 1971, 84 percent of agricultural land was in private farms.

[5] In the latter case one now speaks—somewhat inelegantly—of "marketizing" the command economy.

areas. The line dividing the two is not a sharp one and nothing will be gained by splitting hairs.

There were two major reforms, apart from the original Yugoslav one: in Czechoslovakia (effective at the start of 1967) and in Hungary (1968). Only the Hungarian major reform has survived, though; it will be discussed at length in the next chapter. The Czechoslovak reform, after an exciting brief life, slid back into a minor reform by 1970, following the return to power of conservative political forces in the wake of the Soviet invasion of the country in August 1968. We thus turn to the content of the minor reforms.

Since a cardinal fault of the traditional Soviet-type system has been universally recognized to be its overcentralization, even the minor reforms paid considerable attention to this problem. A typical solution has been to reduce the number of mandatory targets for enterprises, and to some extent to replace more specific targets with more general ("synthetic") ones. Thus, the number of physical production targets was often reduced, output targets converted into sales targets (so as to forestall production of goods that no one wanted), and the importance of profit as a success indicator was usually much enhanced. All this, of course, gave the firms some more leeway for decision-making (though often not very much more, as we shall see). Similarly, management was given some more leeway with regard to the use or disposal of the firm's internal resources: labor, inventories, and so forth. However, for antiinflationary reasons strong control continued to be exercised over wage rates and the total payroll. Enterprises also obtained more freedom to undertake their own capital investments, either from retained profits and depreciation reserves or from bank credit.

Although these measures did moderately enlarge the firm's scope for action and therefore can be qualified as having been mildly decentralizing, another important move (which often preceded the reforms) complicated the picture in this regard. This is the agglomeration of enterprises, either into super-enterprises (as, say, in Czechoslovakia) or into "association," which often also became super-enterprises in effect if not in name. The associations bring together all or most of the firms in a given branch or subbranch of industry, and are charged with a wide range of the most important decisions, such as choice of technology, investment, distribution of products among the constituent firms, and so forth. The associations or super enterprises thus represent a certain centralization on the lowest tier of the economic hierarchy, but at the same time also a degree of decentralization in that they would assume some of the functions that had hitherto been exercised by the central planners and ministries. The latter result has often been welcomed by the central authorities in that it tended to unburden them of a great deal of detailed work.

The minor reforms also brought some significant changes into the nature of economic information. Thus, although prices remained largely under strict central control (for the danger of inflation persisted) and therefore continued to be cost-based rather than demand-determined, the costs now came to include some elements that previously had been dogmatically ignored. Chief among these have been interest on capital (though still not under this name) and in some cases differential rent for natural resources. Wholesale prices have been recalculated not only to include interest and rent, but also to reduce the great dispersion in profit margins in industry; the latter, an important practical purpose insofar as the new incentive schemes have been typically geared to profitability (on which more presently). On the other hand, for political reasons, retail prices for goods and services were hardly touched by the reforms. With many wholesale prices and farm prices having risen, subsidies to certain consumer goods (especially meat) have tended to go up sharply. This additional financial burden on the treasury has perhaps inhibited the further rationalization of wholesale prices (which would mean even greater subsidies), and has consequently also limited the effectiveness of the reforms.

Not least in importance are the measures pertaining to the strengthening of incentives at the enterprise level. Typically, they provide for larger allotments out of profits to three kinds of funds: investment at the enterprise's discretion, general benefit to the staff (for example, housing, recreation), and monetary rewards paid directly to individuals (premia, bonuses). The heightened emphasis on premia and bonuses is part of the overall tendency under the reforms to strengthen the reliance on material incentives. And although this is true of workers and employees at all levels, the chief beneficiaries are, of course, those who have the greater say in the performance of enterprises, namely, the managerial and technical personnel.

Such are the main provisions of the minor reforms in a nutshell. Our summary necessarily overlooks differences between the various countries, some of which are not insignificant.[6] Thus the East German reform (the so-called New Economic System), delegated considerable powers to the associations (V.V.B.s in Germany) and assigned relatively high importance to profitability for the enterprises under the associations. At the other end of the spectrum, the Soviet reform provided a minimal degree of decentralization, gave little scope to the associations until 1973,[7] and in fact did little to raise the importance of profit as the firm's goal.

It is at least as important to note what the minor reforms did not change as what they did change. They left the hierachical structure of economic administration and management essentially intact; they retained the crucial role of

[6] A very readable account of the state of reforms at the turn of the decade will be found in Michael Kaser and J. G. Zielinski, *Planning in East Europe: Industrial Management by the State* (London: Bodley Head, 1970). A more rigorous and more recent treatment of several of the reforms, including the Yugoslav but excluding the Soviet, is in Morris Bornstein, ed., *Plan and Market: Economic Reform in Eastern Europe* (New Haven: Yale University Press, 1973). Very useful also is the compendium of the Joint Economic Committee of the U.S. Congress entitled *Economic Developments in Countries of Eastern Europe* (Washington: U.S. Government Printing Office, 1970).

[7] See note 9, Chap. 6, p. 98.

physical production targets, even if their number was reduced in some cases; they left prices almost as rigid and centrally controlled as before; and (in accord with our definition of "minor reform") they did not introduce the market mechanism to any significant extent. Furthermore, they did not abolish the central allocation (rationing) of producer goods, which would have been difficult to carry off successfully with wholesale prices still rigid and unresponsive to demand. They did not appreciably alter the role of money and finance, which remain "passive" rather than "active."

In short, the minor reforms may have had a beneficial effect in that they abolished some of the least-justifiable constraints on the firms' actions (within the framework of the command system) and gave management more freedom and personal incentive to use the firms' internal resources to greater effect. In the first few years, they probably did have a positive effect on efficiency and growth, though this is still moot. Yet they did not significantly change the whole pattern of relations within the economy: between demand and supply, among enterprises, and between them and their superiors. Consequently, they do not seem to have markedly alleviated the operating problems of Soviet-type economies, or to have helped them to adjust to intensive (as against extensive) growth, or to have raised their ability to earn hard currency through exporting.

But the minor reforms raise an even more fundamental question: *Could* they succeed? Is such a "halfway house" viable? The reason for doubt on this score rests on the notion of alternative coordinating mechanisms.[8] As the minor reforms have indeed decentralized some significant functions, such as current production and some investment decisions, they have also weakened the coordination of the whole economy by means of the command (administrative) principle. But what is there to ensure that they will be coordinated in any other way, in that nothing—meaning specifically the market mechanism—has filled the gap? As a result, with time the imbalances and disproportions are likely to accumulate, production and investment are likely to move in directions not fully desired by the leaders or planners, and the pressure to improve coordination will mount. Barring major (marketizing) reforms, which are foreclosed primarily on political grounds, the only course is to recentralize, in other words to reverse the minor reform to some extent. It is instructive to note that by the early seventies several of the countries that had had minor reform—Bulgaria, East Germany, the USSR—had partially reversed them, in the sense of restricting in one way or another the scope of decision-making by the individual enterprise.

CUBA

In its short history to date, communist Cuba presents important lessons for the comparative study of economic systems in general and communist

[8]See Chap. 2.

economic systems in particular. In some major respects it bears greater resemblance to Communist China than to Eastern Europe and the USSR, a resemblance that we inquire into in the next section.

There is no space here to take up many of the most important aspects of Cuba's economic history since 1959: the development strategy, the closely related problem of foreign trade and of Soviet economic support, the U.S. embargo on trade with Cuba following that country's expropriation of American property in 1960. We will refer to these matters only in passing as we consider the problems that are of more central concern to the theme of this book, such as the organization of the economy and the various crucial economic institutions, the nature and role of planning and of the market, the related questions of management and finance, and last but not least, the specific Cuban methods of eliciting the compliance and commitment of the individual. We must also note that while the Cuban regime has concentrated on building a new type of egalitarian society and a new kind of unselfish man, it has also been concerned with the industrialization and development of the economy. The two goals have frequently come into mutual conflict, which in part explains the alternation of several socioeconomic stages in a little over a decade.[9]

Fidel Castro and his followers took power at the very start of 1959. It was only somewhat later that they began to call themselves "communist" or to nationalize property on a large scale. By late 1960 all large agricultural estates (which had been important in Cuba) and all important nonagricultural firms, both domestic and foreign-owned, had been taken over the state.[10] The National Institute of Agrarian Reform (INRA) was established in June 1959, acting as the chief instrument of state control over agriculture since. Lately, about 70 percent of cultivated land has been in state farms, where the labor force consists of hired workers. About 30 percent of the cultivated area is in private farms, which are also closely controlled by INRA and are responsible for compulsory deliveries to the state at low prices. Cooperative (collective) farms and communes are now of negligible importance in Cuban agriculture.

In industry, the nationalized firms were merged in late 1960 and early 1961 to form large so-called consolidated enterprises that united firms in the same or similar lines of production. Later, large enterprises were also created on the vertical rather than the horizontal pattern, in other words, firms at successive stages of production were combined.[11] Some of these enterprises are quite large in relation to the total economy.

Although by 1961 the market mechanism was already largely destroyed

---

[9]A very useful survey and analysis of the Cuban experience (to 1970) is the collective volume entitled *Revolutionary Change in Cuba* (Pittsburgh: Pittsburgh University Press, 1971), of which Carmelo Mesa-Lago is editor and chief author. It will be hereafter cited as *Revolutionary Change*.

[10]The remaining private establishments outside of agriculture were nationalized in 1968 during the so-called Revolutionary Offensive, a phase that marked the most leftward swing of Cuban domestic policy.

[11]Cf. the contribution of Roberto M. Bernardo to *Revolutionary Change*, pp. 185 ff.

or severely impaired, a new set of institutions to replace it was not developed at once. It is widely recognized that there was more confusion than system until 1963, even if some Soviet-style instruments of coordination and planning (such as material balances) began to be introduced in early 1961, and the Central Planning Board (JUCEPLAN) had been already in existence since March 1960. In those early years a number of eminent foreign experts—Soviet, East European, and Western Marxist—were recommending the adoption of the Soviet-style economic system in Cuba, but the leadership was not eager to do so. One of the reasons was its critical stance toward the Soviet structure of incentives for and controls over the individual producer, which in turn was part of a fundamentally different view in regard to the relation between man and society. What the Cubans saw in the USSR did not correspond to their conception of either a socialist society or socialist man.

Incentives and Rewards

The values that have been emphasized in the Cuban ideology are those of social and economic egalitarianism, of placing the society and the collective above the individual, and of unselfishness on the part of the individual in his everyday relations, and especially at work. Social egalitarianism has meant minimizing the differences in social worth between groups of the population: persons with different occupations and levels of skill and training, rural and urban dwellers, men and women, blacks and whites, and so forth. The economic corollary of this has been a relatively egalitarian wage and income structure.[12] Clearly, neither an egalitarian structure of rewards nor a high degree of social equality would be promoted by a structure of wages and salaries that relied heavily on differential material (monetary) rewards. In addition, material incentives appeal to man's selfishness and acquisitiveness, making it much more difficult to reeducate the citizenry so as to create the New Man. Awareness of the Soviet and East European experience only tended to reinforce the convictions of the Cuban leadership on this score. In terms of Etzioni's terminology (Chapter 2) this meant a minimal reliance on remunerative controls that bring about a calculative response on the part of the individual, replacing them with normative controls that stimulate moral involvement and eagerness to contribute one's efforts to society. Thus, "moral incentives," comprising various honorific titles and awards (medals), are supplemented by the manipulation of ideological symbols. The symbols, it must be noted, are not only socialist or communist, but also conspicuously nationalistic and patriotic. The third kind of control over the individual, coercive control, is, of course, not part of the "moral incentives," and

[12]The new values are described in the contribution of Jose A. Moreno to *Revolutionary Change*, pp. 471 ff. Excellent discussions of the debate over the new values, and of some of their implications for economic institutions, will be found in Silverman's "Introduction" to Bertram Silverman, ed., *Man and Socialism in Cuba* (New York: Atheneum Publishers, 1971), pp. 3–28, and in Carmelo Mesa-Lago, "Ideological, Political, and Economic Factors in the Cuban Controversy on Material versus Moral Incentives," *Journal of Interamerican and World Affairs*, 14:1 (February 1972), pp. 49–111.

its effects may well be countersocial (alienative). In any event, however, it has played an important role in the Cuban picture along with normative control.

The opposition to material incentives applies as well to the remuneration of managerial and administrative personnel. Indeed, given the responsible and skilled functions that such personnel perform, the material rewards paid to them would be especially high, and so naturally would be a serious offense against egalitarianism, while it is precisely the more responsible employees who should set the example of unselfish service to society. It seems that the Cuban regime has been successful in markedly reducing—if not entirely eliminating—social inequalities.[13]

However, the process of replacement of moral incentives and other controls for material incentives has not been either smooth or uncontroversial in Cuba. Until 1966 there was no unanimity on the question within the leadership. The primacy of moral incentives was argued by a faction led by Ernesto (Che) Guevara against considerable opposition. In those years, the wage and salary structure was hardly very egalitarian. Even disregarding agriculture, where wages were quite a bit lower, the lowest monthly wage for a manual worker was one-tenth as large as the highest salary for technical or executive personnel.[14] Even more indicative of the importance of material incentives until 1966 was the widespread application of piece-rate pay in industry.

It was only in August 1966 that Fidel Castro himself came out for the Guevara position in regard to incentives and greater equality of earnings, and the corresponding policies came to be consistently applied. The trend was greatly reinforced in March 1968, when the so-called Revolutionary Offensive was launched. At this point, piece-rate wages, overtime pay, and other incentive payments were to be eliminated, while simultaneously the range of free public goods, social services, and free personal services (including some passenger transport and housing) was greatly widened.

The reasons for this turn of policy in the Guevarist direction are probably complex, having to do with both domestic and internal circumstances, both economic and political. An economic explanation that has been advanced[15] stresses two factors. The first is the necessity to shift urban labor to agriculture in the wake of the shift in development strategy that once again emphasized the production and export of cane sugar. Such a shift of labor was difficult to undertake by means of wage differentials, for it involved transferring manpower from what generally have been higher-paid jobs to lower-paid jobs. Second, there had taken place a sharp decline in the availability of consumer goods, leading to greater resort to formal rationing (already in effect since 1962), which

[13]Cf. Nelson Amaro and C. Mesa-Lago, "Inequality and Classes," in *Revolutionary Change*, pp. 341 ff.

[14]Cf. Carmelo Mesa-Lago, "Labor Organization and Wages," in *Revolutionary Change*, pp. 209 ff.

[15]Silverman, *Man and Socialism*, pp. 18 ff.

inevitably meant a decline in the appeal of additional money earnings. Under these conditions material incentives were likely to be both ineffective and inflationary, and the turn of policy toward patriotic and other ideological appeals and toward moral incentives is therefore understandable. At any rate, the period 1966–70 stands out as the peak of the "left" policy in regard to incentives and economic equality in Cuba; though, unfortunately, there seem to be no comprehensive data to indicate the degree to which wages and earnings were levelled. The same period also witnessed growing concern on the part of the regime with insufficient commitment by many workers toward production, as evidenced by absenteeism, shirking of work, insufficient intensity of effort on the job, and the like. Evidently, neither the moral stimuli nor the so-called communist consciousness (*conciencia*) that was to bring out spontaneous commitment to work were sufficient to maintain reasonably high labor productivity. The response from above, especially from 1968 on, was to turn increasingly to various forms of mobilization of labor through administrative pressure, social pressure, and coercive measures. These methods reached a high point at the time of the all-embracing campaign to meet a highly ambitious sugar-production target in 1970, and it was the failure of this campaign that brought about the next important turning point in the evolution of the Cuban economic system.

It must be noted that the Soviet and East European experts and leaders were very skeptical of the Cuban rejection of material incentives, regarding it as a utopian policy that could have only negative effects on productivity. The concern of the Soviets in this matter has been more than just theoretical, since they have been, so to speak, underwriting the Cuban economy by means of large economic aid. The worse the Cuban economy performed, the costlier it was to be for the Soviets.

Centralization

The opposition to material incentives seems to have been the major motive behind the development of a distinctive, highly centralized structure of organization of the economy, the *sistema presupuestario* (or "system of budgetary finance," as it is sometimes rendered in English). Begun as early as 1960 by Guevara, and the subject of considerable controversy for several years, it remained the dominant form of organization and management throughout the sixties, even while undergoing some evolution in detail. In Cuban parlance, budgetary finance is contrasted with "self-finance," the latter being basically the traditional Soviet system of economic organization and management, the *khozraschet* system.[16] Note that the system of budgetary finance is *more* centralized than the *khozraschet* system.

Under budgetary finance, the individual (consolidated) enterprise has no financial autonomy, and hence virtually no managerial autonomy of any kind.

136   [16]See p. 100. There is, however, some similarity between Cuban "budgetary finance" and Soviet "War Communism."

Indeed, the whole nationalized sector of the country is thought of as a single huge firm run from the center. All of the money receipts of the individual enterprise are turned over to the National Bank for the account of the national budget (hence the name of the system). All of the enterprise's monetary requirements, whether for current or capital outlay, are doled out to it by the budget. While enterprises exchange goods for money, the money is for accounting purposes only; it is not "active" in the sense of guiding decisions. Prices are fixed and based on production cost, with little reference to demand. They are not important as signals. The enterprises receive directives for output and inputs in physical terms, and are judged primarily on the basis of technical criteria.[17]

The system of budgetary finance seems to have been prompted by a high order of faith in the rationality of central planning based on purely technical considerations, reinforced by disdain for the market, money, and finance as holdovers from capitalism. Yet, fundamental seems to have been the notion that only such a highly centralized system is compatible with the rejection of material incentives for management. For any lesser degree of centralization, any greater leeway for managerial decision, requires some device to ensure that the managers will indeed take and carry out the right decisions. This in turn means a significant role for profits at the enterprise level, and material incentives for managers to ensure that the enterprise earns the profits. But under the system of budgetary finance, where managerial autonomy is at a minimum, it seemed possible to rely primarily on the management's (and workers') communist consciousness, supplemented by moral incentives.

From the beginning, budgetary finance displayed the shortcomings that one would expect of a highly centralized system, especially one that lacks the proper financial instruments to reveal inefficiency and to relate production to requirements, and inevitably tends toward excessive bureaucratization. Magnifying these difficulties was a general shortage of technicians (in large measure owing to their emigration after the revolution), the basic mistrust of them owing to the persistence of a "guerrilla mentality," and, of course, also such things as inexperience with planning at the center and the shortages of many resources.

Because of initial disappointments with it, by 1964 budgetary finance was partly replaced in various sectors of the economy with the rival system of self-finance. But within less than two years, as the political climate was turning "left," it came back into its own. At the same time, for the sake of efficiency, it was somewhat modified in the direction of greater control by the enterprises over their own working capital. But basically the high degree of centralization continued.

As in the case of moral incentives, the system of budgetary finance met

---

[17]Bernardo, in *Revolutionary Change*, pp. 185 ff. A very good analysis of the issues pertaining to "Economic Organization and Social Conscience: Some Dilemmas of Cuban Socialism" will be found in the essay under this title by Bertram Silverman in J. Ann Zammit, ed., *The Chilean Road to Socialism* (The Institute of Development Studies, University of Sussex, England, 1973), pp. 391 ff.

with little favor on the part of the Soviets. It is not clear, however, whether or not it was primarily their influence that led to the turn of policy in 1970. At any rate, in a famous long speech on July 26, 1970, Castro himself severely criticized the very costly attempt to produce a record sugar crop in that year, and went on to criticize many of the fundamental institutions of the Cuban economy as well. In December of that year a Soviet-Cuban Scientific, Technical, and Economic Cooperation Commission was formed, through which Soviet influence in the Cuban economy was presumably enhanced.

At this writing it is still too soon to obtain a clear impression of the latest (post–1970) phase of the Cuban economy. But there is little doubt that a decisive turn back—away from Guevarist economic policy in regard to both incentives and economic organization—has been taken. Material incentives have been brought back, while rational economic management and financial controls are again in vogue. A sharp increase in productivity is the objective. This latest swing of the pendulum underscores anew the conflict between revolutionary values and economic imperatives in a society that is trying to "build socialism and [full] communism at the same time."

CHINA

Another communist society where revolutionary values and the needs of economic growth have tended to bring about an alternation of systemic phases has been that of the People's Republic of China (PRC).[18] In both countries the present regimes came to power as a result of indigenous guerilla action and with no, or almost no, assistance from Moscow. This fact contributed to a sense of political independence and ideological self-assurance that, sooner or later, led to a negative attitude toward the Soviet economic model by both regimes (and to an open break with the USSR on the part of China). Ideologically, both have been critical of Soviet reality from the "left"; that is, they have been critical of the inequality of income distribution and of the high degree of bureaucratization in the USSR. Thus, they have tended to develop their own distinctive institutions, among them a relatively greater emphasis on moral incentives and labor mobilization, and a smaller stress on material incentives (even if in both countries deeds have not always corresponded to words in these matters). In the process, both Cuba and China have gone through several phases

[18]Hereafter, "China" will mean the PRC, which is also colloquially known as "Communist China" and "Mainland China." It is not to be confused with the Republic of China, since 1949 limited to the island of Taiwan (Formosa), over which the PRC claims sovereignty but lacks control. Taiwan has a capitalist market economy that has been very successful in terms of economic growth. Thus, between 1957 and 1970, its gross domestic product increased at an average annual rate of almost 9 percent, and on a per capita basis, at almost 6 percent, both very high rates by world standards and much higher than those in the PRC.

in their relatively short histories under communist rule, oscillating between positions further from (on the "left") and closer to the Soviet system.

Needless to say, there are also very important differences between the two countries. Although both have histories of semicolonial status (whatever this much-abused phrase may mean), their historical, political, and cultural backgrounds could hardly have been more different. In both area and population China is almost one hundred times as large as Cuba, and its resource endowment is immeasurably greater and more varied. On the other hand, while Cuba was already relatively quite advanced and fairly modernized at the time of the communist takeover, China was one of the world's poorest and least industrialized major countries.

It is useful to contrast China's and the Soviet Union's economic condition on the eve of their respective First Five-Year Plans, China in 1952 and the USSR in 1928.[19] China's population was almost four times as large as Russia's, but her nonagricultural labor force and her urban population were only two to two and a half times as large. The number of scientifically and technically trained people was extremely small in China. On a per capita basis, her production of grain and cotton was only half as much, and of livestock products only about one-third as much as in the USSR. China's per capita output of electric power was only 37 percent as large, and the per capita output of major industrial materials and manufactured consumer goods ranged from one-tenth to one-half as large as Russia's in 1928. The production of machinery and equipment was virtually negligible. In sum, Russia had had her industrial takeoff decades before the communists took power; not so China. Clearly, it was to be much more difficult to mount a major industrialization drive in China than it had been in the Soviet Union (where it was difficult enough).

Objectives

Rapid industrialization has, in fact, been second to none as a policy objective for the Chinese regime from the start, albeit tempered by other goals. As in the Soviet case, this objective has been pursued for a variety of reasons, such as the construction of a highly productive socialist society, the raising of the population's living standards from very modest levels, and—last but not least—national pride and military power. The last two reasons are not to be overlooked. There was always a very strong nationalist component in the Chinese communist ideology, one that greatly facilitated its appeal to broad peasant masses during the guerilla war period, especially during the war against Japan (1937–45). Later, the nationalist appeal was also to become of prime importance in the conflict with the Soviet Union, a conflict that incidentally also

---

[19]This is well done in two works: Alexander Eckstein, *Communist China's Economic Growth and Foreign Trade* (New York: McGraw-Hill Book Co., 1966), Chap. 2, and K. C. Yeh, "Soviet and Communist Chinese Industrialization Strategies" in Donald W. Treadgold, ed., *Soviet and Chinese Communism: Similarities and Differences* (Seattle: University of Washington Press, 1967), pp. 327–50.

greatly reinforced the urgency to build up industrial capacity for defensive purposes. No better illustration of this can be offered than the relatively quick acquisition of capability to produce nuclear weapons, with all this implies for the creation of an advanced industrial and scientific base. The same considerations of national pride and military need have pushed China in the direction of a good deal of industrial self-sufficiency, which could be attained only with great effort.

In the Chinese case, much more than in the Soviet case, the drive for rapid industrial growth has been pursued jointly with what might be called (for lack of a better expression) revolutionary social objectives, such as the reeducation of man in the direction of greater social consciousness and subordination of self to the group, a relatively egalitarian distribution of income, and the provision of a floor, however modest, to the individual's material circumstances. An important aspect of this policy has been a significant reduction in the role of remunerative controls (material incentives) and a corresponding elevation in the roles of normative controls, coercion, and moral incentives.

We will return to this aspect of policy toward the end of our discussion of the Chinese economic system. At this point let us at least take note of the fact that, as in Cuba, the twin objectives—rapid industrialization and just-mentioned social goals—have been in some conflict with one another. What is more, diverse elements within the Chinese communist leadership (despite the overall primacy of Mao Tse-tung) have apparently differed as to how the twin objectives might be best reconciled at particular points in time. Consequently (and probably for other reasons as well), the Chinese economy has gone through several major phases since 1949, marked by sharp changes in policy in transition from phase to phase, and at times also by considerable political upheaval and occasionally violence. The observer's task in understanding and describing the institutions of the Chinese economic system is therefore greatly complicated because there have been in effect not one but several Chinese economic systems in the brief span of a quarter century. The pages to follow will present the chief characteristics of each of the several phases, and conclude the section with a discussion of two of the major issues that have run through all these phases, the issues of organization and of incentives.[20]

a. 1949–52. Reconstruction and consolidation. Policy during this first phase after the establishment of the PRC in October 1949 necessarily had to attend to the reconstruction of facilities damaged by many years of war, by

[20]The periodization here corresponds closely to that in Jan S. Prybyla, *The Political Economy of Communist China* (Scranton, Pa.: International Textbook Co., 1970, paperback), a useful text that is organized chronologically and gives considerable attention to the political side of the economic history of the PRC. A shorter and also very useful survey is to be found in Arthur G. Ashbrook, Jr., "China: Economic Policy and Economic Results, 1949-71" in U.S. Congress, Joint Economic Committee, *People's Republic of China: An Economic Assessment* (Washington: U.S. Government Printing Office, 1972), pp. 3–51. Note the useful tabulation of swings in policy on p. 4.

massive Soviet dismantling in the major heavy-industry region, Manchuria, and by the collapse of normal economic relations owing to hyperinflation and political chaos. But beyond this, the new regime proceeded with the consolidation of its control of the country and the transformation of ownership of economic units. In the latter instance, most important was the land reform of 1950, which confiscated most of the holdings of landlords and some of those of rich peasants, and distributed the land to poorer peasants and landless laborers. Note that at this point agriculture was not yet socialized (collectivized); this was to come in 1955–56.

Socialization in the other producing sectors proceeded faster than in agriculture, but was far from precipitous. By 1952, 36 percent of the wholesale trade volume and 58 percent of the retail volume were still in private hands, as was half of industrial output (both private factories and individual artisans) and half of motor transport.[21] Indeed, private firms and joint state-private firms were to continue to exist, though of declining importance, for quite a few years yet. During this period production recovered rapidly.

b. 1953–57. The First Five-Year Plan. The first Chinese FYP was drawn up on the Soviet model with Soviet expert assistance, and the period witnessed institutional transition to an economic system very close to the Soviet Industry and other modern production sectors, finance, agriculture, and various other parts of the economy were largely patterned after the Soviet example. Private activity was largely eliminated by 1956 (faster than the FYP anticipated), especially with the collectivization of agriculture along Soviet lines. There is, however, considerable doubt that the FYP had actually been fully drawn up at the start of the period. Many of the preconditions, such as a developed national statistical system, were only being established or were still lacking on the eve of the plan period. A comprehensive plan seems to have gone into effect only in 1955, thus covering only the second half of the quinquennium.

It was during this period that large-scale Soviet deliveries of machinery and equipment and technical assistance for Chinese industrialization began, a factor of great importance for the industrial takeoff, even if the amount of credit extended by the USSR was relatively small. The growth of production during the five years was very high: The output of modern industry nearly doubled in the five years, and GNP increased by a third or more.[22]

c. 1958–60. The great leap forward. Quite suddenly in the middle of 1958 the Chinese economy was turned onto a radically different course, the so-called Great Leap Forward (GLF), involving both a radically new strategy

---

[21]The progress of socialization is conveniently summarized in Li, Choh-ming, *Economic Development of Communist China* (Berkeley: University of California Press, 1959), pp. 12–24, especially the table on p. 16.

[22]Western estimates (for industry, by K. Chao); such estimates are conveniently summarized in Eckstein, *Communist China's Growth*, Chap. 3. A very convenient reference book for such statistical data as were available at the time of its publication is Nai-ruenn Chen, ed., *Chinese Economic Statistics: A Handbook for Mainland China* (Chicago: Aldine, 1967).

of development and radically new institutions. The reasons for the GLF are still not very clear. It seems that the leadership was not satisfied with the pace of development, especially in agriculture (where it was rather modest during the first FYP), and came to regard the Soviet strategy of industrialization with the attendant institutions as not suitable for the more backward conditions of China. The political divergence between Peking and Moscow had already begun, even if it was not to be made public for another few years.

Under the GLF extremely high and utterly unrealistic targets were set for the output of key commodities, both in agriculture and in industry. But even more striking were the means. These included: the mass mobilization of underemployed labor to construct and operate small, primitive production facilities; a high degree of decentralization of the whole economy but under very close party supervision and direction (the party itself being, of course, centralized); deemphasis of material incentives; and the organization of agricultural activity in so-called people's communes. The communes were huge units comprising on the average almost 5,000 households. Each commune could thus mobilize a large amount of labor for internal purposes or for public works. Internally, material incentives were minimized and distribution according to need was to be stressed, the latter to the point of free meals in communal dining halls. In both town and village, an atmosphere of feverish activity took over, political direction took precedence over technical and professional management (the "red" over the "expert"), and economic calculation was thrown to the winds.

For more information on this fascinating episode the reader is referred to the specialized literature.[23] Suffice it to say here that in terms of production the results were disastrous. After an initial jump, the output of the major industrial and agricultural commodities slumped badly, bringing the population to the brink of starvation and inflicting a severe setback to the industrialization program. A further severe blow was administered to the Chinese economy in the middle of 1960, when in consequence of the rapidly deteriorating relations between the two countries the USSR suddenly withdrew all its technical assistance personnel, which had been widely engaged in the Chinese industrialization program. The exact amount of the setback is difficult to ascertain owing to the statistical secrecy that accompanied it, and various Western estimates arrive at different figures, but on the whole they do agree that the GNP of the PRC did not reattain its 1959 level until the mid-sixties, and on a per capita basis, until the end of the sixties or the beginning of the seventies.

d. 1961–65. Recovery and readjustment. To pull the economy back up, the regime abandoned most of the characteristic features of the GLF and returned in part to the previous system. The feverish pace abated. Material incentives were reintroduced, although without going all the way to Soviet practice in this regard. The "expert" regained some of his position as against the "red."

[23]For a very concise analysis see Eckstein, *Communist China's Growth*, pp. 29–37. A more extensive treatment is in Prybyla, *Political Economy*, Chap. 8.

Many of the primitive industrial undertakings started under the GLF were now abandoned. The communes remained, but their more extreme features were eliminated. A policy of "agriculture first" was launched, which at once admitted the damage done to this sector under the GLF and stressed the need to build it up as the basis for the coming resumption of rapid industrialization. Industry was in part reoriented to serve agricultural recovery.[24] Planning remained on a year-to-year basis. There was considerable decentralization of economic administration to the provincial and local levels, and small-scale private activity was once again permitted and even encouraged.

e. 1966–69. The great proletarian cultural revolution. Again, suddenly, a new radical turn in domestic politics took place in the spring of 1966, the so-called Great Proletarian Cultural Revolution (CR). Its main thrust was to revive the primacy and force of revolutionary values, with emphasis on mass mobilization and normative controls, reduction of the role of material incentives, great equality of income, and a general ascetic outlook toward material welfare. The causes of the CR are no more clear than those of the GLF; no doubt bitter dissension within the leadership added vehemence and violence to the CR, if it was not the sole cause. Adulation of Mao's person reached new heights, and "Mao's thoughts"—collected for popular consumption in the famous little red book—were to furnish answers to all problems. In the process, the government bureaucracy was badly shaken, and the Chinese Communist party was virtually destroyed as an effective force on the local and provincial levels. The party's place was taken by the so-called Revolutionary Committees, in which army officers often occupied key positions.

The effects of the CR on the economy were substantial. Industrial production dropped[25] in 1967 to recover only in 1969, although agriculture seems to have suffered little (in contrast to the experience under the GLF). But, perhaps the most profound and most lasting damage was inflicted on higher education, because much of the disruptive activity and violence took place at universities and otherwise involved the students.

f. 1970. Another readjustment and the Fourth FYP. Once again the pendulum swung in the now familiar way. After the CR, material incentives were strengthened, the political fever subsided, and something like normalcy returned, and economic calculation and rational decision-making have been rehabilitated. The Fourth FYP (1971–75) was launched, a fact that in itself betokens stabilization and renewed emphasis on production. In an important sense, therefore, the trend since 1970 in China—as in Cuba, it will be recalled —has been toward the orthodox Soviet economic system. Though not primarily

---

[24]However, the expansion of defense industry was also stressed in this period, owing to the acute deterioration of relations with the USSR and the war in Vietnam. The first Chinese atom bomb was exploded in October 1964.

[25]By 10 to 20 percent between 1966 and 1967, to recover only in 1969, according to various Western estimates.

economic in nature, but equally significant of the change in climate, have been the developments in international relations since 1971: the establishment of diplomatic contacts with the United States, a more open posture toward the West in general, and the PRC's entry into the United Nations. However, extreme hostility toward the USSR remains.

Results

It is not easy to appraise the performance of the PRC in terms of economic growth, if only because the statistical data are exceedingly scanty (especially so since the end of the fifties, although there may be a return to greater publication of data in the seventies). Thus, independent Western estimates can have only a low degree of accuracy and are likely to vary substantially, which is indeed the case. But they do agree that overall economic growth, as measured by the average annual rate of increase of the national product, has been relatively moderate for the whole period since 1952. Because the population has probably increased quite rapidly, perhaps by two or more percent per year (another statistical question mark), the rate of per capita growth of the national product seems to have been quite modest, though significant. The First FYP saw the fastest growth; the rates after 1957 are probably considerably lower. Industrial output has naturally grown much faster than the whole national product. Yet, whatever the exact figures might be, there is little question that the PRC has not been among the most rapidly developing countries of the underdeveloped world, if the fifties and sixties are taken together.[26]

A closer look brings out certain contrasts. On one hand, agricultural production has only kept up with population growth at best (since 1952), leaving per capita consumption at very modest levels indeed. On the other hand, industrial production has probably increased at a respectable rate (though numerical estimates vary widely), and, what is more, a substantial modern industry has been built. That last is particularly evident in military hardware and outer-space exploration, but can be observed in many civilian industries as well, serving both investment and consumption. Much was done in developing the modern transport network. A sizeable research and development effort seems to be in progress, a good part of it, of course, related to the military program. Lastly, China has also engaged in furnishing foreign aid by way of large construction projects in some underdeveloped countries.

The relatively modest overall growth is doubtless explainable by historical circumstances: the initial poverty of the PRC, and particularly the great difficulty of expanding agricultural production in an overpopulated and as yet little-

[26]More moderate estimates of overall and industrial growth are to be found in T. C. Liu and K. C. Yeh, "Chinese and Other Asian Economies: A Quantitative Evaluation," *American Economic Review* 63:2 (May 1973), pp. 215–23; and in Alexander Eckstein, "Economic Growth and Change in China: A Twenty Year Perspective," *China Quarterly* (May–June 1973), pp. 211–41. Higher growth estimates are given in Dwight H. Perkins, "An Economic Reappraisal," *Problems of Communism*, 22:3 (May–June 1973), pp. 1–13; and in Rawski's article cited in note 28, below.

modernized agrarian setting in which the population is overwhelmingly rural. It is certainly also partly due to the large diversion of resources to defense. But it is probably in significant measure due as well to the turbulence of the brief history of the PRC, as has just been sketched out.

At the same time, the present regime in China would most likely insist that the numerical record of growth addresses itself to only some of the goals it has been pursuing, and that it overlooks the equally important social goals: the reeducation of man, the reformation of society, and the maintenance of an egalitarian distribution of material benefits. To these we will return.

Organization and Institutions

It is clear from the foregoing that the Chinese economic system has changed too often and too radically to permit a brief summary statement regarding its organization and institutions. Our attempt is, therefore, limited to the two more recent periods of relative stability, that of 1961–65 and that which began around 1970 and is currently under way. This choice is prompted by two considerations: first, we will be looking at what is in effect at this writing (though it would be foolhardy to rule out another major turn of events in the Chinese economy in the near future), and second, because relatively more is known of the way in which the economy functioned during these two periods than during the two major "leftward" swings of the pendulum, i.e., during the GLF and the CR.

Although in very broad terms there is considerable similarity between the organization and administration of industry (and other modern sectors) in China and in the Soviet Union, such differences as can be noted on the whole suggest greater flexibility of organization and administration in the former than in the latter. The most important industrial enterprises are under central control, but the rest of industry is under provincial and local subordination. (It must be noted though that many of the provinces of the PRC are larger in population than the individual countries of Eastern Europe, excepting the USSR.) Likewise, the determination of prices is in large measure decentralized to the regional level.

Small-scale firms, often utilizing primitive techniques and the abundant unskilled labor, are much more prevalent in China than in the USSR, and seem to operate with considerably greater suppleness and initiative. The most important producer goods are allocated, whether by central or regional authorities. The overall system appears to be basically a command system, but with relatively greater freedom of action at local levels, and with more of a (legal) market nexus than in the Soviet economy. Coordination and enforcement of priorities in the economic sphere, and even direct intervention in management, by the Communist Party (and after the CR, by the Revolutionary Committees) have been more pervasive in China than in the USSR.

As a result, the Chinese economy seems to operate at least as well as the Soviet in those areas where short lines of communication and speed of adjustment are important, as, for instance, in the supply of consumer goods of variety and quality to the population. At the same time, it does not seem to be immune to the usual defects of the Soviet-type command economy, such as fragmentation of decisions, local autarky, waste of inputs, hoarding of materials, and resistance to innovation at the operating levels.[27]

Incentives and Controls

As noted, the aim of the Chinese leaders has been the industrialization of the country *together* with the transformation of society and of man. Man is to be socially conscious and guided by the needs of society, the immediate group, and his fellow man. He is to give his best to his work, guided by concern for the common good rather than material incentive. He is to abandon selfishness and acquisitiveness. The distribution of material benefits is to be relatively equal— thus, it is hoped, equalizing the social worth of individuals—and a floor is to be provided for every person's standard of living. At the same time, in society at large, the age-old distinction between town and country, industry and agriculture, and mental and manual labor are to be erased. These are, of course, more or less the characteristics of the ideal Marxian society, the ultimate historical stage of full communism, except that in Marx the stage is to be attained only after the productive capacity of the economy has developed so far as to ensure abundance of material goods. The last is, of course, at least as distant a goal for China as it is for the vast bulk of mankind today. Yet the Chinese leaders have insisted that the pursuit of the social aims must accompany industrial development, lest the very process of industrialization and raising the material well-being of the population compromise the building of a socialist—and ultimately, communist—society. They are convinced that the Soviet Union has made this fatal mistake by relying primarily on material incentives in order to bring out economic performance from its population, and has thereby taken the "capitalist road" of selfishness and inequality, rather than the true socialist road.[28]

Yet it would be quite incorrect to infer from this that material incentives do not find an important use in the PRC, or that the distribution of income is not without a significant degree of inequality. (We refer here to the above-mentioned two recent periods of relative stability. There is no doubt that during the

[27]The Chinese economy during the 1961–65 period is treated at length in the following major works (in addition to those already cited): Audrey Donnithorne, *China's Economic System* (London: George Allen and Unwin, 1967); Nai-ruenn Chen and Walter Galenson, *The Chinese Economy Under Communism* (Chicago: Aldine, 1969); Dwight H. Perkins, *Market Control and Planning in Communist China* (Cambridge, Harvard University Press, 1966); and U.S. Congress, Joint Economic Committee, *An Economic Profile of Mainland China*, 2 vols. (Washington: U.S. Government Printing Office, 1967). For a concise treatment of the post–1970 period see Dwight H. Perkins, "Plans and Their Implementation in the People's Republic of China," *American Economic Review* 63:2 (May 1973), pp. 224–31.

[28]Cf. Charles Hoffman, "The Maoist Economic Model," *The Journal of Economic Issues*, 5:3 (January–March 1973), pp. 28–30. The main thesis of this article, however, is that economic growth has been faster than had been estimated by most Western specialists.

GLF and CR the role of material incentives was sharply curtailed and inequality of earnings must have been appreciably reduced, even if we lack any firm data for these instances.)

To take nonagricultural labor first, the information brought back from China in the mid-sixties and again in the early seventies by the more skilled and perceptive visitors indicates that in a *given* factory the ratio of the highest wages of blue-collar workers to average wages and to the lowest wages (excluding those of apprentices) have been roughly 3:2:1. The ratio of the highest salary, usually received by the top technical or managerial personnel, to the average wage or salary in the same factory has been of the order of between 2:1 and 3:1 (and 4:1 to 7:1 in relation to the lowest wages).[29] These are ratios in a given factory. Since the pay scales are not the same for different enterprises, the spread of wages and salaries in a given locality, let alone in the whole country, must be substantially greater. These are not insignificant differences in pay, and the resultant inequality of earnings may be not much smaller than that in Soviet industry.

We should, however, take note of a few additional factors. In China, in contrast to the USSR, top managerial personnel does not receive any bonuses for good performance, though the lower levels of management and the rank and file personnel do. This probably tends to cut off the "upper tail" of the industrial earnings structure, compared to the Soviet case. On the other hand, there are in China, as in the USSR, large bonuses for innovation, invention, and technical improvement. Further, on the equalizing side, in China certain basic consumer commodities (grain, edible oil, cotton cloth, coal) are rationed to the nonagricultural population and sold at relatively low prices, while other important services (medical, educational) are extended free or nearly so. There is an extensive social security system that is quite advanced for a country at the low economic level of China. Lastly, it should be noted that the supply of consumer goods for sale to the public is quite good in terms of variety, quality, and availability—compared, say, to most other communist countries. Thus, the Chinese worker who responds to material (monetary) incentives finds many things to buy with his additional earnings.

In sum, the distribution of nonagricultural earnings for a country as poor as China appears to be relatively not too unequal, with a definite floor to the lowest incomes and with a developed social security system to protect against adversity. This is a major achievement, even if the degree of income inequality or the role of material incentives is not nearly as insignificant as the official pronouncements would lead us to believe.

[29]Cf. Charles Hoffman, *Work Incentive Practices and Policies in the People's Republic of China, 1953–1965* (State University of New York Press, 1967), Barry M. Richman, *Industrial Society in Communist China* (New York: Random House, 1969), pp. 798 ff.; A. Doak Barnett, "There are Warts There, Too," *New York Times Magazine*, April 8, 1973, pp. 103, 104.

In the agricultural communes—actually after the GLF run more like collectives than like communes—we find the same general picture. Material incentives are definitely employed and appear to be important, and income differentials are probably significant, both within and between individual communes.[30] But perhaps the clearest example of the use of material incentives in regard to peasants is the policy of permitting the cultivation of private plots, the produce of which can be sold in the open market for the peasant's own account as well as consumed in his household.

However, it is also clear that the authorities do not rely on material incentives alone to elicit performance and deploy and redeploy labor. Indoctrination and close administrative control (often what we would regard as coercive in nature) have been in continuous use in the relatively "stable" periods let alone during the brief "leftward" swings. These means are used to bring about compliance and good performance on the job. They are also very much used to redistribute labor between firms, industries, and (especially) localities. Since much of the spatial redeployment of labor has been movement from towns to the villages, it probably would have required very large monetary inducements, with attendant inflationary dangers, to bring it about by means of material incentives. We have seen the same problem already in the case of Cuba; and as in Cuba, it may well be that the Chinese denigration of material incentives is at least in some measure a case of making an ideological virtue out of an economic reality.[31]

CONCLUDING REMARKS

In this and the preceding chapters we have examined two very different kinds of attempts to modify the traditional Soviet-type economy. These are, first, efforts in the Soviet Union and in several East European countries to make their economies more responsive to demand, foreign as well as domestic, and more conducive to innovation, by diminishing the high degree of centralization of economic decision-making, while essentially retaining the command principle. As part of such "minor reforms" (and even more of the "major reforms," in which the command principle has more or less given way to the market mechanism, as described in the next chapter) there has been a reaffirmation of the dominant role of material incentives in motivating the individual to do the economy's work. The second kind of modification of the Soviet model, in the Chinese and Cuban cases discussed in this chapter, has been a marked attenuation—though far from complete elimination—of material incentives, combined (at

[30]In both agriculture and industry there is the practice of determining the rate of an individual's pay according to his political attitude as well as on more directly economic grounds. It is not clear how this works, although one would expect that the practice might bring in both simulation by the worker and arbitrariness on the other side.

[31]The author is indebted for this observation to Dr. Christopher Howe (London).

least in the Cuban case) with a much more pronounced centralization of economic decisions. The attenuation of material incentives has been accompanied by intense political indoctrination of and widespread administrative (coercive) controls over labor, in order to bring about the needed deployment of manpower. A major end of this policy has been to narrow the dispersion of earnings and to reduce social differences.

In either case the full returns are not yet in. But if a provisional observation is to be ventured, it is that in both cases there seems to have been a drift back to the traditional Soviet system. East European minor reforms (including the Soviet one) have been subject to "creeping recentralization," as the need to husband scarce resources by centralized administrative means in the absence of a market mechanism tended to reassert itself. This was especially marked whenever the pressure on available resources mounted, as happened in the late sixties and early seventies.

In the Chinese and Cuban cases the need to better husband resources was also apparently a major reason for muting, around 1970, the emphasis on normative ("ideological") controls over producers—which in any case hardly could have been long maintained at the high pitch of the late sixties in both countries —and for giving more scope to material incentives and to the Soviet way of managing things generally. However, administrative controls over labor still remain strong in both countries, compared to the USSR. Neither continuous feverish political manipulation of the population, nor for that matter widespread coercive controls, are conducive to efficiency and initiative in the economy. Because China—and even Cuba—still have far to go to reach high levels of economic well being, and in any case find their resources under constant heavy pressure to meet many immediate objectives, the recent observed trends in both countries are consequently not surprising. In other words, an egalitarian distribution of earnings is one of the most difficult ends to promote in relatively poor countries, especially when they are undergoing rapid structural change, even under the most propitious political conditions.

149

The Socialist

Market Economy

CHAPTER EIGHT

THE EARLY THEORIZING

The idea that a socialist economy, one in which means of production are publicly owned, can also be a market economy was slow in maturing. Its intellectual origins lie, first, with those neoclassical economists of the late nineteenth and early twentieth centuries, mostly nonsocialist, who insisted that the "economic problem," the best use of available resources for society's ends, was formally the same regardless of who owned the productive assets, and would be solved with the aid of prices, wages, the interest rate, and so on, under socialism as well as under capitalism. Second, they lie with those socialist economists of democratic inclination—in Germany, England, and the United States in the twenties and thirties—who were searching for a reply to the taunts from antisocialist economists (the most famous being Ludwig von Mises) that socialism would be incapable of efficient resource allocation for lack of meaningful prices freely forming in the market.[1] The end result was the so-called "competitive solution," a *model* of a perfectly competitive socialist economy that, like the model of a perfectly competitive capitalist economy, achieved static efficiency by means of the market mechanism. In this model, individual socialist firms would com-

[1]For an historical survey of these strands of socialist thought see Carl Landauer, *European Socialism: A History of Ideas and Movements*, Vol. 2 (Berkeley: University of California Press, 1959), pp. 1643 ff. Landauer himself is one of the pioneers of the idea of market socialism.

pete with one another within a market economy, while the allocation of re-sources (except for the overall rate of saving) would be ultimately determined via freedom of household choice.

The advocates of the competitive solution soon found themselves in a lively polemic not only with antisocialists but also with more authoritarian socialists. To the latter, competition and the market mechanism represented everything that socialism had traditionally stood *against*; nor did they put much stock in consumer sovereignty. Instead, they preferred the "centralist solution," a close cousin to the planned command economy that the USSR was introducing at the time.[2]

The advantages that, for instance, Oskar Lange in his celebrated essay[3] claimed for the model of the competitive socialist economy over its capitalist counterpart were these: (1) a more just distribution of income owing to the elimination of private property incomes, and for the same reason a more meaningful pattern of effective demand for consumer goods; (2) more opportunity to take account of externalities; and (3) stabilization of the economy at high employment by bringing the rate of saving into equality with the rate of investment. In Lange's model, a Central Planning Board sets prices so as to equate demand and supply, while the managers of individual socialist firms and industry planners push production of every good to the point where its marginal cost equals its price. This ensures that every unit of every resource is used to the maximum satisfaction of effective demand.

The rule for (static) efficiency—output where marginal cost equals price—had actually been developed by Abba P. Lerner, who in a major work[4] that appeared some years after Lange's essay, presented a model that differed from Lange's in at least two important respects. Lerner avoided price setting by a Central Planning Board and instead left the process to the free market. Second, he stressed that private or public ownership mattered little from the point of view of allocative efficiency, except where subsidization was necessary on static efficiency grounds.

---

[2]A well-known analytical survey of the literature is Abram Bergson, "Socialist Economics" in Howard S. Ellis, ed., *A Survey of Contemporary Economics* (Philadelphia: Blakiston [for the American Economic Association], 1948), pp. 412–48. Nearly twenty years later Bergson published a rather reserved reappraisal of market socialism; see his "Market Socialism Revisited," *Journal of Political Economy* 75, no. 5 (1967), pp. 655–73.

A stimulating recent discussion of the "socialist controversy" can be found in Benjamin N. Ward, *The Socialist Economy* (New York: Random House, Inc., 1967), Chapter 2.

[3]"On the Economic Theory of Socialism" in Oskar Lange and Fred M. Taylor (Benjamin E. Lippincott, ed.), *On the Economic Theory of Socialism* (Minneapolis: University of Minnesota Press, 1938), pp. 99 ff.

[4]*The Economics of Control* (New York: The Macmillan Co., 1947). This is one of the most readable of the important economic treatises published in recent decades.

MARKET SOCIALISM IN EASTERN
EUROPE SINCE THE WAR

The first socialist market economy to make its appearance in the real world following these debates[5]—that of Yugoslavia—developed quite independently of this theorizing. Instead of succeeding a mature capitalism, it arose in a country that had hardly known capitalism, as a reaction to a Soviet-type command economy. In other words, the "market socialism" was to be a fundamental improvement on nonmarket socialism, not on market capitalism; it was to be the means to a more perfect socialism.

World War II brought a communist regime to Yugoslavia. However, unlike those in other East European countries, this regime was not imposed by the conquering Soviet Army but won its own victory in a most difficult war against many internal and external enemies. The victorious military leader and the president of the postwar gŏvernment, Tito, proved to be too independent-minded for Stalin. The two fell out over who was to be boss within Yugoslavia and in June, 1948, broke completely with each other.

Until then the Yugoslavs had been second to none among the Soviet satellites in faithfully copying Soviet economic institutions and methods. The rift with Stalin gave them the opportunity to take a more detached look at the system they had only recently transplanted. They found it wanting on many scores; inefficient (as discussed in the preceding chapter), neglecting the consumer, over-centralized, overbureaucratized, and affording no opportunity for the individual worker to feel meaningfully involved in the production process. The last fault, "alienation," had traditionally been one of the main charges thrown out against the capitalist economy by Marxists; it seemed incongruous that a socialist economy should suffer as much from it. Lastly, they found that the collectivization of agriculture was highly unpopular with the peasants and a fetter on farm production.

The distinctive economic system that Yugoslavia developed in the early fifties, after much trial and error, aims at a relatively high degree of decentralization of economic activity as a way of combating bureaucratization and affording maximum opportunity for producers' participation in economic decisions,

[5]Actually, there had already existed a workable socialist market economy before the debate reached its high watermark—the Soviet economy under the so-called New Economic Policy (NEP) from 1921 to 1928. Under the NEP, all large-scale economic activity was conducted by the state, agriculture was private, and there was some small-scale private enterprise in trade, manufacturing, and so on. The state exercised close overall control over the whole economy, but the command principle even within the state sector was secondary to the market mechanism. The NEP was highly successful in achieving full recovery for the Soviet economy from its virtual paralysis in 1921. See V. N. Bandera, "The New Economic Policy (NEP) as an Economic System," *Journal of Political Economy*, 71, no. 3 (1963), pp. 265–79.

while at the same time preserving its socialist aspects and speeding the development of what is still a relatively backward economy.

It was only a decade and a half later, as part of the wave of economic reforms in Eastern Europe in the sixties, that other communist countries undertook to "marketize" their command economies. As we already saw in the preceding chapter, at the beginning of 1967 Czechoslovakia adopted a market-socialist system, and exactly a year later Hungary followed suit. But, as we also saw, the Czechoslovak reform withered after the Soviet invasion of that country in August 1968, after a time being reduced to just another minor reform in Eastern Europe. By contrast, the Hungarian market economy was spared such a fatal political blow and is now, like the Yugoslav market economy, very much a going concern. We shall take a look at the two separately in this chapter, taking note at this point of the important fact that there are some major differences between them (the most important of which pertain to internal arrangements within the enterprise and to the degree of socialization in agriculture).

YUGOSLAVIA

Ownership and Management

In 1953 after permission was given to peasants already in collectives to leave them, the private sector in agriculture increased from three-fourths to over 90 percent, measured in terms of arable land, later gradually declining to 85 percent (in 1970). The remaining 15 percent of arable land is occupied by state farms and collectives. Private farms are normally limited to ten hectares (24.7 acres) in size, a substantial amount by Yugoslav standards, but are otherwise not restricted in their operation. Private enterprise is also permitted in small-scale production and trade outside agriculture, though no more than five persons may be employed by a private employer (not counting family members).

With these exceptions, all enterprises are publicly owned, and it is in this "socialist sector" that one of modern Yugoslavia's most distinctive institutions —so-called *workers' management*[6]—is found. The basic idea is that the workers (including white-collar employees) of an enterprise, though not its legal owners, have the ultimate authority for its affairs as well as a financial stake in the results of its operation. In this manner the socialist ideal of industrial democracy is to be realized, the "alienation" of the worker from his place of work is to be minimized, and at the same time the constructive energies of the workers are to be enlisted for their own and the social good.

Of course, workers' management cannot be meaningful unless the enterprise itself enjoys a good deal of autonomy. In the Yugoslav case this is achieved by relating the firm to the economy by means of the market mechanism rather

[6]Also frequently called "workers' self-management."

153

than by a Soviet-style command hierarchy. Within the individual enterprise, there is a management board consisting of the enterprise's own workers elected by and responsible to a workers' council, which in turn is elected by and responsible to the totality of the enterprise's employees. Day-to-day management is, however, up to a manager ("director"), who at once reports to the management board (of which he is a member) and overrules it in the event of conflict with law. He is hired and fired by the workers' council.

In order to give the enterprise and the individual worker a powerful incentive to produce and to do so prudently and efficiently, the workers' earnings, determined according to rates set by each workers' council, come from the enterprise's net income. (Wages as such are no longer paid, though the state does guarantee certain minimum earnings.) A part of the enterprise's net income may be reserved at its own discretion (and with the encouragement of tax laws) for internal investment.

What is the objective of a worker-managed enterprise in Yugoslavia? Is it to maximize the total profit of the enterprise, as might be the case with any enterprise in a market economy? Or, since presumably the workers have the last say in formulating the firm's policy, is it to maximize profit (and hence presumably earnings) *per worker*? If the enterprise cannot vary the size of the labor force, the two goals, of course, amount to the same thing. But the Yugoslav enterprise *can* take on additional workers and (though this is harder) dismiss part of its work force. In this case the two goals do not lead to identical results. Specifically, if the firm maximizes profit per worker, and if there are diminishing returns to labor (as there usually are beyond some point), then it will tend to have a smaller work force and to produce a lesser output than if it aimed to maximize total profit. Since the issue was first rigorously formulated in 1958 by an American student of the Yugoslav economy, Professor Benjamin Ward,[7] it has received a fair amount of attention in theory. However, such empirical evidence as is available on the actual behavior of the Yugoslav firm gives no clear indication as to what its principal objective is. There is no doubt that profits are very important to it, but it is not obvious whether the firm maximizes total profits, or profits per worker, or some combination of the two, or something else. (It will be recalled that straight profit maximization need not accurately represent the objective of the "capitalist" firm, either.)

Establishment of New Enterprises

If each enterprise is run by its workers, how can one come into existence before it has hired any workers? Sometimes, a new enterprise is "spun off" by an old one. Or a group of persons may band together to found a new enterprise, provided the initial capital can be raised from some governmental source. In

[7]Cf. Benjamin Ward, "The Firm in Illyria: Market Syndicalism," *American Economic Review*, 66, no. 4 (1958), pp. 373–86. He developed his ideas much further in his *Socialist Economy* (cited in note 2), Chapters 8 through 11.

the case of major, important new ventures, the initiative may come from the federal or republic (state) government, which would also advance the necessary funds. But most commonly the impulse comes from the commune (local government), which may have one or more motives to establish a new enterprise: fiscal (since the profits of enterprises are a major source of revenue for the communes), to relieve local unemployment, to supply the commune's population with needed goods or services, and even for sheer prestige. In this case, the initial capital comes from resources at the commune's disposal and from various investment banks and government funds.

Once an enterprise becomes established it naturally becomes subject to the usual internal arrangements, workers' management. Yet this may also mean that the person(s) or organization or enterprise that launched the new firm loses control of it soon after it is established, which may be a deterrent to the promotion of new enterprises in some instances. But in terms of our discussion in Chapter 2 we find that in the Yugoslav economy—in contrast to the Soviet-type economy —there is a good deal of possibility for self-organization, in other words, for creative, decentralized institutional response to particular economic needs as these make themselves apparent.

The Market

The market mechanism in Yugoslavia operates on the whole along familiar lines. To begin with, there is a high degree of freedom of consumer choice and of choice of job, so that the economic behavior of households is essentially the same as in other systems where freedom of household choice obtains. (In fact, Yugoslavia is the only communist country in which freedom of choice of job extends to the possibility of seeking employment abroad, which is practiced on a large scale. In the early seventies, nearly one million Yugoslavs out of a nation of about twenty million were working abroad, mostly in Western Europe, and their remittances have been a very important part of Yugoslavia's hard currency earnings.)

As for individual enterprises, they are also largely guided by market signals, primarily prices, in determining their decisions with regard to outputs, inputs, technology, and investment. And in turn, the activities of the totality of firms are coordinated primarily by the operation of the market mechanism. All this of course is in sharp contrast to the way a command economy functions.

It is interesting to note that in the more than twenty years that the Yugoslav economic system has been in existence, the long-term tendency has been to allow an increasing role to the market mechanism, as against administrative controls. (An important exception has been the persistence of price control owing to chronic inflationary pressure, on which more presently.) To be sure, this tendency for fuller "marketization" has been one of the most intense domestic political issues, nor has it proceeded smoothly at all times. But, given the basic commitment to *market* socialism, it has been a consistent tendency,

155

in the sense that the broader the scope of operation of the market mechanism, the more efficiently can it function. The other side of this phenomenon has been the growing autonomy of the individual enterprise, especially as it pertains to the possibility to retain larger proportions of new income for investment by and within the enterprise.

In one very important area of the economy, however, the market mechanism has been significantly restricted; this is the area of capital flows. In other words, the capital market is—still?—only very rudimentary. True, there is a well-developed commercial banking system, as there are savings banks for household savings, but there is little by way of financial institutions that would redistribute funds between enterprises on a long-term basis. The restrictions may have been chiefly of an ideological kind, out of fear of replicating "capitalism" too much. But efficiency in production requires efficiency also in the flow of investible funds, so that the establishment of a more developed capital market is very much in the "logic" of the situation, even if not entirely viewed with favor.

Being a market economy, the Yugoslav economy is subject to virtually all the hazards and problems of one. Thus, there is an ever-present danger of monopoly with the undesirable effects of high prices for consumers, excessive earnings by the *workers* of the monopolistic enterprise (and, one might add, by the local commune), and misallocation of resources. This danger is greatly enhanced by the fact that the country is relatively small and cannot afford too many firms in industries with important economies of scale, while competition from abroad may be ineffective because of the chronic shortage of foreign exchange to pay for imports. Although fully cognizant of the problem, the Yugoslav authorities have not yet taken very determined steps to combat monopoly and other restrictions on competition.

Another serious problem has been presented by strong inflationary pressure, a concomitant of the rapid economic expansion. In order to contain it, the authorities have frequently seen fit to resort (among other measures) to extensive price control. Whatever its advantages for combating inflation and its merits, price control interferes with the operation of the market mechanism, throws demand and supply out of balance, and tends to distort the direction of investment. These effects prompt additional controls, and the decentralized nature of the whole system is thus threatened. However, price control is generally regarded in Yugoslavia as an emergency measure and not, as in the USSR, a permanent feature of the system.

Labor; Earnings; Unemployment

Owing to the system of workers' management, the labor market in Yugoslavia exhibits some distinctive features. Because there are nominally no wages, there is also no formal price for labor; but workers are obviously guided in their choice of jobs by earning prospects in different enterprises. On the demand side, as we have seen, enterprises may tend to take on too few additional workers so as to avoid spreading their net incomes too thin; they may also be reluctant to fire employees even when economically advisable, because this may create awkward problems with the worker-managed firms.

Because workers are paid shares of the net income of their respective enterprises instead of wages and salaries, it is quite common for the same kind of work to be remunerated very unequally in different enterprises, depending of course on the overall financial success of each enterprise. Although this is in accord with the philosophy of workers' management and may have positive incentive effects as well, the inequalities in earnings are not always perceived as equitable. They may thus complicate the operation of the labor market and place a burden on political institutions.

The existence of workers' management in a socialist economy does not rule out conflicts of interest between minorities and majorities within enterprises, or between enterprises and society as a whole. Probably no economic system ever can, even under more affluent and democratic conditions than obtain in Yugoslavia. This raises the problem of trade unions and strikes. At first glance it may seem that there is no place for either in a system of workers' management. But in fact, labor unions do exist in Yugoslavia and are fairly important nationally, though wage bargaining with individual enterprises is not one of their significant functions. Rather, on the plant level they sometimes handle the grievances of individual workers or groups of workers. On the national level, they have at times pressed hard and with some success for an increase in the share of national income allotted to private consumption. There are also occasional strikes that are aimed by workers against their own managements or by whole enterprises against the central authorities (since the latter, despite the high order of economic decentralization, do affect the fortunes of enterprises through control of taxes, prices, and investment funds).

There has been appreciable unemployment in Yugoslavia in the face of chronic inflationary pressure. Much of it is "structural," occasioned by the difficulty of absorbing large numbers of village migrants who often lack the requisite skills.

Planning; Stabilization

As Yugoslavia shifted from a command economy to a market economy the role of planning changed fundamentally. The one-year plans, which carried the detailed directives for the economy in the Soviet manner, lost their purpose and disappeared. The five-year plans remained but with the growing importance of the market changed more and more into "indicative" plans—combinations of particular government programs and forecasts for the rest of the economy to effect expectations. Thus, planning in Yugoslavia is much more similar to that in France than to that in the USSR, although in the relative extent of its publicly owned sector it is much closer to the latter than to France. The crucial consideration, however, is not "socialism" but the degree of decentralization in the economic system, that is, the existence of a market economy. But, as in any market economy, short-range stabilization of employment and, especially, prices is also an important concern in Yugoslav policy.[8]

Despite rapid growth in recent years, Yugoslavia is still a relatively poor, predominantly rural country, with economic (and cultural) contrasts that are as striking as in any other European country. The north exists on a Central European level of industrialization and wealth; the south is still on a "Balkan" level. Ever since the end of World War II, the communist regime's primary goal has been to industrialize and modernize the country, especially its backward regions, speedily and within a socialist framework. Since the early fifties, this framework has been the distinctive one that we have been describing in the present chapter.

Consequently, in drawing up the five-year plans, Yugoslavia's leaders and planners have striven for very high rates of overall and (particularly) industrial growth, rising technological levels, a rapidly increasing standard of living, and —not the least—preferential development of the backward regions. (The regional economic policy, however, has been the subject of intense political controversy that has badly strained the political unity of the country.)

Summary Appraisal

Since the early fifties, Yugoslavia has developed a highly distinctive economic system—a socialist market economy with workers' management and planned economic growth—which, though far from perfect, is clearly workable and possesses some marked advantages over the Soviet-type system. Among the latter we may list: (1) thanks to the market mechanism, better and faster mutual adjustment of demand and supply, greater attention to the needs of the consumer within the limits of resources allotted to consumption, and much wider scope to local economic initiative (whether by the enterprise or by the commune); (2) correspondingly, much less administrative pressure by the authorities on all facets of economic activity, as well as more relaxed (though still authoritarian) political control over the society in general; (3) avoidance of the oppressive and wasteful system of collectivized farming; and (4) a significant measure of industrial democracy within the socialist enterprises. Welfare-state measures have been introduced on a considerable scale.

But there are also many problems, as we have repeatedly noted. Many of them derive at bottom from the backwardness of the country and from the great contrasts among its regions. As a result, and given the governing ideology, it has been found necessary to reserve strong central controls in order to maintain high rates of investment, to limit consumption, and to favor the development of the more backward regions. National purposes and decentralized interests and initiative have often conflicted (as of course they do in other systems,

[8]We may note here that Yugoslavia has employed something similar to the Swedish system of investment reserves; see p. 86.

too). For these reasons, as well as because of the novelty of the whole system, there have been numerous and frequent revisions of institutions and policies, which have added both to the problems of the economy and to the difficulty of appraising its merits and weaknesses.

On the whole, the Yugoslav regime has not been too doctrinaire in economic matters, compared with other communist regimes. Although it has permitted small-scale private enterprise even outside of agriculture, it has also tended to restrict its operation by taxes and other means so that the supply of many goods and services has been impaired to the inconvenience of the consumer.

One of the most striking achievements of the Yugoslav economy has been its extremely fast growth, among the very fastest in the world. Between 1950 and 1970 the gross national product tripled, implying an average annual rate of growth of some 5.6 percent (and about 4.5 percent per capita). Over the same twenty years, industrial production quintupled (8.4 percent per year) and agricultural output increased 2.2-fold (4 percent per year, or 2.8 percent per year per capita).[9] Personal consumption also has increased sharply. Among the factors that explain this impressive record are: the high rate of investment; the direct initiative of the central authorities in carrying out capital formation plus the strong decentralized drive for investment (as already mentioned); and the large flow of labor to the cities from the villages, where it is in surplus. One must also mention foreign aid: $2.25 billion from the United States up to mid-1964, and a smaller but substantial amount from other Western governments and from international institutions.

With all its defects and handicaps—inadequate competition on the domestic market, price control, foreign exchange control, and so forth—the market mechanism in Yugoslavia seems to have functioned reasonably well in bringing forth not only growth but also technological and organizational innovation, satisfaction of consumer demand, and flexible adaptation to export requirements. In these three respects the Yugoslav economy has clearly functioned better than have the command economies of the East European countries (although most of them are considerably more developed than Yugoslavia).

But the pride of the Yugoslav official ideology has been the institution of workers' management. That workers' management "works," in the sense of being a viable and functioning system, is evident from the foregoing. But it is far from clear how close it comes to its own ideal of industrial democracy. In theory, management is ultimately responsible to the workers, and major policy decisions in each socialist enterprise are made by the workers' councils. All this is made possible by the autonomy of the enterprise within a market-economy

[9]These are Western estimates; the gross national product here corresponds to the "Western concept." See: J. T. Crawford, "Yugoslavia's New Economic Strategy: A Progress Report," in U.S. Congress, Joint Economic Committee, *Economic Developments in Countries of Eastern Europe* (Washington: U.S. Government Printing Office, 1970), Table 1, p. 613. The source gives series through 1968; they are here extrapolated to 1970 on the basis of official data. Note that these independent estimates of growth are close to the official ones, allowing for difference in concept of national product.

context. Yet many questions remain. To what extent is the manager actually responsible to the workers' council? In any case, in the larger enterprises, does not the power really lie with some "insiders"? And if power is in fact broadly diffused among the workers, how competent are they in such a relatively backward country to exercise it well? Is economic efficiency best served by workers' control over the director, or might there not be a golden mean in this regard that would balance efficiency against industrial democracy (workers' management)? Might there not also be a similar conflict between growth and industrial democracy?[10]

One difficulty mentioned in the previous pages has already led to an important modification of the Yugoslav system. It will be recalled that the fact that workers are the residual beneficiaries of their firms' successes and failures has brought about considerable inequality in earnings of persons doing essentially similar work but employed in different firms. This has not only contributed to income inequality but has also placed strain on the labor market and on social and political harmony. Consequently, measures were introduced in 1972 to significantly limit, by means of complicated formulas, the distribution of larger earnings to workers. If these measures succeed in their purpose, they will doubtless also in some respects limit the enterprise's autonomy and the decision-making scope of its personnel.

In Yugoslavia there is also the matter of the influence of the League (party) of Communists. The party apparently does not as a rule interfere directly in the affairs of the individual enterprise, but it can and probably does exert influence through key personnel, trade unions, the commune government, and other channels.[11]

The Yugoslav system is significant not only by virtue of its distinctiveness but also—perhaps even more so—because it serves as a living and workable model of an alternative socialist system for the Soviet-type economies of Eastern Europe. And in fact, the abortive major reform of the Czechoslovak economy for a while took a Yugoslav-style course, with regard to both the market and workers' councils. Both fell victim to the return of conservative elements to power following the Soviet invasion of the country in 1968. The Hungarian major reform took a different course: marketization but no workers' management. To this experience we now turn.

---

[10]Some of these questions have their counterparts in regard to stockholders' control in capitalist corporations. By way of mental exercise, the reader may wish to compare and contrast the relations between the Yugoslav enterprise and their workers and capitalist corporations and their stockholders, in theory and practice.

[11]There is now a fairly large literature on the Yugoslav economic system in the English language. Some of the more important works are listed in the "Selected Readings" at the end of this book. In addition, the reader may wish to consult the following two articles: Egon Neuberger and Estelle James, "The Yugoslav Self-Managed Enterprise: A Systemic Approach," and Svetozar Pejovich, "The Banking System and Investment Behavior of the Yugoslav Firm," both in Morris Bornstein, *Plan and Market: Economic Reform in Eastern Europe* (New Haven: Yale University Press, 1973).

HUNGARY

The Hungarian economic reform is of outstanding interest to students of economic systems. A major reform in our terms, it went into effect on January 1, 1968, and virtually overnight transformed a Soviet-type command economy into a socialist market economy. As we have already noted, this was not the first case of "marketization" of a Soviet-type economy, but it is nonetheless a unique case in some important respects. Although Yugoslavia marketized its economy nearly two decades earlier, it did so after only a few years of experience with the Soviet system, and carried the process through much more gradually. Moreover, as we saw in the preceding section, the institution of workers' management is an integral feature of the Yugoslav socialist market economy; it is not so in Hungary. Czechoslovakia, too, attempted a major reform at about the same time as Hungary, but had to abandon it for political reasons, as already mentioned.

The degree of success of the Hungarian reform is in some dispute at this early point, less than six years from its onset. Nonetheless, it stands as an instructive example both of the creation of a socialist market economy in Eastern Europe, and of the many political constraints that attend such a transformation and inevitably impinge on its success.

Intentionally given the modest name of the New Economic Mechanism (NEM) in order to dispel any implications of simultaneous political change, the Hungarian reform was carefully and ably prepared by a group of economists and other specialists with the backing of top party leaders. It was synchronized with a wholesale price reform that made prices more flexible and more responsive to demand, as would be required for the operation of the newly recreated market mechanism.

Objectives and Constraints of the NEM

The objectives of the Hungarian reforms were essentially the same as everywhere in Eastern Europe, as listed in Chapter 7; namely, greater efficiency of resource use in general, stimulation of technological advance and innovation, better satisfaction of consumer needs in both variety and quality of goods, and greater effectiveness in exporting in order to earn foreign exchange, especially hard (Western) currency.

The last reason is especially important. Hungary is a small country and is rather poor in natural resources. The rapid expansion of industry and other sectors since World War II has sharply increased her requirements for imported fuel, raw materials, semimanufactured goods, and many types of equipment. In addition, consumer demand for imported commodities, or goods produced

161

from foreign materials, has been also rising. Altogether, before the reform, exports or imports amounted to some 20 to 30 percent of GNP,[12] one of the highest ratios in Eastern Europe, and fairly high even by world standards. About two-thirds of this trade was—and continues to be—with the other countries of Eastern Europe, especially with the USSR, whence most of Hungary's imported raw and basic commodities come. But it was in the trade with the Western countries that Hungary, like her Eastern neighbors, had been experiencing the most acute shortage of foreign exchange. This called for more exports to the West, which, however, in the opinion of the reformers were handicapped (under the old system) by the insufficient incentive to produce for and sell in Western markets, by technological backwardness, and by the clumsiness of the Soviet-style monopoly of foreign trade.

So much for the objectives of the NEM. To achieve them by reforming the whole economy would not have been easy in any case even in the absence of severe political constraints. The marketization of a Soviet-type economy sooner or later involves a wide-ranging and in some respects profound alteration of the fabric of the whole society. It is likely to change the role of the ruling party in the society to the extent that formerly this role substitutes for certain functions of the absent market mechanism in the Soviet-style economy,[13] and is therefore unwelcome to some elements within the Communist Party. It elevates even further the importance of material incentives; hence, it may conflict not only with some aspects of the socialist ideology but also with the interests of those who expect to be in lesser positions to take advantage of the new incentives. The major reform greatly widens the autonomy of enterprises; thus, it calls for managerial talents different from those that had been successful hitherto. Not all managers may welcome it, therefore. It is likely to redistribute income, status, and power in many other respects as well. Fundamentally, the reform cannot be successful unless it reallocates resources, which is the economist's euphemism for a process that has its very unpleasant features: the closing down of factories, unemployment and loss of earning power for many people, hardship for some localities, and so forth. And there is also considerable danger of inflation as consumer demand is allowed greater freedom of expression in both consumer and producer goods markets.

These negative prospects also defined the political constraints under which the government proceeded to carry out the reform. It was careful not to fire any significant number of managers who were clearly unsuited for the new conditions, lest this powerful group be unduly alienated. Unemployment would affect and alienate much larger numbers; fear of it occasioned a series of policies that often restrained the full realization of the NEM (as we shall see). Equally important, any significant rise in consumer prices was ruled out, owing to the memory among the people of two hyperinflations within the past fifty years.

162

[12]The exact figure depends on methods of estimation, price adjustment, and other technicalities.
[13]See above, pp. 102–04.

Lastly, the reform had to bring about significant economic improvement in the short term in order to be "sold" to the public over the longer run. These have indeed been very serious constraints on the freedom of action of the regime in bringing the NEM into being.

Provisions of the NEM

Briefly, the reform consisted of the following measures.[14] As already mentioned, prices were recalculated and *in part* set free to move. At retail, prices were freed entirely for commodities and services accounting for about one-quarter of consumer outlay; allowed to move between set upper and lower bounds for another quarter; and fixed or subjected to ceiling levels for the remaining half. At wholesale, for domestically produced basic materials, prices accounting for only about 30 percent of sales were set free; but for manufactured goods, prices accounting for nearly 90 percent of sales were set free. At the same time, and most significantly, materials allocation for producer goods was eliminated, except for a handful of commodities, which suggests that the new prices were not too far from equilibrium levels.[15]

A most important price to be set was the exchange rate—or to be exact, two separate sets of exchange rates, against Eastern and Western currencies. The values of foreign currencies in terms of Hungarian money, the forint, were sharply raised to bring them closer to equilibrium levels.[16] But equilibrium levels were not reached, necessitating a complicated system of subsidies to export industries and various methods to limit the demand for foreign currency by means other than its price.

Enterprises are rather free to decide on the mix of inputs thanks to the virtual disappearance of materials allocation. In one respect there is tight control, however; namely, in respect to wages, and for anti-inflationary reasons. Because of high aggregate demand (on which more below) and generally low resistance of Hungarian firms to wage demands—labor unions, incidentally, have somewhat gained in autonomy since the onset of the NEM—there has been concern from the start with the prospect of a wage-push inflation. The policy adopted has been one of limiting the percentage by which a firm's average wage may rise in a given year. Like all microeconomic solutions to macroeconomic problems, it is not very satisfactory in that it weakens the firm's incentive for efficient operation and in this way, in the long run, tends to aggravate the

[14]An authoritative description of the reform by a group of leading Hungarian economists is Istvan Friss, ed., *Reform of the Economic Mechanism in Hungary* (Budapest, 1969). Two very good analytical accounts are: Bela Balassa, "The Economic Reform in Hungary," *Economica* (February 1970) pp. 1–22; and Richard Portes, "Economic Reforms in Hungary," *American Economic Review*, 60, no. 2 (May 1970), pp. 307–13.

[15]In fact, as will be mentioned presently, the sellers' market persisted and often rationing was taken over by the producers.

[16]In line with the greater shortage of hard currency, value of the U.S. dollar was raised much more (in forint) than that of the transferable ruble, the unit of payment among East European countries.

very macroeconomic problem that it aims to solve. In the specific Hungarian instance, it is also a significant restriction on the firm's freedom of action, and so contravenes the spirit of the NEM.

A key measure was to free enterprises almost completely of compulsory production targets (plans). Instead they are left to make profit, it being presumed that in doing so they will be serving the interests of the country. (This presumption of the coincidence of particular (firm) and social interest is one of the most fundamental philosophical departures of the NEM, or any major reform, from the traditional Soviet-type system. Note, however, that the Hungarian socialist market economy is hardly a *laissez-faire* economy.) To induce management to pursue profit, it is allowed to keep a predetermined substantial percentage for its own use. Part of this retained profit, also predetermined, can be applied to investment in the firm. The other part is distributed to the work force as bonuses, by far the highest bonuses going to the decision-makers themselves, the management.

One consequence of this arrangement is that about one-half of all investment is undertaken on enterprise decision and initiative, in contrast to the Soviet-type economies where the fraction is tiny. This lends considerable flexibility to the Hungarian economy and may in the long run be one of the most significant effects of the NEM.

In the absence of directive targets, one-year plans have lost most of their operational importance. The five-year plans, however, have greatly gained in relative importance, in that it is they that represent the guidelines for the economy's development and structural change. In other words, Hungarian plans have become more like the Yugoslav and even the French ones—indicative rather than imperative. From this it should not be inferred that the government and the planners do not keep rather close control of the economy. The methods, however, tend to be more macroeconomic and more fiscal and financial than in the traditional command economy. Banks have increased considerably in importance as institutions that regulate the economy, as money has become much more "active."

Simultaneously with the above-described measures, somewhat greater scope was given to private enterprise (though it is still limited to very small-scale activities), and to the agricultural cooperatives (collectives). These are significant measures.

Some Problems of the NEM

We have already noted the eagerness of the Hungarian leaders to avoid any significant unemployment under the NEM, and at the same time to show good economic results in the short run. These concerns have dictated a policy of maintaining a high level of aggregate demand, which has indeed been successful in maintaining full employment and in ensuring profitability to all but a very few firms. But although these effects have been desirable in themselves,

they have also led to some serious difficulties. The high level of aggregate demand has given a new lease on life to the sellers' market that was inherited from
the preceding era, with the attendant problems of shortages (often handled by
informal rationing by the producers), weakened incentives to produce and to
innovate, and all the other well-known manifestations. Because of the sellers'
market, and the inflationary pressure that underlies it, it has been difficult to
proceed much further with the liberalization of prices and foreign trade. The
closely related high demand for labor has occasioned the microeconomic wage
control, some of whose consequences we have already noted. In turn, the price
and wage controls have seriously hampered the operation of the market and
slowed down the desirable restructuring of the economy.[17]

Another legacy of the past is industrial organization. At the time of the
introduction of the reform, Hungarian industry was highly concentrated, each
branch of production being monopolized by one or, at most, very few firms. This
structure was not changed, although competition is essential for proper functioning of a market economy.[18] It was hoped that competition would come from
abroad, but the shortage of foreign exchange has so far prevented any significant
effect from this side. Hence, the Hungarian economy is highly uncompetitive, for
all this implies. A consequence is additional reason or excuse for price regulation.

A serious problem is the prevalence and growth of subsidies, which place a
heavy burden on the budget and keep the market from allocating resources in a
more efficient way. The subsidies are primarily in two areas of the economy:
very large ones on some consumer goods (meat, housing, passenger transport),
prompted by the political imperative to keep retail prices and rates from rising,
and also the large subsidies to export industries that we have already noted.

Yet another major issue is that of income inequality. It had been widely
felt by the reformers that material incentives were insufficient and, hence, rewards too equal. The NEM has had some antiegalitarian effects such as boost-
ing managerial earnings and incomes from private activity. Public dissatisfaction
followed and was openly voiced (though obviously not on the part of those who
had gained), which forced the government to lower the maximum limits for
managerial bonuses and, in November 1972, to adopt the policy of restricting
the prices charged and the profits earned by the more profitable enterprises.
Whatever the social and political benefits of these measures, there is no doubt
that they tend to constrict further the operation of the market mechanism. They
may also significantly reduce managerial incentives for efficient operation.

[17]Two very good recent Western discussions along this line are David Granick, "The Hungarian
Economic Reform," *World Politics*, 25, no. 3 (April 1973) pp. 414–29; and Richard Portes, "Hungary:
The Experience of Market Socialism" in Zammit, *The Chilean Road to Socialism* (The Institute of Development Studies, University of Essex, England, 1973), pp. 367–89. Granick on the whole takes a
more pessimistic view of the successes and prospects of the NEM than does Portes. See also the very
useful Hungarian collection, a sequel to the Friss volume cited in note 14: Otto Gado, ed., *Reform of
the Economic Mechanism in Hungary: Development 1968–1971* (Budapest: 1972).

[18]Thus, at the end of 1970, there were only 812 enterprises in all Hungarian industry, 291
of which employed 74 percent of the industrial labor force.

These are all important problems. Yet one more ought to be mentioned and even singled out: the problem of the accountability of the firm's management in a system of market socialism. In fact, it exists under capitalism as well, insofar as ownership and control are separated (Chapters 4 and 5), and moreover, insofar as society demands an additional measure of responsibility from management (see Chapter 9). Under socialism the problem takes a particular form because accountability of management to any capitalist owner(s) is ruled out from the start. And yet, to the extent that the firm has significant autonomy of decision, as it must by definition in a socialist *market* economy, the management cannot be left responsible only to itself.

The Yugoslavs have attacked this problem ingeniously by means of the institution of workers' management. In theory, management is responsible to the workers[19] (though in some regards to the broader society as well), while in turn the workers' desire for income provides the economic drive for management. At the same time, the alienation of workers from their place of employment is presumably minimized, for even if the workers do not nominally own the firms, they run them. So much for theory. Reality, as we saw in the preceding section of this chapter, corresponds to the theory to some degree. We have also noted that management's responsibility to the rank and file may impair efficiency (if there is a reluctance both to hire and to fire labor), and may cause insufficient retention of the firm's net income for investment in the firm because the rank and file may prefer to take it as their earnings now. Finally, and quite importantly, the system of workers' management often results in very unequal earnings by workers in different enterprises, because the firms' net incomes (profits) are at the mercy of the market.

These difficulties associated with workers' management may have been sufficient for this solution to accountability to be rejected by the authors of the Hungarian reform.[20] Instead, they subordinated enterprises to ministries. Managers are thus responsible upward, to the state, and not downward, to the workers. This has its own problems, though. One is that the ministries may not be very sympathetic to the whole reform, to the market, to firm autonomy, and to reducing the monopolistic structure of industry.

Another potential difficulty is that labor may not feel that sense of participation in economic decision-making which social ideology would seem to prompt. Indeed, while the command economy had already polarized manage-

---

[19]It will be recalled that "workers" here stands for the whole work force of the firm.

[20]There may very well have been another major reason. As Yugoslav experience has shown, workers' management is a source of independent power in a society that undermines the monopoly of political power held by the party in a communist country. Little wonder, therefore, that the Soviet leaders are implacably opposed to workers' management in their own country and in other countries within their sphere of influence, such as Hungary.

ment and labor, it had brought them into conflict directly because management had almost nothing to give that labor might want from it. Nearly all power to dispense benefits rested with the central authorities. But with the advent of market socialism of the Hungarian variety, the firm is autonomous enough to be the target of labor's demands. Thus, industrial conflict becomes a real possibility, and more than just a possibility if the existing trade unions (still under close party control) continue to assert themselves or if other bargaining bodies are formed by the workers themselves.

Summing Up

In sum, the Hungarian reform of 1968 has brought into being a distinctive economic system, one of market socialism, but without the workers' management feature that characterizes the similar Yugoslav system. It appears to be a workable system (so long as the USSR tolerates it), despite the many problems that we have mentioned. But its accomplishments in the first few years in terms of growth, efficiency, consumption levels, and export efficacy, are not yet very conspicuous.

CONCLUDING REMARKS

The Yugoslav and Hungarian cases are the only contemporary instances of marketized Soviet-style economies, but they are not necessarily the only cases of what might possibly be characterized as market socialism in the contemporary world. In many noncommunist underdeveloped countries the state is a dominant producer, at least in the modern sector. In some West European countries, as we have seen, such as Italy and Austria, state-owned firms play large roles in industry and finance, and usually dominant roles in transportation and communication. Then there is the unique case of Israel, with a sizeable state-owned sector and a similarly large production sector owned by the trade-union federation (the Histadrut), not to mention the well-known communally organized farms, the *kibbutzim*.[21]

But analysis of even just the two cases presented in this chapter does bring out some significant observations regarding the problems of market socialism. One of its most fundamental problems is that of the accountability of the firm's management. In the absence of private owners, to whom will the managers answer? They can answer to the government, as in Hungary; but then it may be difficult to ensure the high autonomy of the firm that efficiency and initiative in

[21]For lack of space we cannot take up the important Israeli case. The interested reader is referred, *inter alia*, to the following two brief accounts: Haim Barkai, "The Kibbutz as Social Institution," *Dissent*, Spring 1972, pp. 354–70; and J. Y. Tabb and A. Goldfarb, "Workers' Participation in Management in Israel," *Internation Institute for Labor Studies, Bulletin No. 7* (June 1970), pp. 153–99.

a market economy demand. And this may not further the ideals of industrial democracy and nonalienation of the workers from the work process. Also, as in Hungary, a simultaneous policy of ensuring continuous very high employment and holding earnings differentials in check, although most attractive ends in themselves, may well impair the market economy's efficiency if not its viability.

On the other hand, managers may be made accountable to the workers (employees) in the given firms, as in Yugoslavia. This facilitates the ensurance of a very high degree of autonomy for the firm, but may create other significant problems, as we have seen in this chapter. One of them is the following: to make the workers the ultimate decision-makers in the firm it is necessary to motivate them by allowing them to share significantly in the firm's net income. They become residual beneficiaries, and the firm becomes a kind of producers' cooperative. As with such cooperatives generally (the collective farm of the Soviet and East European type), there is likely to be a very considerable inequality in earnings per worker between firms, an inequality that indeed has a tendency to grow. This, in turn, creates serious problems in the labor market, affects efficiency, and—last but not least—contributes to social and political tensions. We have noted the Yugoslav's recent attempts to deal with this problem, but such attempts must perforce be at the expense of both the firm's autonomy and the interests of the better-off workers. We have noted other problems of Yugoslav market socialism as well.

To mention these dilemmas of both the Hungarian and the Yugoslav economies is not to fault market socialism as a system. All economic systems have their major problems; there are no ideal systems in reality.

Systems and People

CHAPTER NINE

THE INDIVIDUAL AND SOCIETY

Economic systems are for people. The issues of market against command, centralization or decentralization, planning or no planning and what kind of planning, controls and what kinds of controls —all these issues directly or indirectly bear on the fundamental question of the relationship of the individual or the group, on one hand, and the larger group, the society, and the state of which they form a part, on the other hand.

The individual's freedom and dignity within the economic order is in large measure a function of the alternatives open to him for his own deciding. Even if his decision is virtually predetermined by economic circumstances, as is a poor man's spending much of his income on basic food, the mere fact that he has at least some options contributes to the upholding of his individuality. (Anyone who has eaten Army rations for many months would most probably agree!) At least as important is the freedom of choice of job, and perhaps even more, the freedom to quit a job. Little wonder then that all the three main types of economic systems we have examined—advanced capitalist, Soviet-type, market socialist—share the institution of freedom of household choice, although they do differ fundamentally regarding the individual's place in society. The impairment of this freedom of choice as regards both the job (and place of residence) and consumption was among the more resented features of Stalinism, and the peasants' virtual attachment to collective farms is still greatly resented.

Freedom to operate one's own business or farm falls in the same

169

category; and even if most people in an advanced economy would not and could not do so, the substantial existence of such opportunities in itself adds to the quality of the economic and social order. In any case, the tendency toward private enterprise is not easily stamped out even by protracted indoctrination and outright prohibition, as the experience of the Soviet Union demonstrates, and measures to enforce such prohibition only add to the tensions between the individual and the state. Some of the East European countries are allowing a limited scope for private activity, thereby affording both a safety valve for such tension and a source of needed goods and services for the consumer.[1]

But most individuals in the advanced economies are not their own bosses; instead, they are employed, usually by large private or public organizations. They must confront other large and powerful organizations in addition to their employers: labor unions, professional associations, and especially the state at its several levels and in its many manifestations. In this environment the individual's or minority's protection at bottom rests probably on nothing more tangible than the acceptance of the democratic spirit and rules of the game by all concerned. But proper institutions help to hold up this slender reed. In one well-informed opinion the following are the minimal requirements of a "democratic industrial society":

—there should be as many power centers as possible, consistent with the effective functioning of society;
—these power centers should be roughly balanced in strength and should be independent of one another;
—the participants in each power center (union members, stockholders) should be able to exert at least a minimum of control over the leadership;
—each power center should have an adequate judicial system (grievance machinery) to protect the rights of the participants;
—necessary government controls in the economy should be concentrated on procedures rather than on substantive issues; for example, instead of regulating prices or wages the government should seek to regulate mergers or the process of collective bargaining.[2]
—basic protection against risks of economic instability (unemployment) or personal misfortune (sickness) through private insurance or social security enlarges the individual's range of effective choice and enables him to assert his individuality.

The other side of the coin in the relationship between the individual and society is the individual's motivation to perform and to comply, so that the social fabric may cohere and the social order may function. In Chapter 2 we discussed

[1]We have already noted in Chapter 7 that most of the agriculture in Yugoslavia and Poland is under private operation.

[2]Clark Kerr, "An Effective and Democratic Organization of the Economy," in The American Assembly, The President's Commission on National Goals, *Goals for Americans* (Englewood Cliffs, N.J.: Prentice-Hall, Inc., paperback, 1960), pp. 149–62. (The whole volume is a convenient collection of the objectives of what might be called the "mainstream" of informed American opinion of its time.)

at some length the problem of motivation and its relation to incentives and social control over the individual; in later chapters (especially 6 through 8) we looked at certain attempts to change human motivation, to create a New Man. This is not the place to go over this ground again. Suffice it to recall that the attempts—even in Cuba and China—to do away with material incentive have not been entirely successful, and that too often the alternative has turned out to be, in good part, compulsion and coercion.

THE ECONOMIC UNIT AND SOCIETY

Division of labor in the economy necessarily raises the question of harmony between the behavior of the economic unit, on one hand, and the objectives of the larger organization or the whole society, on the other. (For the moment, we take the nature of the objectives of the larger organization or of the society and the political process that determines them as given.) The problem is obviously of crucial importance in a market economy, capitalist or socialist, where the individual economic unit is accorded considerable autonomy of deciding and acting. But in fact, as we have already glimpsed, it is perhaps of even greater importance in the Soviet-type command economy, owing to the greater demands placed by organized society on the economic unit while denying a socially constructive role to the primacy of the profit motive.

Laissez faire is dead. We no longer assume, if we ever did, that the unhampered activity of every private economic unit brings about the best of all possible worlds. The market mechanism is not faultless and the modern state—itself far from infallible—intervenes in a myriad of ways (as we saw in Chapters 4 and 5): to take care of externalities, to regulate monopoly, to forbid outright many acts that are deemed to clash with the public interest, to stimulate other activities, to redistribute income and wealth after the market has done its distributing, and at times even to ration scarce goods in accordance with social priorities, and to engage in outright production. But, everything considered, there is still a basic presumption in the market economy of lack of conflict between the particular lawful act of an economic unit and the public interest.[3]

For this presumption to be valid, at least five conditions must be met. First, the unit's objective(s) must be in harmony with society's objective(s). In a market economy, the most common objective of the individual firm is profit (though, as we have seen, it would be wrong to think of at least the larger firms as being straight profit maximizers). Since profit is the difference between value produced and value used up, it is thus the first approximation to net value created. And

[3]For a clear and nontechnical statement of the basically technical problems of control under decentralization in large organizations (of which the market economy is a conspicuous instance) see Kenneth J. Arrow, "Control in Large Organizations," *Management Science*, 10, no. 3 (April 1964), pp. 397–408.

since increasing net value created comes very close to increasing the national income, which is what all societies desire, profit-making is therefore (in principle) usually assumed to be a socially legitimate objective for the individual economic unit in a market economy.[4]

This is also why nearly all the proposals for reform of the Soviet-type system aim to supplant value of output by profit as the socialist firm's "success indicator." As the Soviet economy has learned from bitter experience, to downgrade profit is to upgrade waste. For this reason the Soviet Union itself has lately accorded a slightly greater role to profit in economic decision-making, while those communist countries that have carried economic reforms considerably further—and certainly the "marketizers," Yugoslavia and Hungary—have stressed profit-making much more. Interestingly, the slogan of those reformers in the USSR who would upgrade the resource-allocative role of profitability in the Soviet economy is: "What is advantageous for society must be made advantageous also for the enterprise!"

Yet the converse does not necessarily hold; what is profitable or otherwise advantageous for the economic unit need not be advantageous for society, either under capitalism or under socialism, and either in a market economy or in a command economy. This depends, among other things, on the quality of the information. Do the prices that enter into decisions approximate the relative scarcities of the goods from a social standpoint?—always remembering that the scarcities are relative to the ends to which society wishes to put its resources. This is not to argue for a perfectly efficient allocation of resources in the textbook sense, an ideal state of things that is neither attainable in reality, nor necessarily more desirable than some of the other desiderata, such as distributive equity or growth (see Chapter 1). But "bad" prices can cause serious problems, among which is the likelihood that they will lead to administrative rationing of resources, which in turn is often costly in both economic and political terms. The quality of the information is our second condition for harmonizing the behavior of the unit with the goals of society.

The third condition is that of the unit's sufficient overview. It must be able to perceive (whether in the form of price signals or otherwise) the effects of its actions or inaction *and* it must be able to relate these effects to its own "success indicator," say, profit. This is, of course, the problem of externalities, already mentioned by us in Chapter 4 and to which we will return in a moment.

Fourth, there is the dual problem of the decision-maker's accountability and of the mainspring of his action. In regard to accountability, the basic dilemma is that if the economic unit (firm) is to be enterprising and efficient it must enjoy a high degree of autonomy, in which case, if it is large and important enough, it develops its own power and momentum and is no longer easily amenable to adequate control by *any* authority. We have encountered this problem

[4]The reader is reminded of the distinction between profit-*making* by enterprises and profit-*taking* by owners.

in the form of separation between ownership and management in the large corporate capitalist firm, in the nationalized firm, in the worker-managed Yugoslav firm, or in the hierarchically supervised market-socialist firm in Hungary. On the other hand if the control is very stringent, as in the Soviet-type command economy, the result is patently detrimental to efficiency and initiative on the firm level. There are probably better and worse solutions to this dilemma under specific circumstances, but it is difficult to expect that it permits of highly satisfactory solutions in the real world.

Closely connected with the decision-maker's accountability is his motivation and incentive for action. Cultural norms,[5] professional standards, the nature of the system, and the specific structure of the available rewards all play a role here, but the fact is that we really do not know too much about the forces that motivate managers and other decision-makers in the various economic systems. If it is the expectation of gain, there is the difficult problem of relating the gain to the unit's—and society's—benefit, and of making sure that both the short-run and the long-run benefits enter the picture in proper combination. If it is not primarily material gain, then the safeguarding of society's interest may be even more difficult, because the translation of signals into economic action may be even more uncertain. Again, in principle the problem cuts across all modern economic systems, as we have had occasion to note.

Fifth, and also related to the issue of accountability, is the containment of economic power within its proper bounds. In a competitive system, and not only under the Utopia of perfect competition of the textbook, this function is exercised by competition to a considerable extent. Yet adequate competition is neither possible nor desirable everywhere; hence, the problem is always with us to greater or lesser degree. It links up closely with microeconomics, for the intensity of aggregate demand in large measure determines how keen will be the competition between sellers or between buyers. (Our discussion of the Hungarian sellers' market is a case in point.) Where competition among producers or sellers is explicitly and emphatically rejected, as in the state sector of the Soviet-type economy, the problem of power, and of its control by the administrative hierarchy, is especially acute.

Externalities; Social Responsibility

We have already seen that the market produces the undesirable economic phenomena that economists call externalities, and that social action is necessary to counteract them.[6] But it seems that command economies—specifically, the Soviet-type economy—are prone to produce similar effects, although one might have thought that the absence of major private property and the centralization

---

[5]Cultural conditioning of managers, as well the industriousness of the labor forces, are among the most important assets of the more highly industrialized societies. One effect is to reduce the productivity and efficiency implications of the ownership factor—whether private or public.

[6]See above, pp. 34–35, 66–67.

of decisions in the Soviet-type economy would have forestalled their appearance. The explanation is essentially twofold. First, the commitment to rapid, forced industrialization has focused attention and resources on the sheer quantitative expansion of production, and has therefore diverted attention and resources from the protection of the environment and similar socially desirable activities. In a sense, the *whole system* has failed to "internalize" the costs of environmental disruption, so that the high degree of centralization of economic decisions has been immaterial (and perhaps harmful). On the intermediate and local levels —the ministry, the trust, the firm—the neglect of externalities was ensured by the structure of "success indicators" and the great stringency of resources. Second, some of the specific institutions of the Soviet-type economy have tended to aggravate the problem. For instance, the absence of private property in natural resources has promoted their wasteful use because no one in particular suffered the loss, and the failure to price natural resources at all[7] made them appear expendable. (These problems are being recognized increasingly now by Soviet economists.)

Some of the just-mentioned institutional defects that aggravate the incidence of external diseconomies can of course be corrected or alleviated. But the fact remains that externalities are probably unavoidable under any economic or social system if the matter is left to the economic decision-makers alone. It is inconceivable that the economic process could be so centralized as to permit the "internalization" of all social costs—and if it were, it would probably be very inefficient on other scores. The more promising possibilities rather lie in other directions. One of them surely is the diminution of a sense of urgency, whether for private gain (as under a regime of private property) or national economic growth (as in the communist lands and in many another underdeveloped country today); in other words, a change in social values and even possibly ideology. The second and closely related direction of change must be toward effective social control of business—socialist, nationalized, as well as private business. It would take us too far afield to discuss the various instruments of such social control of business in regard to externalities, instruments such as taxes, fees, subsidies, and outright prohibitions and compulsions. Suffice it to mention here that a system such as the Soviet, in which (as we have seen) firms are not very sensitive to cost, is in effect deprived of a set of efficient devices for the social control of externalities.[8] And behind this approach is of course the whole political process that will lead to social control in the area of externalities; here, too, the Western democracies need not be at a disadvantage compared to the dictatorial governments in the communist world.

An even broader question, of which the social handling of environmental disruption is a part, is that of the social responsibility of the businessman, or,

[7]See above, Chapter 6, p. 101.

[8]Cf. Larry E. Ruff, "The Economic Common Sense of Pollution," *The Public Interest*, 19 (Spring 1970), pp. 69–85.

more generally, the economic decision-maker, whether in a private or public organization. This has become a widely debated issue in the West, and particularly in the United States, in recent years. The proponents of greater social responsibility of business (or of the corporation, as the authors usually put it) hold that large-scale business is too important a social force to remain aloof from the social problems of the time and place. It has the responsibility to be aware of and sensitive to the needs of the community and society, and to go a long way (within the limits of each firm's resources, of course) to help solve these problems. Business should exercise its initiative and employ its skills in this regard. Naturally, such activity will be costly, but the costs ought to be perceived as investment in better relations with the social environment, goodwill, and often higher profits in the future.

The nub of the controversy is whether the socially beneficial activity of business will or will not significantly reduce profits in the long run. Because the primary function of business is to serve the economy by pursuing profitable activities,[9] any outlay of a social character that will eventually be repaid in greater profits is clearly not very controversial. Here, the question is one of correct information and judgment, rather than principle. But what if the social outlay is not likely to be repaid even in the long run? The proponents of greater corporate social responsibility will often say that up to a point business should still bear the cost as part of its wider social role, and may also point to the likelihood that society may force business to do what it refuses to do voluntarily in any case.

Opponents of greater corporate social responsibility argue along the following lines: that it is the social function of business to do its own business and not to solve a wide range of social ills; that by trying to do the latter it will only carry out its own function less well, and society will be the loser to this extent; that the more socially conscious businessmen will tend to lose out in economic competition with the more callous ones, which is hardly just; that the business firm need not have the proper information as to what social activities are socially desirable and to what extent; that the firm only places itself at the mercy of various pressure groups in the community and perhaps even exposes itself to blackmail through boycotts of its products, and so forth; and, last but not least, that leaving the solving of many of our ills to business is simply a way for organized society to shirk its own responsibilities—that is, the job should be done by government.[10]

---

[9] As stressed earlier in this chapter.

[10] The literature on "corporate social responsibility" is large. A convenient survey can be found in Clarence C. Walton, *Corporate Social Responsibilities* (Belmont, Ca.: Wadsworth Publishing Co., 1967, paperback). A sympathetically favorable view is taken by Dow Votaw and S. Prakash Sethi in their *The Corporate Dilemma: Traditional Values versus Contemporary Problems* (Englewood Cliffs, N.J.: Prentice-Hall, Inc., 1973, paperback). A classic statement in opposition to the assumption of social responsibility by business is in Milton Friedman, *Capitalism and Freedom*, (Chicago, Ill.: University of Chicago Press, 1962) pp. 133 ff.

The issue of the social responsibility of the economic decision-maker arises in all economic systems. It is no less poignant in a socialist economy, and is in some ways more acute in the command economy. The last is so because of the nature of the success indicators for the firm or higher economic unit, which, as we have seen, does not sufficiently take into account society's needs. Thus, the Soviet manager who produces goods of inferior quality or inadequate variety, or hoards materials, is often following the prescribed success indicators but is hardly acting in a socially responsible manner. Indeed, he is frequently reminded of this. Thus, the nature of the problem of social responsibility is relative to the systemic features of the economy (and, naturally, also to the values held by the community). In a communist country, the institution that has the primary function of imbuing decision-makers with a sense of responsibility and monitoring their actions in this regard is the Communist party. It is one of the party's most important functions, which it clearly derives from the nature of the economic system, another important instance of political and economic institutions reinforcing one another.

CONVERGENCE?

The three major economic systems we have examined in this book arose in response to the challenges of industrialization and industrialism. Though they may have closer-range goals, such as military capability and national power, they all strive for material abundance based on modern technology. Is it likely that they will grow increasingly similar? Will some sort of relatively uniform "industrial society" emerge eventually? The question of "convergence" of the different economic (and political) systems has been receiving increasing attention in recent years.

Let us mention, first, that the very idea of convergence is abhorrent to those on the extremes of the ideological spectrum. Or, to be more exact, they speak in terms of the *sub*mergence of the *other* system, not a convergence of two or more systems.[11] Thus, the official Soviet position asserts that talk of "convergence" and of a uniform "industrial society" is just another anticommunist propaganda trick to divert attention from the inevitable, ultimate victory of

---

[11]The distinction between "submergence" and "convergence" in this context has been introduced by Zbigniew Brzezinski and Samuel P. Huntington, *Political Power: USA/USSR* (New York: The Viking Press, 1964); pp. 419ff, which is a thorough review of the convergence theory. The evolution of each *political* system in its own way rather than convergence, despite certain growing economic similarities, is the thesis of Brzezinski and Huntington. Jan Tinbergen's "Do Communist and Free Economies Show a Converging Pattern?" *Soviet Studies*, 12, no. 4 (April 1961), pp. 333–41, leans more on the side of convergence; he is answered by Knud Erik Svendsen, "Are the Two Systems Converging?" *Ost-Okonomi*, no. 3 (December 1962), pp. 195–209. See also Peter Wiles, "Will Capitalism and Communism Spontaneously Converge?" or, *Encounter* (June 1963), pp. 84–90.

communism throughout the world. And there are some in the capitalist world who aver that socialism and communism are inherently so evil and unworkable that it is only a matter of time before the communist regimes collapse and their countries revert to capitalism. In other words, communism will "bury itself," perhaps with a little assist from the outside. So much for "submergence."

Now, of course, there is a good deal to the convergence theory. Industrialism and its concomitants—such as urbanization, widespread education and technical competence, higher consumption levels—impose their stamp on outlooks, values, behavior patterns, and even forms of economic organization. Many of the problems of industrialized societies are similar, as we saw in the preceding section of this chapter, and there may be some similarity in the responses. As the economy grows more complex, technology more sophisticated, and the consumer's needs more demanding—and as at the same time the need for brute mobilization of resources becomes less pressing—the market mechanism becomes ever more attractive in relation to command. Ideological fervor flags with the passage of time; life grows more comfortable. Is it thus not possible that other Soviet-type economies will with time follow the examples of Yugoslavia and Hungary (and the aborted one of Czechoslovakia) and will "marketize" themselves? And that the Chinese and Cuban economies will move even closer to the Soviet model from their respective positions on the "left"?

But if command may give way to the market mechanism with time, is it not also true that in the capitalist world the market mechanism is increasingly being "tamed" in the social interest by the government by means of national economic planning of one kind or another, not to mention the myriad of controls of all kinds? And are not the capitalist countries moving more and more in the direction of the welfare state, to some extent following the example of the Soviet Union? Is not all this indication of ultimate convergence?

Whether it is or not depends on what one means by the term. The organization of industry, the behavior of management, the provision of social security, rising standards of living—these are very important factors, and they certainly have their impact on cultural, social, and political dimensions of the country, but need they be decisive in all important respects? One can point to Japan, which has succeeded superbly at the Western game of industrialization, but which has not traded all its distinctive institutions for Western-style ones. Generally speaking, in all systems existing institutions develop extremely strong staying power, especially if they are buttressed by vested interests, as they often are. And the more concentrated the power, as in the communist countries, the stronger the resistance to change. We have already seen (Chapters 7 and 8) how difficult it is to reform a command economy, and how short-lived partial reforms can be. We have also witnessed some levelling off of the appeal of national economic planning in the Western market economies, not to mention the widespread disappointment with the effects of postwar nationalization in Western Europe. In short, only the passage of a good deal of time will tell how much convergence there will be, economically and politically, between the various economic systems.

LOOKING AHEAD—
RICH AND POOR

While the Soviet-style East hopes for less rigid economic control by central authorities, and while the West is searching for more effective forms of social control and direction of the economy, both sides are beginning to look forward seriously to the problems of higher productivity. To be sure, most of the communist East, even omitting the communist countries of Asia, is still very far from abundance, still very poor by Western standards, and still struggling to provide adequate food and shelter for its populations. Nonetheless, the problems of forthcoming automation of production (only beginning there) and its effects on employment, of the direction in which mass consumption (still in its infancy there) should go when it comes, of public versus private services, and so forth, are being increasingly and perhaps not prematurely discussed by Soviet and other East European economists.

Much more pressing are the problems of increasing affluence and approaching abundance in the West. It may be paradoxical to speak of the problem of abundance in the United States while the country is still not rid of poverty, but actually it is the realization of potential abundance that makes the persistent pockets of poverty both economically and politically intolerable. Clearly, we shall have to do much rethinking of our institutions and values as the economy's productivity continues to grow at a sound pace. Already we are devising new techniques—mostly new forms of partnership or cooperation between the federal government, private industry, and the autonomous universities—in various frontier areas of technology and production, such as atomic energy, space exploration, and the use of artificial satellites for communication.

Should we de-emphasize sheer production growth and concentrate on shifting resources in favor of the public sector in order to redress the balance between "private affluence and public squalor," as John K. Galbraith has forcefully argued?[12] Or should the U.S. do the redressing while simultaneously forcing greater economic growth, because growth strengthens America for both internal and international tasks, as the Swedish economist Gunnar Myrdal has countered?[13] Should the federal government guarantee a substantial minimal income to every citizen regardless of what he contributes to production, because abun-

[12]*The Affluent Society.*

[13]*Challenge to Affluence* (New York: Pantheon Books, 1963). See also his *Beyond the Welfare State* (New Haven: Yale University Press, 1960).

dance will enable it and the need for markets require it?[14] Above all, how shall we, as individuals and as a society, make sure that the increased outpouring of material goods and the lengthening hours and years of leisure become a blessing and not a curse? What are the implications for our political and economic systems, our ideologies, our ethics, our myths, and our politics?

Most of the world's countries and people are far removed from such worries. They face the real "economic problem"—how to make do with scanty resources and how to increase them at a pace that is not intolerably slow. Few are the underdeveloped countries that have not expressed their intention to industrialize and develop, but their industrializing ideologies and the institutions they use or intend to use for the purpose vary greatly. The various economic systems in the advanced countries present themselves as models of industrialization. Yet we can expect only very few to opt definitely for either the "Western" (let alone the strictly American) economic system, or, outside the communist world, for the Soviet system, or, for that matter, for the Yugoslav model (though it has elicited some interest in a few underdeveloped countries).

To begin with, capitalism has a bad name to many people in the underdeveloped countries. It is associated in their minds with colonialism, imperialism, great differences in income and wealth, class tensions, lack of national solidarity, and so on. Others may dislike it precisely because of its association with political democracy. At least the phraseology if not the policy of many underdeveloped countries is thus anticapitalist, although in some instances socialism is preached while capitalism is being effectively practiced (for example, in India). In some cases "socialism" is simply a fashionable euphemism for political dictatorship. But the fact remains that, call it socialism or controlled (planned) capitalism, the role of the state in most of these economies is likely to be relatively high, if only because domestic private interests are likely to be too weak to accumulate the capital and to foster the industrialization that the political leaders (and often the population at large) deem required. On our part, it behooves us little to insist that the underdeveloped country copy our own institutions of industrial capitalism as closely as possible when their conditions and values are usually radically different from those we encountered and espoused in the nineteenth century.

But although usually assigning a large role to the state and to economic planning, the noncommunist underdeveloped countries are not copying the Soviet—or, for that matter, the Chinese—model of industrialization, either. For some it is unpalatable because of its attendant political repression and human sacrifice. For others it is unfeasible because their regimes could not institute the political controls implicit in the model even if they wanted to. For many it is irrelevant, because even with Soviet-style political controls they could not

<hr>

[14]Robert Theobald, "Abundance: Threat or Promise," *The Nation*, May 11, 1963. See also his *The Challenge of Abundance* (New York: Potter, 1961; Mentor paperback, 1962).

achieve anything like the Soviet rates of growth in view of their backwardness and lack of resources. Of the last, some may be watching Communist China's progress, which is still very much in the balance. Theirs are the really hard choices to make; they can use not only our example and our help but also our understanding.[15]

[15]The writing on economic development is by now enormous. For an eloquent analysis of the relation between economic development and choice of political system see Robert L. Heilbroner, *The Great Ascent: The Struggle for Economic Development in Our Time* (New York: Harper & Row, 1963; Torchbook paperback, 1963); and his *The Making of Economic Society* (Englewood Cliffs, N.J.: Prentice-Hall, Inc., paperback, 1962), Chap. 7.

Selected Readings

Not much is written on economic subjects that in one way or another is not relevant to the study of economic systems. Clearly, one must be very selective. On the other hand, there are so many good and germane books now available in paperback form, including many of those cited in this work, that it is possible to build up a decent library in the field with a few visits to bookstores and a relatively modest outlay of cash.

The reader is invited to follow up the numerous references in our footnotes; we shall avoid duplicating them here. Since the present volume is brief, mention should be made of more voluminous systematic treatments of the subject. William N. Loucks, *Comparative Economic Systems*, 7th ed. (New York: Harper & Row, 1965), is a veteran and venerable textbook, having held the field since 1938. It is particularly strong on institutional description. Carl Landauer, *Contemporary Economic Systems* (Philadelphia: J. P. Lippincott Co., 1964), also ranges broadly and is particularly strong on various aspects of socialism and planning. George N. Halm, *Economic Systems: A Comparative Analysis*, rev. ed. (New York: Holt, Rinehart, & Winston, 1960), emphasizes the contrast between market and command economies. Lynn Turgeon, *The Contrasting Economies: A Study of Modern Economic Systems* (Boston: Allyn & Bacon, Inc., paperback, 1963), is a sector-by-sector comparative analysis of the Soviet and American economies. Allan C. Gruchy's *Comparative Economic Systems* (Boston: Houghton Mifflin Co., 1966) is a comprehensive text with somewhat of a historical perspective. A recent and promising entry in the textbook field is John E. Elliott, *Comparative Economic Systems* (Englewood Cliffs, N.J.: Prentice-Hall, Inc., 1973).

The following are useful collections of readings: Morris Bornstein, *Comparative Economic Systems: Models and Cases* (Homewood, Ill.: Richard D. Irwin, Inc., 1970); Marshall I. Goldman, *Comparative Economic Systems: A Reader* (New York: Random House, Inc., 1971); and Wayne A. Leeman, *Capitalism, Market Socialism, and Central Planning* (Boston: Houghton Mifflin Co., 1963); and Jan S. Prybyla, *Comparative Economic*

Systems (New York: Appleton-Century-Crofts, Inc., 1969. The textbooks and collections of readings generally contain substantial bibliographies.

Highly recommended is the most readable work by Lloyd G. Reynolds, *The Three Worlds of Economics* (New Haven: Yale University Press, paperback, 1971). The three worlds are the developed capitalist, the underdeveloped noncommunist, and the communist; they are discussed from the standpoint of economic organization, policy, and theory. Equally stimulating and almost as widely ranging is Benjamin Ward's *The Socialist Economy: A Study of Organizational Alternatives* (New York: Random House, Inc., 1967).

A landmark in the serious literature on postwar capitalism is Andrew Shonfield's *Modern Capitalism: The Changing Balance of Public and Private Power* (New York: Oxford University Press, 1965, paperback), to which the student is advised to refer. Covering a similar range of topics is the brief text by Philip Klein, *The Management of Market-Oriented Economies: A Comparative Perspective* (Belmont, Ca.: Wadsworth Publishing Co., Inc., 1973, paperback).

Some monographs treating aspects of organization are highly suggested for the understanding of economic systems, even if they do not directly address themselves to such. We may mention, for instance, the following: Tom Burns and G. M. Stalker, *The Management of Innovation* (London: Tavistock, 1961); Alfred D. Chandler, Jr., *Strategy and Structure* (Cambridge: M.I.T. Press, 1962); and Anthony Downs, *Inside Bureaucracy* (Boston: Little, Brown & Co., Inc., 1966, paperback). In addition, the standard literature on organization theory is very helpful to the student of economic systems.

Frederick Harbison and Charles A. Myers, *Management in the Industrial World: An International Analysis* (New York: McGraw-Hill Book Co., 1959), does just what the title says, not omitting the USSR. More specifically, the following two books compare managers and management in the West and in the USSR: David Granick, *The Red Executive: A Study of the Organization Man in Russian Industry* (Garden City, N.Y.: Doubleday & Co., Inc., 1960); and Richard N. Farmer and Barry M. Richman, *Comparative Management and Economic Progress* (Homewood, Ill.: Richard D. Irwin, Inc., 1965). Jesse W. Markham has edited and contributed to a very useful collection on *The American Economy* (New York: George Braziller, 1963), while Calvin B. Hoover is the editor of *Economic Systems of the Commonwealth* (Durham, N.C.: Duke University Press, 1962). Also note Rudolf Frei, ed., *Economic Systems of the West*, 2 volumes (Basel: List Gesellschaft, 1957, 1958).

P. Sargant Florence, *Industry and the State* (London: Hutchinson's University Library, 1957), is a concise introduction to the relations between the two in Britain and elsewhere. David McCord Wright, *Capitalism* (New York: McGraw-Hill Book Co., 1951; Gateway paperback, 1962), is a sympathetic analysis. Friedrich A. Hayek, *The Road to Serfdom* (Chicago: University of Chicago Press, 1944; also paperback), is a controversial classic defense of free-market capitalism. In a similar vein is Wilhelm Roepke, *Economics of the Free Society* (Chicago: Henry Regnery Co., 1963). The symposium edited by Shigeto Tsuru, *Has Capitalism Changed?* (Tokyo: Iwanami Shoten, 1961), consists mostly of Marxist contributions of various shades plus J. K. Galbraith's reaffirmation of his theory of countervailing power. (See also the references scattered through Chapters 4 and 5.)

Insofar as the individual countries or types of economic system are concerned, the reader is urged to consult the references in the respective chapters of this book for further reading suggestions.

Index

183